Dan Hotka

Toad for Oracle®

UNLEASHED

 800 East 96th Street, Indianapolis, Indiana 46240 USA

Toad for Oracle® Unleashed

ISBN-13: 978-0-13-413185-6
ISBN-10: 0-13-413185-1

Library of Congress Control Number: 2015906538

Printed in the United States of America

First Printing July 2015

Trademarks

All terms mentioned in this book that are known to be trademarks or service marks have been appropriately capitalized. Sams Publishing cannot attest to the accuracy of this information. Use of a term in this book should not be regarded as affecting the validity of any trademark or service mark.

Warning and Disclaimer

Special Sales

For information about buying this title in bulk quantities, or for special sales opportunities (which may include electronic versions; custom cover designs; and content particular to your business, training goals, marketing focus, or branding interests), please contact our corporate sales department at corpsales@pearsoned.com or (800) 382-3419.

For government sales inquiries, please contact governmentsales@pearsoned.com.

For questions about sales outside the U.S., please contact international@pearsoned.com.

Editor-in-Chief
Mark Taub

Executive Editor
Greg Doench

Development Editor
Susan Brown Zahn

Managing Editor
Kristy Hart

Project Editor
Elaine Wiley

Copy Editor
Paula Lowell

Indexer
Ken Johnson

Proofreader
Debbie Williams

Editorial Assistant
Michelle Housley

Cover Designer
Alan Clements

Senior Compositor
Gloria Schurick

Contents at a Glance

Introduction xi

1   Getting Started 1

2   Fast Track 25

3   Working with SQL 43

4   Schema Browser 69

5   Working with Data 93

6   Working with PL/SQL 121

7   Miscellaneous Tools 157

8   Getting Started with Toad Automation 171

9   Database Administration 191

10   Toad as a SQL Tuning Tool 227

Index 251

Table of Contents

Introduction .... **xi**

Who Should Read This Book xi

Why This Book Is Unique xii

How This Book Is Organized xii

1 Getting Started **1**

Introduction to Toad 1

    Toad Release History 2

    Toad Editions and Suites 3

    Prerequisites and Installation 5

Running Toad the First Time 8

    Oracle Client Software 9

    Database Connections 10

    Introduction to Main Screens 16

    Basic Toad Customizations 18

Common Newbie Questions 21

    Can Toad Do That? 21

    Toad versus Database Security 22

    Sharing Toad Options Settings 22

    Help—Toad Running Slowly 22

Summary 23

2 Fast Track **25**

Organizing Connections 25

Toolbars and Menus 30

Keyboard Shortcut Keys 33

Startup Windows/Screens 34

Startup Files, Scripts, and Actions 36

Advanced Toad Customizations 37

Sharing Toad Settings 40

Summary 41

3 Working with SQL **43**

Editor Window 43

SQL Editor Output Area 48

Object Describe 51

Toad Insights 57

Code Snippets 58

SQL Recall 60

Auto Replace 63

Query Builder 64
Summary 68

4   Schema Browser 69

Configuring the Schema Browser 69
Creating and Editing Objects..................................... 76
Printing Data Using FastReport 79
Using the Reports Manager... 85
Summary 91

5   Working with Data 93

Reviewing Data Grid Options...................................... 93
    Filter/Sort the Table Data 97
    View/Edit Query 99
    Show/Hide Columns 100
    Show Detail Dataset 100
    Calculate Selected Cells................................... 101
    Export Dataset 102
    Refresh Dataset 103
    Cancel Query Execution or Fetch.................... 104
    Add/Delete Rows 104
    Row Set Navigation Buttons 105
    Edit Row Set Control Buttons 105
    Commit/Rollback 105
    Bookmark Navigation....................................... 105
    Single Record Viewer....................................... 105
Save Data in Various Formats 106
Master Detail Browser 111
ER Diagrammer 113
HTML Documentation Generator 115
Summary 119

6   Working with PL/SQL.. 121

Using the Editor 121
Using Code Templates 127
Project Manager... 132
Using Code Snippets 133
Code Shortcuts 135
Code Analysis... 139
Using the Debugger... 142
    Basic Debugging 142
    Advanced Debugging Techniques.................... 148
Using the PL/SQL Profiler 153
Summary 156

7   Miscellaneous Tools **157**

     Code Road Map 157

     External Tools 160

     Compare Files 163

     TNS Editor 164

     Script Manager 165

     UNIX Monitor 167

     Summary 169

8   Getting Started with Toad Automation **171**

     Command Line (Legacy) 172

     Automation Designer (Future) 180

     Summary 190

9   Database Administration **191**

     Health Check 192

     Session Browser 194

     Database Browser 197

     Simple Export 202

     Data Pump Export 205

     Tablespace Management 210

     Generate Database Script 212

     Generate Schema Script 214

     Compare Databases 216

     Compare Schema 218

     Analyze All Objects 220

     Rebuild Multiple Objects 223

     Summary 224

10   Toad as a SQL Tuning Tool **227**

     Toad and Explain Plans 227

     SQL Statistics 231

     Toad and SQL Trace 233

         Toad and TKPROF 238

         Toad and Trace File Browser 241

     Statspack Interface 243

     AWR Browser 245

     Toad and the PL/SQL Profiler 246

     Toad and the SQL Optimizer 248

     Summary 249

Index **251**

About the Authors

Bert Scalzo is a Database Expert for HGST (a Western Digital company) and was formerly at Dell Software as a member of the Toad dev team for 15 years. He has worked with Oracle databases for more than two decades. Mr. Scalzo's work history includes time at both Oracle Education and Oracle Consulting. He holds several Oracle Masters certifications and has an extensive academic background—including a BS, MS, and PhD in Computer Science, an MBA, plus insurance industry designations. Mr. Scalzo is also an Oracle ACE.

Mr. Scalzo is an accomplished speaker and has presented at numerous Oracle conferences and user groups, including OOW, ODTUG, IOUG, OAUG, RMOUG, and many others.

He has written several books and numerous articles, papers, and blogs for the Oracle Technology Network (OTN), *Oracle Magazine*, *Oracle Informant*, *PC Week* (eWeek), *Dell Power Solutions Magazine*, *The LINUX Journal*, LINUX.com, Oracle FAQ, and Toad World.

http://bertscalzo.com/

Dan Hotka is a Training Specialist and an Oracle ACE Director who has more than 37 years in the computer industry, and more than 31 years of experience with Oracle products. His experience with the Oracle RDBMS dates back to the Oracle V4.0 days. Dan enjoys sharing his knowledge of the Oracle RDBMS. Dan is well published with 12 Oracle books and well over 200 published articles. He is frequently published in Oracle trade journals, regularly blogs, and speaks at Oracle conferences and user groups around the world.

Dan Hotka, Author/Instructor/Oracle ACE Director

www.DanHotka.com

Dan@DanHotka.com

DanHotka.Blogspot.com

Dedication

To my past and present miniature schnauzers Ziggy, Max, and Dexter—the three most wonderful four-legged kids that any parent could ever have. ☺

And to my wife Susan who's always jealous of my many book dedications solely to the dogs...

Bert Scalzo, PhD

This book is dedicated to my grandson Riggs, without whom my family would not be the same. Here's to the next generation!

Dan Hotka

We Want to Hear from You!

As the reader of this book, *you* are our most important critic and commentator. We value your opinion and want to know what we're doing right, what we could do better, what areas you'd like to see us publish in, and any other words of wisdom you're willing to pass our way.

We welcome your comments. You can email or write to let us know what you did or didn't like about this book—as well as what we can do to make our books better.

Please note that we cannot help you with technical problems related to the topic of this book.

When you write, please be sure to include this book's title and authors as well as your name and email address. We will carefully review your comments and share them with the authors and editors who worked on the book.

Email: errata@informit.com

Mail: Addison-Wesley/Prentice Hall Publishing
ATTN: Reader Feedback
330 Hudson Street
7th Floor
New York, New York, 10013

Reader Services

Visit our website and register this book at informit.com/register for convenient access to any updates, downloads, or errata that might be available for this book.

Introduction

IN THIS CHAPTER

▶ Who Should Read This Book

▶ Why This Book Is Unique

▶ How This Book Is Organized

A complete rewrite of the popular but dated *TOAD Handbook*, this book covers the very popular Toad for Oracle database management and development tool. It covers all the popular and key features of Toad, including many features that are new additions to Toad version 12.5. Moreover, this book offers numerous Toad tips and tricks, with ample expert advice and techniques—without focusing on any particular version of the Oracle database. Readers should be able to identify and readily adapt these "best practices" to their daily use of Toad.

Who Should Read This Book

This book should benefit all Toad users. It is ideal for a wide range of users, from those who are new to both Oracle and Toad, to very sophisticated or experienced users of Toad. Furthermore, this book attempts to address the specialized needs for three key database personas: database administrators, database application developers, and data/business analysts. In truth, Toad has so many features and offers so many benefits that no one book can realistically hope to fully cover them all. Thus, each chapter focuses on a particular functional or task-related area, covering it in depth with illustrations, tips, and techniques from Oracle and Toad experts.

This book is ideal for the following types of readers:

▶ The power user who wants easy access to data, help with SQL, and help with occasional coding assignments

▶ The user who wants to increase his or her productivity while using the Oracle RDBMS

▶ The IT professional who is already familiar with Toad but needs help with its extended features

▶ The developer who wants to do something specific but cannot remember how

▶ Any Toad user who wants to learn how to take advantage of Toad's newly introduced features

Why This Book Is Unique

This book doesn't make assumptions about readers' prior Toad or Oracle administrative or development background, so it presents the full range of tips and techniques applicable to these tools. The main goal of this book is to illustrate the use of Toad and to serve as a handy reference for anyone using the Toad database tool. To this end, the book is liberally illustrated with working examples of all topics covered.

This book is intended to be a complete, single source of information, usage, tips, and techniques for the Toad tool. It focuses on the following topics:

▶ Toad installation and setup

▶ Development of PL/SQL and SQL statements and scripts in an easy-to-use and intuitive environment

▶ Tuning SQL and debugging PL/SQL

▶ Modeling any user's schema

▶ Routine and advanced DBA tasks

▶ Exporting of data into various formats

▶ Additional features such as ER diagrams, trace file analysis, tablespace management, object management, and the ability to add your own favorite editors and programs. This book includes a chapter on Toad as a SQL tuning tool, something Toad is very good at.

How This Book Is Organized

The chapters are organized as follows:

▶ Chapter 1, "Getting Started," discusses the various versions and editions of Toad, and how it is packaged and sold. This chapter also details the installation and prerequisites for the computing environment that will run Toad. This chapter has a nice section on using Toad for the first time. The goal of this chapter is to jumpstart your learning process and make you productive with Toad ASAP.

▶ Chapter 2, "Fast Track," is a fast track to customizing Toad at startup, navigating the menus, learning the key shortcuts, and customizing Toad for your personal preferences.

► Chapter 3, "Working with SQL," is all about the SQL Editor and working with SQL. This chapter shows a number of ways of creating SQL without doing much typing at all. This chapter shows how to set up your own personal code shortcuts, and illustrates how to use the SQL Recall (SQL history). This chapter concludes with how to create SQL via mouse operations using Query Builder.

► Chapter 4, "Schema Browser," covers saving, formatting, and reporting on data from about any data grid. The focus of this chapter is the Schema Browser and how to best configure it for your personal preferences, as well as how to work with the data in any data grid. This chapter concludes with a nice walkthrough of the FastReport feature built into Toad, a nice report writer.

► Chapter 5, "Working with Data," finishes the discussion on working with data grids, showing the data relationships and how to see them, generating SQL from the relationships, and more.

► Chapter 6, "Working with PL/SQL," is for the PL/SQL developer. Toad is rich with development features such as code templates, code snippets, and more. This chapter covers the PL/SQL Debugger and PL/SQL Profiler that are built into Toad.

► Chapter 7, "Miscellaneous Tools," illustrates the team-building features built into Toad.

► Chapter 8, "Getting Started with Toad Automation," explores using the Automation Designer or Toad's own programming language to automate repetitive tasks.

► Chapter 9, "Database Administration," is for the DBAs using Toad. This chapter covers the database health check, how to monitor sessions and databases, tablespace maintenance, reporting, and more. Toad is an excellent Oracle administration tool.

► Chapter 10, "Toad as a SQL Tuning Tool," covers how to set up and use explain plans in Toad, illustrates useful hints, and reviews how to turn SQL Trace on/off via a number of mechanisms (for a session or for an individual SQL), and explores both the TKProf interface (the old and true character-mode trace analyzer) and Toad's own trace file browser that allows you to quickly find the problem SQL.

We hope you enjoy using this book as much as we have enjoyed writing it.

Bert Scalzo

Dan Hotka

CHAPTER 1

Getting Started

IN THIS CHAPTER

▶ Introduction to Toad
▶ Running Toad the First Time
▶ Common Newbie Questions

This chapter provides a complete introduction to Toad. It starts by covering everything you need to know in order to select the correct product offering/version, fulfill all of its installation prerequisites, and install it successfully. This chapter also illustrates what you need to know to launch it, connect to a database, and begin using Toad's basic features. Finally, it answers the most common *newbie* questions.

Introduction to Toad

Welcome to the wild and wonderful word of Toad. There are a lot of things you'll need to know before installing and using the product. Even though Toad is just a Microsoft Windows application with a standard Windows installer, there are some significant, non-obvious things to appreciate before beginning your journey.

While some experienced Microsoft Windows and Oracle database users might already know all the issues covered in this section, nonetheless it is worth reviewing to prevent any potential headaches or *gotchas*. For those not quite as comfortable with Microsoft Windows or the Oracle database, this section will be absolutely critical for your success and even satisfaction. Many Toad users have initially found the product difficult due to a lack of this knowledge. Most have eventually said "Wow, that was really easy once someone explained it!"

Toad Release History

Toad has been around for almost two decades. It started as freeware built by one lone Oracle user who hated using the command line in SQL*Plus—and no graphical tools were available. Around 1997 Toad and that developer were acquired by Quest Software (now Dell Software). Thus began its commercial journey.

During those two decades there have been many Toad, as well as Oracle, database releases. Some important interdependencies exist among all of those releases. Knowing what version of Toad works with which version(s) of the Oracle database is one example—that is, compatibility. Then there's what version of Toad supports which Oracle database version's new features—that is, support. Figure 1.1 shows the history timeline for both products' versions. You can learn a lot from this diagram.

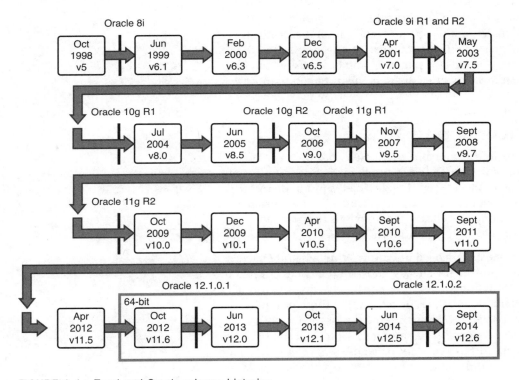

FIGURE 1.1   Toad and Oracle release histories

Note that Figure 1.1 entirely answers the *support* question. If the Toad release precedes the Oracle release in question, then obviously there's no way that version of Toad can support the new database features. So, for example, a fair number of people are still using Toad 9.7, mostly because they did not pay for maintenance (that is, support) and thus were not entitled to updates. However, the same people also tend to be using Oracle 11g R2 or 12c. Because Toad 9.7 was released before either of those Oracle versions, such users won't be able to use Toad to leverage 11g R2 or 12c features. In general, Toad support for new database version features will be either the first or second Toad release after the database release. In fact, Toad 10.1 supports Oracle 11g R2, whereas Toad 12.1 supports Oracle 12c (i.e., 12.1.0.1).

However, Figure 1.1 does not answer the *compatibility* question. Other mitigating factors come into play; specifically, the local PC's installed Oracle client version(s) (covered later in this chapter) and Toad's *data access* component, which communicates to the database via that client. So, for example, Toad 9.7 may yield an error about an unrecognized client version if your Oracle client is 12c, which the old *data access* component won't recognize. Likewise, Toad 12.6 may yield an error about a deprecated client version if your Oracle client is 9i, which the database no longer supports. The first is a Toad error and the second is an Oracle error.

So here's some advice about compatibility. If you're using a really old version of Toad, then you'll need an Oracle 9i, 10g, or 11g client (which can be recognized by the *data layer* component). However, then connecting to newer database versions with deprecated 9i or 10g clients may fail. If instead you're using a newer version of Toad and newer database versions (that is, 11g or 12c), then you should use the latest and greatest Oracle client (that is, 12c, but 11g will work as well). But if you're using a newer version of Toad with older versions of Oracle database, then you'll need an older Oracle client. Finally, if you're using a newer version of Toad with both current and older versions of Oracle database, you may need two Oracle clients—one for old versus new database versions. This is all rather complex, so Table 1.1 better illustrates these rather intricate and obtuse interdependencies.

TABLE 1.1   Toad versus Oracle Compatibility

Toad and DB Versions	Old Client	New Client
Old Toad/Old DB	OK	Unrecognized
Old Toad/New DB	Deprecated	Unrecognized
New Toad/Old DB	OK	Deprecated
New Toad/New DB	Deprecated	OK

Finally, note back on Figure 1.1 that 64-bit support was added beginning with Toad 11.6. This is further explained later in this chapter in the "Oracle Client Software" section.

Toad Editions and Suites

One quite common issue that confuses most new (and even long-time) Toad users is knowing what edition they have purchased—and thus what features they have. Many people seem to wrongly assume that there is just one form of Toad that costs $975, and that singular Toad gives you every feature possible. In reality a great many Toad offerings called editions and suites are available. They include the following:

▶ Toad for Oracle Base Edition

▶ Toad for Oracle Professional Edition

▶ Toad for Oracle Xpert Edition

▶ Toad Developer Suite for Oracle

▶ Toad DBA Suite for Oracle

▶ Toad DBA Suite for Oracle—RAC Edition

▶ Toad DBA Suite for Oracle—Exadata Edition

The Base edition is the foundation for all other editions and suites. It generally possesses just the basic, core features and functionality. That's not to say that it's *crippleware*. Many people find the Base edition more than sufficient for most normal database tasks, such as working with SQL or PL/SQL and browsing their database objects. Naturally, due to the lowest cost, this is a popular edition.

The Professional edition includes all the features in the Base edition, plus adds database import/export support and Code Analysis (formerly called CodeXpert). Years ago Professional also added the PL/SQL Debugger, but that feature has since moved down into the Base edition. Code Analysis is the big item here. It enables automated PL/SQL code reviews and rates the code using well-established software engineering metrics. Many larger shops use this to reduce coding defects.

The Xpert edition includes all the features in the Professional edition, plus adds integrated, push-button SQL tuning and the standalone, full-featured SQL Optimizer product. The integrated tuning within Toad's SQL Editor is sufficient for most basic needs. When the SQL is more complex or you want far more control (that is, options) while tuning, you can invoke SQL Optimizer, which finds every combination of SQL variations yielding the same results but with different and hopefully better run times.

For each of these three editions, there is also an optional DB Admin Module that costs extra and adds numerous DBA features. Some people attempt to administer their database using just the Base edition, and for some it's sufficient. For more complex DBA tasks users have two options: Oracle Enterprise Manager (OEM) or Toad's DB Admin Module. Many choose the latter so they can perform all their tasks using just the one tool. Just the additional database object types supported, database browser, database health check, compare schema with full sync capability, and multi-schema compare/sync warrant the extra cost.

As for the various Toad Suites, they are an entirely different animal altogether. They bundle in other standalone tools along a theme: code developer versus DBA. The Developer suite contains Toad Xpert plus Code Tester for automated unit testing and Benchmark Factory for stress testing. The DBA suite contains Toad Xpert plus DB Admin Module, Spotlight for diagnostics, and Benchmark Factory for workload replay. Finally, the DBA suites for RAC and Exadata merely add Spotlight diagnostic support for their namesakes. Many people find Spotlight alone worth the price of the DBA suite because it is licensed by seat and not database server, enabling you to monitor any database having performance problems.

Finally, people often say, "I don't know which Toad edition or suite we bought. Is there a way to find out?" For suites the answer is to look on your Windows Start menu for entries named Dell and/or Quest Software. Under those you will find entries for the names of the products that have been installed. If you see Code Tester, then you have the Developer suite. If you see Spotlight, then you have the DBA suite. If all you have is Toad and SQL Optimizer, then you have the Xpert edition. If all you see is Toad, then simply invoke Toad's Main Menu → Help → About to display the splash screen, which displays your version and edition licensing information as shown in Figure 1.2.

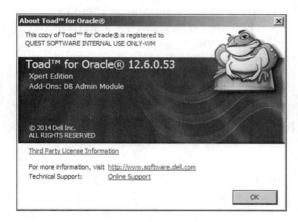

FIGURE 1.2   Toad's About screen

Prerequisites and Installation

Toad is a Microsoft Windows program that can be installed and runs on just about any current version of Windows, including:

- ▶ Windows XP (32-bit and 64-bit)

- ▶ Windows Vista (32-bit and 64-bit)

- ▶ Windows 7 (32-bit and 64-bit)

- ▶ Windows 8 (32-bit and 64-bit)

- ▶ Windows Server 2003 (32-bit and 64-bit)

- ▶ Windows Server 2003 R2 (32-bit and 64-bit)

- ▶ Windows Server 2008 (32-bit and 64-bit)

- ▶ Windows Server 2008 R2 (64-bit)

▶ Windows Server 2012 (64-bit)

▶ Windows Server 2012 R2 (64-bit)

What about older versions such as Windows 95, 98, and 2000? Will Toad install and run on those operating systems? For older versions of Toad the answer is "maybe." However, for newer versions of Toad the answer is a definitive "no." Windows 95 and 98 have limited Graphics Device Interface (GDI) resources, which causes problems with Toad displaying its screens. Windows 2000 lacks support for current Microsoft .NET versions required by Toad suites and any edition above Base, so old Windows versions are definitely out.

What about newer versions such as Windows 8.1 and 10? Will Toad install and run on those operating systems? Unfortunately, Toad's development team cannot afford to perform quality assurance (QA) testing for every Windows version. Hence newer versions such as Windows 8.1 and 10 are not yet certified. Furthermore, as the latest new Windows versions are added to the supported list, others such as Windows XP and 2003 may have to fall off. That's just the natural progression of things.

As with most Microsoft Windows applications, installing Toad is rather simple and straightforward. First you download the desired edition or suite EXE file for normal graphical interface installs or the MSI file for remote, unattended installs. Most people will download and run the EXE file for a typical, graphical Windows install experience. Note that both 32- and 64-bit versions are available of all downloads. Figure 1.3 shows the Toad 12.6 EXE installer files.

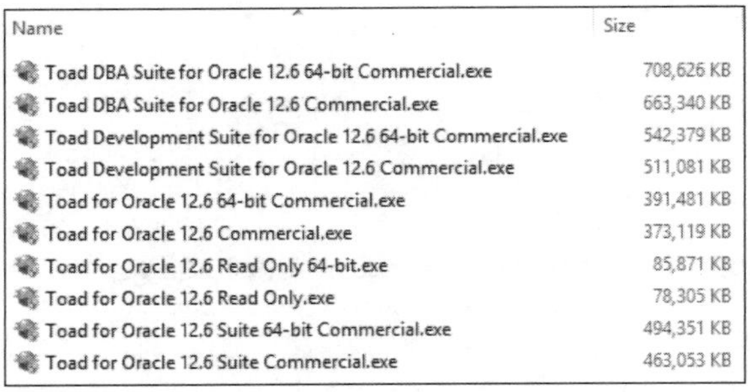

Name	Size
Toad DBA Suite for Oracle 12.6 64-bit Commercial.exe	708,626 KB
Toad DBA Suite for Oracle 12.6 Commercial.exe	663,340 KB
Toad Development Suite for Oracle 12.6 64-bit Commercial.exe	542,379 KB
Toad Development Suite for Oracle 12.6 Commercial.exe	511,081 KB
Toad for Oracle 12.6 64-bit Commercial.exe	391,481 KB
Toad for Oracle 12.6 Commercial.exe	373,119 KB
Toad for Oracle 12.6 Read Only 64-bit.exe	85,871 KB
Toad for Oracle 12.6 Read Only.exe	78,305 KB
Toad for Oracle 12.6 Suite 64-bit Commercial.exe	494,351 KB
Toad for Oracle 12.6 Suite Commercial.exe	463,053 KB

FIGURE 1.3   Toad 12.6 installer files

When you run the Toad installer, one of the first questions it will ask is for your license key as shown in Figure 1.4. You do not have to enter it at this point. If you do, then that license will automatically be applied to each product installed. If you don't, then later when you run Toad and other products such as SQL Optimizer, Benchmark Factory, or Spotlight you may have to enter the key manually. So it takes less work if you enter the license key when the installer asks for it. Finally, note that if your machine already has a valid key registered (such as for a previously installed version) then you will see both a key icon with a green check mark and the message "A Valid Key has been found" as shown at the top of Figure 1.4.

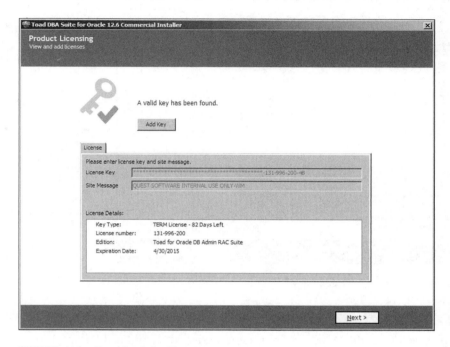

FIGURE 1.4   Toad installer license screen

Next the Toad installer displays a screen where you can see which products that install EXE file contains (see Figure 1.5). In the Windows title bar you can see that this is the installer for the Toad DBA Suite, hence why it lists products such as SQL Optimizer, Benchmark Factory, and Spotlight. You simply check those that you desire to install. However, note that some products will show red stop signs next to the product selection check box on the left and the product description box on the right. The stop signs communicate that those products so marked cannot be installed due to missing prerequisites such as .NET 3.5 and 4.0. If you see such indicators and want to install those products, then you must abort the Toad installer, install the missing prerequisites, and then rerun the Toad installer. After all the prerequisite tests pass, you'll then be able to complete the Toad install process.

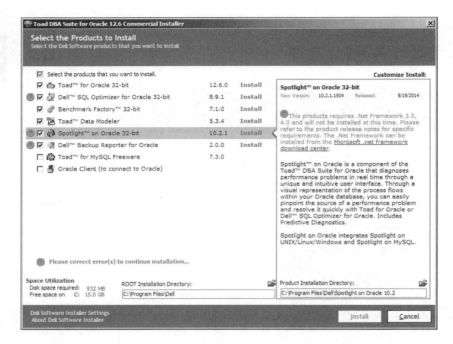

FIGURE 1.5   Toad installer product selection

After the Toad installer completes successfully, you'll find Toad and other product icons on your desktop as well as in the Windows Start menu under entries named Dell and/or Quest Software. There's yet one more key prerequisite necessary, the Oracle Client, which is covered in the following section.

Running Toad the First Time

With Toad now successfully installed, it's time to run it for the first time. This requires installing and configuring the Oracle client, connecting to the desired Oracle database, learning the basic menus and screens, plus making some basic customizations that will make your Toad usage more productive.

These next few sections are critical. Toad must connect to your Oracle database in order for you to work on it. Failure to connect will severely limit which features and functions in Toad will be active. For example, with no connection you cannot browse the database or submit SQL commands to retrieve and display data. Yet as important as connecting to the database is, it's one of the most frequent problems for new users.

Oracle Client Software

Regardless of whether your database is running on a remote server or on your local Windows PC, Toad needs to talk to Oracle's application-to-database communication interface known as Oracle Net Services (also known as SQL*Net). There are no exceptions. Yet many people routinely ask "Can't Toad connect to the database using ODBC?" The answer is "no."

Oracle Net Services functions essentially as a client/server architecture as shown in Figure 1.6. Toad's data access component communicates with the Oracle Call Interface (OCI) to link with Oracle Net Services on the client machine, while the database links with Oracle Net Services on the server machine in the same fashion. Lastly, Oracle Net Services transfers all data back and forth between the client and database server via TCP/IP. Note that the network packets are not, by default, encrypted. You must purchase Oracle Advanced Security to encrypt network traffic among clients and databases.

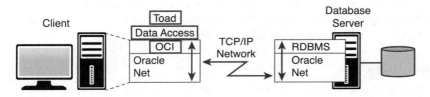

FIGURE 1.6   Oracle Net Services architecture

Oracle Net Services can be installed on your Windows machine in one of two ways: the instant client or a fat, full install. The instant client is merely a 20–60 MB zip file (depending on the client version) of Windows DLL files that you unzip into a directory. You also must include that directory in your Windows PATH environment variable. The full, fat client is a 600–900 MB zip file containing an installer for all the Oracle executables, and DLLs necessary for everything but running a database. This install creates what's referred to as an *Oracle Home*, which are Windows Registry variables that point to the installation. The fat client does not require any inclusion in the Windows PATH environment variable.

When you launch Toad it checks the Windows PATH environment variable for Oracle Net Services DLLs and the Windows Registry for an Oracle Home (in that order). If Toad finds either, then all is well and Toad works as expected. If not, then you will see the error shown in Figure 1.7.

FIGURE 1.7   No Oracle Net Services error

Finally, without exception, the bit size for the Oracle client must match the bit size of the Toad installer that you downloaded and ran. Remember, prior to version 11.6 Toad was 32-bit only. If your Windows is 32-bit, then your only option is the 32-bit Oracle client and 32-bit Toad. However, if your Windows is 64-bit, you have two options: both Oracle client and Toad 32-bit, or both 64-bit. These are the only valid bit size combinations and are better illustrated by Table 1.2.

TABLE 1.2   Toad vs. Windows Bit Compatibility

Windows Bit Size	Toad 32-bit	Toad 64-bit
Windows 32-bit	32-bit client	INVALID
Windows 64-bit	32-bit client	64-bit client

If you violate these valid combinations, then on launch, newer versions of Toad will once again give an error like the one shown in Figure 1.7. However, invalid combinations with older versions of Toad will give a less friendly error message like "cannot locate OCIxxx.DLL" (where xxx is either numbers or blank).

Database Connections

Oracle provides two primary ways or mechanisms for identifying the database you want to connect to: via an alias or direct connect string. Even though these two key connection methods accomplish the exact same thing, most Toad users will find that they favor one or the other. Both have pros and cons; it all depends on your likes and preferences. However, Toad permits using both connection methods if you so desire.

The Toad connection screen will be your first and most important feature to learn and master. You can invoke it either via the [icon] icon on the main window toolbar or by choosing Main Menu ➔ Session ➔ New Connection. The connection screen may appear rather busy or complex on initial inspection, as shown in Figure 1.8. The screen is basically split into two major sides: left and right. The left side displays a simple table of prior successful connections. After you've made a few connections to populate this table, you can then simply double-click on an entry to connect to that database. The right side is where you enter the information to create a new database connection. When you click the Connect button it will both connect to that database and add it to the table for the next time you launch this screen. The right side fields for user or schema and password are for your Oracle database login credentials. Below them is a *tabbed* style area with three tabs: TNS, Direct, and LDAP. You will primarily just use the first two tabs, which equate to the earlier mentioned two primary ways to identify the database to which you want to connect.

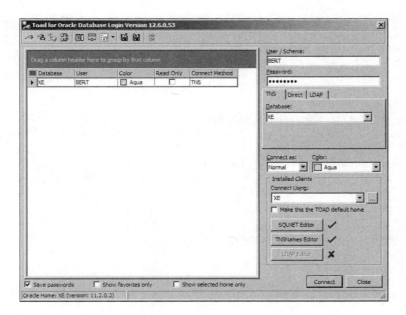

FIGURE 1.8   Toad's connection screen

TNS stands for Transparent Network Substrate, which is simply the fancy name for Oracle's Net Services architecture. And although all peer-to-peer communication is over TCP/IP (refer to Figure 1.6), TNS uses a proprietary protocol. These last two facts are just for the benefit of those interested. You won't care about that during normal day-to-day Oracle database work using Toad.

When you choose the TNS tab, the connection screen's right side will display the fields shown in Figure 1.8. The Database field is a drop-down list that should be pre-populated with known database aliases if you have an Oracle TNSNAMES.ORA file. If you installed the fat Oracle client, then that file should be either in your Oracle Home directory under the \Network\Admin subdirectory or a directory pointed to by the TNS_ADMIN Windows environment variable. If you instead installed the instant client, then only TNS_ADMIN will work because there is no Oracle Home (that is, no registry entries, just unzipped DLL files added to your PATH). The TNSNAMES.ORA file is simply a text file that can be edited with any editor (for example, Notepad). However, Oracle requires a specific and special syntax. If you don't get the syntax right, then the aliases won't be displayed in the drop-down list. Because many people are not experts on this syntax, Toad provides a special

TNSNAMES.ORA-aware screen with a tree view to browse the alias and syntax highlight-ing, as shown in Figure 1.9. You merely click the TNSNames Editor button to launch it. Note that this button will have a green check mark next to it if the file already exists (refer to Figure 1.8) and a red X if not. Also note that it shows you the complete Oracle Home directory string.

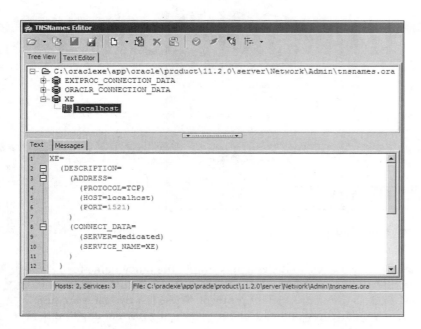

FIGURE 1.9   Toad's Intelligent TNSNames Editor

As you can see in the top half of the screen's tree view in Figure 1.9, I have three database aliases in the browser and an extremely long directory name for my Oracle Home. Note that the directory name starts with oraclexe, which indicates this PC is running a local copy of the Oracle Express Edition database. The bottom half of the screen in Figure 1.9 displays the syntax-highlighting text editor for the top browser's currently selected alias. The Oracle TNSNAMES.ORA syntax requires four things:

▶ The alias name (that is, the short name displayed in the drop-down list)

▶ The network protocol

▶ The network port

▶ The database server's service name for the target database

So in Figure 1.9 the XE database alias points to the localhost database and communicates via TCP/IP on port 1521 to connect to the XE database service. Generally speaking, either the DBA or project lead will supply an initial, default TNSNAMES.ORA file with all the remote server databases with which you should work. You will have to create your own TNSNAMES.ORA file or add new entries to an existing file if using a local database. Finally, note that even though the XE alias points to a local database, it still communicates via TCP/IP.

If you instead choose the Direct tab as shown back in Figure 1.8, the connection screen's right side will not display the Database alias drop-down list but rather fields for the host, port, and database service name. In essence you are simply bypassing doing aliases and just directly entering the same information that would have been in the TNSNAMES.ORA file.

Returning to Figure 1.8, there are three other fields of interest. Note the drop-down list with three values: Normal, SYSDBA, and SYSADMIN. In most cases you should select Normal (the default). The other two are special Oracle connection requests for special DBA privileges for things like starting up and shutting down the database. These should only be selected if you know for a fact you will be doing operations that require such extra privileges. Note that SYSDBA does not mean you are a DBA, contrary to popular belief.

The color drop-down list is a useful, but often overlooked, connection feature. After you select a color (default is none) for a connection, Toad will highlight four items with that color as shown in Figure 1.10 (note that the following list numbers match the numbers called out in Figure 1.10):

1. The connection toolbar icon for that connection

2. The screen toolbar icons for open screens using that connection

3. The child window border for all non-maximized screens

4. The bottom status bar on all windows, maximized or not

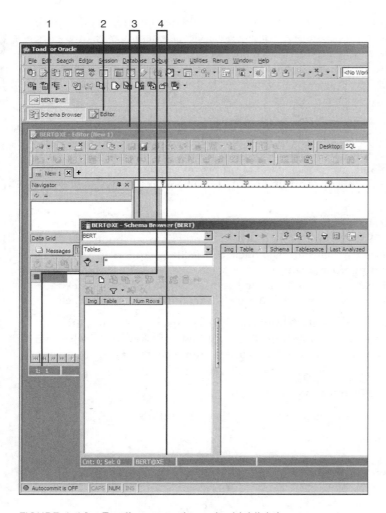

FIGURE 1.10   Toad's connection color highlighting

Returning to Figure 1.8 again, the other field of interest is the Oracle Homes Selector drop-down list. It will display all Oracle Homes found in the Windows registry, valid or invalid (which can occur; don't select those). So how do you discover what Oracle Homes are invalid and possibly correct them? You click the button with three dots to the right of the drop-down list, which opens the Oracle Homes editor shown in Figure 1.11. As you can see there are two Oracle Homes on this PC: the fat client installed first to connect to remote databases, and the fat client installed as part of the Oracle Database Express Edition running locally. Note, too, that the two Homes are for different Oracle versions:

11.2.0.2 versus 11.2.0.4. In general, minor differences like this can be ignored. Remember that, as mentioned earlier in this chapter, you may work with both old and new Oracle databases, which could require multiple Oracle Homes (that is, an old one like 10g for very old database version connections and a newer one like 12c for more current ones). Also note that after you've selected an Oracle Home for a new connection, you can also check the box below it labeled Make this the Toad Default Home as the default for all future new connections. Finally, note that after a connection is established and active and points to a selected Oracle Home, all new database connections must default to that active connection's Oracle Home. Many people ask why. The Toad application can only point to one set of Oracle Net Services DLL files while running. Thus you will need to either disconnect all sessions or restart Toad to switch the selected, active Oracle Home.

FIGURE 1.11   Toad's Oracle Home browser

Lastly, if you enter invalid login credentials or make some other mistake (such as trying to connect to a database that's shut down), Toad's connection screen opens an error screen like the one shown in Figure 1.12 to inform you what's wrong, and in some cases some steps that may help you troubleshoot the problem.

FIGURE 1.12   Connection error for a bad password

Introduction to Main Screens

After a database connection is successfully established, you can then use Toad to perform tasks on that database. While there are numerous Toad screens, reports, and utilities, you will find a small subset to be the primary screens that you use most. In fact, many people use just two Toad screens: the SQL Editor and Schema Browser. Both screens will be covered in full detail in other chapters. This section simply shows you their basics so that after connecting to a database you can see Toad work.

The SQL Editor is by far the single most used screen. It enables you to type in a SQL command such as SELECT * FROM table name, execute that command, and then see the data returned from the database for that command. To launch the SQL Editor you either press the 📝 icon on the main window toolbar or choose Main Menu ➜ Database ➜ Editor. You will see a rather complex and busy screen launch, as shown in Figure 1.13. The screen has three major areas. The upper-left side is the Navigator, which is covered in Chapter 3, "Working with SQL." You can either ignore it for now or click the X in its upper corner to hide it. The upper-right side is the editor text entry area. Here you simply type a SQL command like the one shown. Note that this editor will perform syntax highlighting to make the reading and writing of SQL code easier. After you've typed your SQL command (with or without the semicolon terminator), then press the 📝 icon (first position on the SQL Editor's lower toolbar). This is the "execute statement" function, which is by default also mapped to the F9 key. Either way, Toad will send this command over to the database and then fetch back the data, which is shown in the bottom panel's Data Grid tab. As with the navigator, you can ignore these other tabs for now as they are covered in a later chapter. You've now successfully used Toad to perform your first database action.

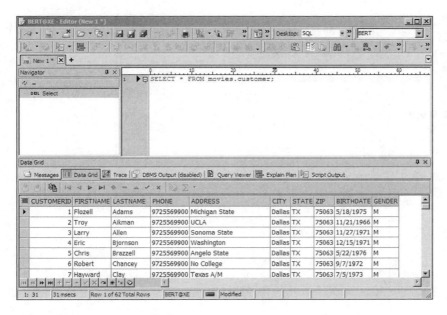

FIGURE 1.13   Toad's SQL Editor

The Schema Browser is the second most used screen. It enables you to visually browse your database objects. Think of it like the Windows File Explorer, but for database objects instead of directories and files. As with the SQL Editor, this screen offers many features and functionalities, which are covered in a later chapter. For now you are simply going to open it and look around, which is a common activity among people working with databases. To launch the Schema Browser you either click the 🗐 icon on the main window toolbar or choose Main Menu → Database → Schema Browser. Once again you will see a rather complex and busy screen launch, as shown in Figure 1.14. This screen has two major areas. The left side has two drop-down boxes at the top. The first drop-down box is for the database user or schema who owns the database objects, in this case MOVIES. The second drop-down box is for the database object type, in this case Tables. Then the lower-left side will display a list of all the object types for that schema. As you can see, there are seven tables, with the EMPLOYEE table selected or highlighted.

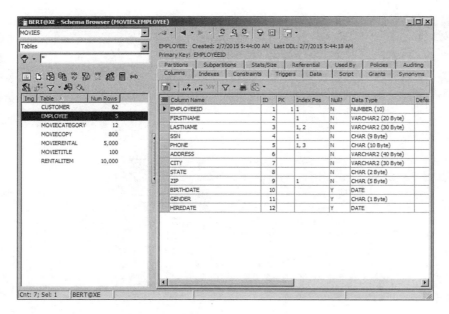

FIGURE 1.14   Toad's Schema Browser

That last part is important, because the right side displays a whole bunch of context-sensitive tabs for that particular object type and specific object. Thus on the right side you see the Columns tab displays information for the twelve columns in that table. The Schema Browser will be covered in more detail in Chapter 4, "Schema Browser," especially what all those right side tabs are for. For now, though, you will want to look at two more tabs: Data and Script. The Data tab displays a data grid much like the SQL Editor, but this one is for all the selected table's data rather than some manually typed SQL command. The Script tab displays a read-only SQL Editor text area (with syntax highlighting), but it is for the SQL command or commands to create that object and its supporting structures. In this case EMPLOYEE would display many commands: one CREATE TABLE, six CREATE INDEX, and one CREATE TRIGGER. You've now successfully used Toad to perform your second database action. In fact you now know the basics for the two Toad screens you'll use most. Some of you may even quit reading the book after just this chapter if the basics for these two screens are all you really need.

Basic Toad Customizations

Now that you've learned a couple screens, you may be thinking that you wish Toad looked and felt differently (that is, you want to customize its appearance and operation). As with the SQL Editor and Schema Browser, this section only covers a couple of the most used basics and leaves the details to later chapters. Remember, this chapter is titled "Getting Started."

As with most modern Windows programs, you can customize the menus, toolbars displayed, and the buttons on those toolbars. If you click the right mouse button while over either the main menu or main window's toolbars you will see the pop-up shown in Figure 1.15. This pop-up permits you to

▶ Select which main window toolbars are visible

▶ Customize main window menus and toolbars

▶ Restore defaults to main window menus and toolbars

▶ Launch the Toad Options screen to define menu shortcuts

▶ Lock the toolbars

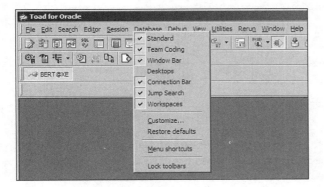

FIGURE 1.15   Customizing menus and toolbars

Most other customizations are accomplished via Toad's Options screen. This screen is arguably the most complex screen within Toad because it has many hundreds of settings to experiment with. These are covered later, but you should feel free after this basic intro to look around a bit and try making some changes, because this screen simply requires time and patience to master. To launch the Options screen you either click the ⊞ icon on the main window toolbar or choose Main Menu ➜ View ➜ Toad Options. You will then see the single most crowded and complex screen launch, as shown in Figure 1.16. The left side displays a tree view of all the option categories you can change. In this case the first editor subcategory for Behavior is selected. Now the right side will change for each and every category or subcategory chosen. Furthermore, many buttons such as Code Templates, Syntax Highlighting, and Key Mapping will launch other screens for yet more options. And some of those suboption screens are as complex as the main Options screen. So clearly there's way too much to cover in this "getting started" chapter. For now we'll simply learn a few that go well with the rest of this quick start tutorial.

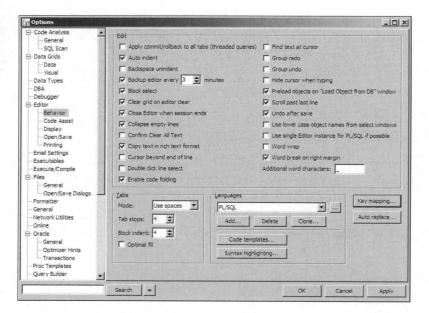

FIGURE 1.16   Toad's Options screen—Editor Behavior

Because this chapter introduced you to the two primary screens the majority of people use most, wouldn't it be nice to make Toad automatically open those two screens on any new database connection? Furthermore, maybe your preference is to have the Schema Browser display in the foreground (that is, up front) with the SQL Editor in the background. Once again you will use the Toad Options screen. However, this time you will scroll to the bottom and select Windows, as shown in Figure 1.17. Note the left side display. The column Auto Open is checked for the Editor (as well as the Schema Browser, which is not in view). The Auto-Open Bring to Front setting is a drop-down list that displays all the auto-open checked screens, and you merely select the one you want to be up front. In this case that is the Schema Browser. Now on any new database connection Toad will open the SQL Editor and Schema Browser, with the latter up front.

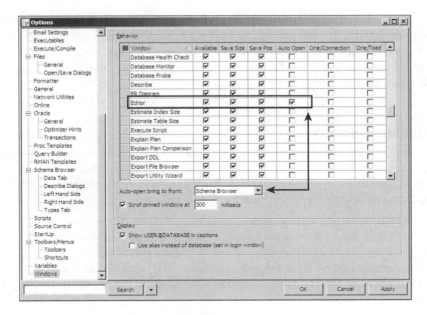

FIGURE 1.17   Toad's Options screen—Windows

Remember, this was a crash course on some basic Toad customizations. Many more customizations are possible, but you now have a grasp on the fundamentals and can customize Toad to taste.

Common Newbie Questions

Toad is a very mature and robust product; hence, it's quite common for those new to the tool to have lots of very basic questions. In fact Toad offers so many features that even long-time users ask these types of questions. I always reply to these people that Toad is so big now that no one really knows everything anymore—in fact often not even the developers who wrote the screens or utilities remember what they coded. So really there is no such thing as a dumb question. Here we'll address the four categories of questions asked most frequently.

Can Toad Do That?

People often ask on the Toad World forums or live at Toad Tips & Tricks sessions whether Toad can do something. Specifically, questions might be something like, "Can Toad version X support this very cool new Oracle feature Y that I'd like to leverage?" or, "Can Toad 12.6 manage AWR snapshots and generate AWR reports?" Another example might be, "Does Toad offer a PL/SQL debugger and profiler?"

The answer to these questions is almost invariably "yes." In fact it's very much like the old Prego spaghetti commercials: "It's in there!" Sometimes locating the desired feature is neither obvious on inspection nor well documented in the online help. But with almost a 20-year history and millions of users, you can be sure that someone has asked for that feature at some point and the Toad developers added it. There are few things that Toad cannot do.

Toad versus Database Security

Probably the most frequent question asked by shops new to Toad is "Will Toad enable my developers or business analysts to do things in the database that they're not permitted to do?" Because Toad is so easy to use and so powerful, some fear that it might allow users to do bad things—like drop a production table or delete all of its data.

The simple answer is "definitely not," because Toad cannot override or supersede Oracle's inherent security. A Toad user has only whatever roles, system privileges, or object grants exist for the user he or she connects as. Thus users can do no more in Toad than they could in SQL*Plus (they simply can do it more easily and faster via Toad). To reiterate, Toad permits database users only whatever rights the DBA has granted them—there are no loopholes or exceptions.

Sharing Toad Options Settings

One of the more common general Toad user questions (after basic configuration and connectivity) is "How can I get the exact same Toad options or settings as my buddy whose Toad works differently (that is, better) than mine?" Another example might be a project manager who wants all his team's Toad users to work the same way. With so many options to set, it simply would be nice to be able to copy them from PC to PC.

Beginning with Toad 12.5, users simply choose Main Menu → Utilities → Copy User Settings. That launches the Copy User Settings screen, which offers a choice for importing and exporting all the options setting files into a single zip file—which you can save as a backup or share with your buddies. For those wondering what this feature does, it simply offers a GUI for the manual method of sharing that Toad users were told to do for years: Copy the files under the directory %APPDATA% \Toad for Oracle\ Client Files.

Help—Toad Running Slowly

It's not uncommon for Windows software to increase in install size and memory footprint over the years—and Toad is no exception. But that does not mean that these newer versions have to run more slowly. The Toad development team takes great pride in keeping Toad expedient as it matures. Thus do *not* simply assume that if your Toad is running slower these days that it's just the "cost of progress."

Start by running the Toad Advisor and see what it turns up. You simply choose Main Menu → Help → Toad Advisor. That launches a simple screen that displays any option settings it thinks are suboptimal. If you agree, then simply double-click on a finding and you will be taken to the Toad Options screen with that field chosen for quick modification. In many cases this simple process can yield great results.

Summary

This chapter provided a fast-track introduction to all things Toad, from its long history to the various editions and suites available—and how they differ. It also covered the installation prerequisites and process. The chapter then covered everything you would need to know to run Toad for the first time, including how to install and configure the Oracle client, connect to the database, a quick overview of the two most used Toad screens, and some basic customizations. Finally, it wrapped up by answering the most common questions asked by new Toad users. In short, this one chapter alone provides all the basic information required to install and begin using Toad.

IN THIS CHAPTER

▶ Organizing Connections

▶ Toolbars and Menus

▶ Keyboard Shortcut Keys

▶ Startup Windows/Screens

▶ Startup Files, Scripts, and Actions

▶ Advanced Toad Customizations

▶ Sharing Toad Settings

The last chapter provided a quick introduction to Toad so that a new user could start using the tool almost immediately. This chapter provides a fast-track introduction for customizing Toad to taste and thus substantially optimizing your productivity. A few people use Toad with just the defaults. Most people take 20–30 minutes to make Toad fit their preferences and needs. This chapter covers the key places where you can make such modifications (and even share them with others).

Organizing Connections

In the last chapter you learned how to perform one of the most fundamental tasks that you'll do over and over again—establish a database connection. Although that task might initially seem straightforward and easy, most people will need to work with dozens to even hundreds of database connections. Thus, organizing the connection screen is one of the first and easiest places to enhance your Toad experience and productivity. It's quite easy and will pay ongoing dividends.

Look at the highlighted section of Figure 2.1, which shows the history of database connections saved. There are ten saved connection rows of data for five distinct users across three different databases. This scenario is not uncommon. In fact you may well accumulate far more saved connections over time. Thus organizing them can be a real time saver. You also may have noticed that Figure 2.1's displayed columns and order are different than yours. Let's start there.

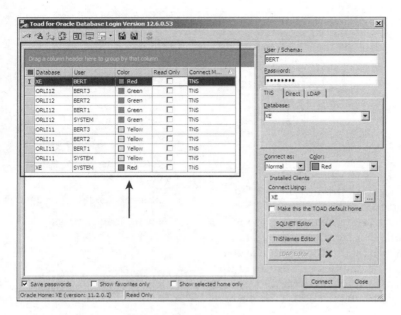

FIGURE 2.1   Organizing the saved connection data grid

One of the first user customizations you'll discover in Toad is that all data grids (that is, spreadsheet-like tabular displays of data) can be modified much like Microsoft Excel spreadsheets. Thus, to resize a column such as Database you move the mouse to the column header's right-hand side border, press the left-hand mouse button, and then drag and drop to resize the column. To instead move a column (that is, reorganize the column ordering), you move the cursor almost anywhere inside the column header, press the left-hand mouse button, and then drag and drop to move the column. To sort upon a column, you move the cursor to most anywhere inside the column header, and left-click the mouse button. An up arrow icon for sort ascending or a down arrow icon for sort descending will appear on the column header's right-hand side as shown in Figure 2.2. Clicking the mouse a second time in the same column header will then reverse the arrow direction and thus the column sort order. Note that this technique only supports performing single column sorting.

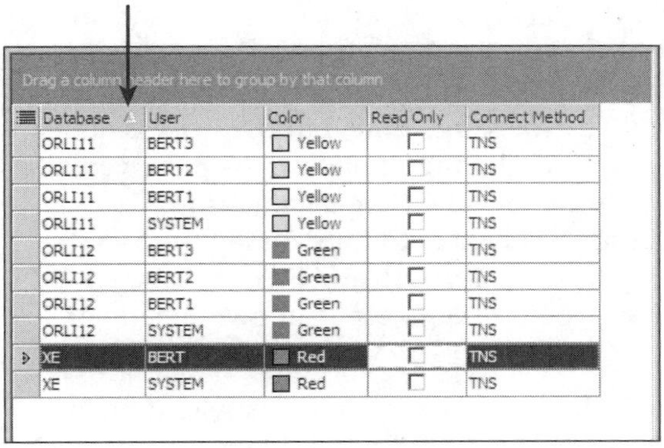

FIGURE 2.2   Sorting the saved connection data grid column

Next, to choose which columns to display (or not), you move the cursor to the column header's upper left-hand corner where the mini-grid icon appears, click the left-hand mouse button, and then select the desired columns to display, as shown in Figure 2.3. Note that you can click the right-hand mouse button to open a pop-up menu for some quick selection choices such as Check all or Uncheck all. Now you will see only the selected columns displayed rather than the default selection. This permits things such as only displaying those columns that will fit in the data grid without causing a horizontal scroll bar control appearing at the bottom of the saved connection data grid. In fact you will quite likely utilize all three of these operations (column reordering, resizing, and display selection) together in order to arrive at your desired saved connection look and feel. For many Toad users, these three operations alone will be sufficient in most cases. For those who desire even more customization, Toad offers three more key functionalities, covered next.

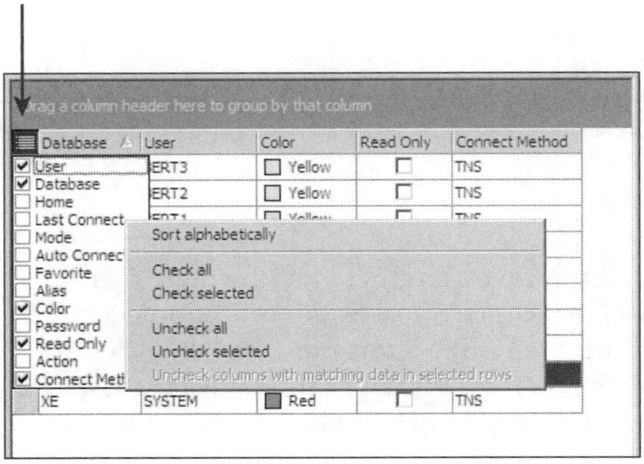

FIGURE 2.3   Choosing the saved connection data grid columns

Sometimes in a data grid you'll want to filter the data (that is, restrict the rows shown in the grid on some condition). Note that this is radically different from, say, adding a WHERE clause on a SELECT that returns data—which is entirely processed on the database server. A Toad data grid filter does essentially the same thing, but the work is done client side after the database returns all the rows. So filtering should not be perceived as the same as a WHERE clause, but as a way to restrict or subset the data returned to you. For example, it might be more efficient while analyzing data to filter on say the STATE column of the CUSTOMER table to show only those in TX, OH, and FL rather than re-executing the expensive query on the server. You'll have to use your own judgment and the context to decide.

There are two ways to invoke Toad's data grid filtering. The first and most visual method is you can move the cursor to the column header's upper right-hand side where the funnel icon will appear (it's not visible until used), click the left-hand mouse button, and then select the desired data values that the filter permits (that is, returns), as shown in Figure 2.4. Note for now the custom option. Second, you can right-click anywhere inside the data grid to open a pop-up menu and then choose Filter Data. Both the aforementioned custom option and the pop-up menu choice invoke a pop-up screen where you can enter far more complex filtering conditions, including things such as parenthetical levels, ANDs and ORs between conditions or levels, and the use of SQL functions.

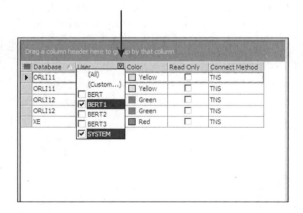

FIGURE 2.4   Filtering saved connection data grid columns

The next two more advanced customizations both involve ways to group your database connections visually. Remember you may well have many dozens or even hundreds of saved database connections after using Toad for even just a short time. Looking back at the last four figures (that is, Figures 2.1 to 2.4), you'll see displayed just above the data grid the following text: Drag a column header here to group by that column. If you use the mouse to select and drag and drop a column such as Database into this area, then the data grid will change to be grouped by that column as shown in Figure 2.5. While this capability might make more sense on other data grids, it's not the most useful for the saved database connection info. In fact with many dozens or more saved database connection entries, this technique just makes the list taller and typically results in the addition of a vertical scroll bar for the data grid. Because many people prefer not to switch to a taller visual style with potentially far more mouse movements required, this technique is not often used on this screen. However, again, for truly more end user database type data, this could well be a useful technique.

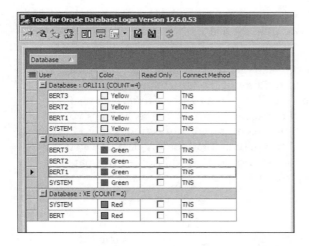

FIGURE 2.5   Grouping saved connection data grid—method 1

The more visually appealing way to group the connection screen data grid is to leverage the visual styles drop-down toolbar icon shown activated in Figure 2.6 and to select whether to display a simple data grid (default) or one with tabs at the top by one of three criteria. Note that Tabbed by Server means the same as group by the database column. Many people find the tabbed grouping easier to read, quicker to navigate, and to just plain feel more natural because Toad's heavily used Schema Browser is primarily a tabbed design. Now note that in Figure 2.6 the database connections are cleanly grouped by database under tabs. Unlike the prior grouping technique, this one doesn't increase the data grid height and thereby increase mouse movements. Although you could argue that changing tabs also requires more mouse movement, it seems to be more acceptable to many users. That acceptance is probably again because Toad pioneered the tabbed visual design concept. So Toad users are accustomed to and seem to just like tabs.

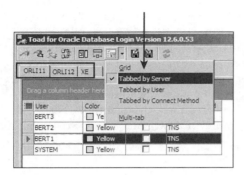

FIGURE 2.6   Grouping saved connection data grid—method 2

Remember that all data grids on any Toad screen operate the same way. So the data grids for the Toad Editor and Schema Browser introduced in the last chapter function identically. Furthermore Toad generally remembers all such data grid customizations so that once made they persist until you change them again. Hence all the techniques you've just learned here for the database connection screen's saved connection data grid except the drop-down visual styles will be utilized throughout Toad for any data grid you may encounter. Note that those using Toad versions prior to 11.0 will not see this data grid consistency as this was a more recent improvement.

Toolbars and Menus

As with most any modern Microsoft Windows application, Toad does enable the customization of both toolbars and menus for the main (that is, parent) window, as well as menus defining your own menu hot keys or keyboard shortcuts. Although many users never utilize this capability, it is one of the easiest ways to organize Toad such that you can locate things and navigate to them far more naturally—thus enhancing your overall productivity. Note that this topic was only very superficially covered in the prior chapter—here we dig into all the fun details.

Toad possesses many capabilities, many of which offer a main menu toolbar if you so desire. But of course turning them all on is probably not very efficient. You might prefer to customize which toolbars are displayed based upon how and what you're going to use Toad for. To do so you simply move the mouse to an open area of the main window's toolbar and right-click to display the menu pop-up shown in Figure 2.7. The top portion of the pop-up shows what menus can be displayed with check marks next to those currently selected. If, for example, you know that you're not going to use nor are interested in Team Coding, then you can simply uncheck that entry so that it's removed from the main menu toolbar. Note the self-explanatory choices near the middle and at the end of the menu for Restore Defaults and Lock Toolbars, respectively.

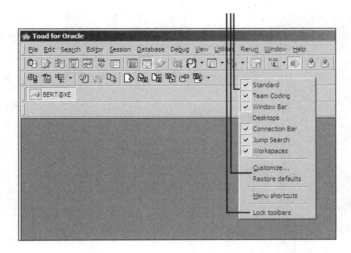

FIGURE 2.7   Customizing toolbars displayed

Now let's make some main window toolbar layout changes by choosing the customize choice in Figure 2.7 in order to launch the Customize pop-up window shown in Figure 2.8. After the Customize window is open you can move and display icons simply by dragging and dropping them:

▶ You can drag and drop additional, new command icons from the pop-up window onto any toolbar in order to add them. In Figure 2.8 the Oracle Parameters window has now been added as the first icon on the main toolbar.

▶ You also can drag and drop currently displayed toolbar icons from any toolbar back into the pop-up window, thereby removing them from that toolbar.

▶ Finally, while the Customize window is open you can drag and drop currently displayed toolbar icons from one location to another, thereby reordering them.

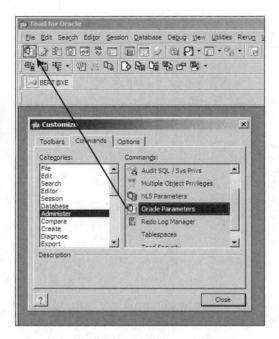

FIGURE 2.8   Customizing toolbars layout—method 1, drag and drop

There's also another, more visual and direct method to enable or disable the currently displayed toolbar icons. Many of the toolbars have a drop-down menu at their far-right end that offers an Add or Remove Buttons drop-down menu as shown in Figure 2.9. When that's activated you can now simply check or uncheck those items to display for that toolbar, the predefined list of all choices that make sense in the context of that toolbar's purpose, or that have been manually added via the Customize pop-up window. Note how Figure 2.9 shows the first choice to be the Oracle Parameters window that we added back in Figure 2.8.

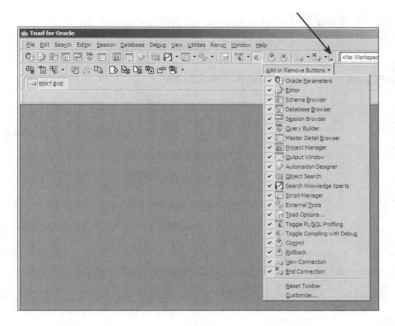

FIGURE 2.9   Customizing toolbars layout—method 2, Add or Remove Buttons menu

Also, for toolbars note that the thick separator bar at the far left of a toolbar can be used to move or relocate that toolbar. When you move the cursor over that thick separator it changes to a crossed-arrow look, which means you can now drag and drop the entire toolbar to a new location.

Keyboard Shortcut Keys

Referring back to Figure 2.7, when you choose Menu Shortcuts it launches the Toad Options screen that we briefly introduced in the last chapter. Note that the focus on the left-hand side tree view is now on Toolbars/Menus → Shortcuts, as shown in Figure 2.10.

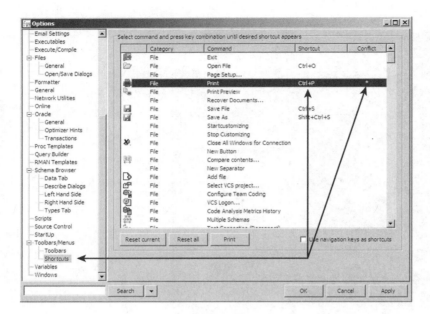

FIGURE 2.10 Customizing keyboard shortcuts

Note that in Figure 2.10 I've chosen to define Control+P as the keyboard shortcut for Print and that it conflicts with some other shortcut already defined as indicated by the asterisk (*) in the last column. Many Toad users spend a fair amount of time performing such keyboard shortcut customizations because they are heavy keyboard users and doing this permits them to work faster and be far more productive. In fact it's not uncommon for Toad users to define all their keyboard shortcuts to match some other environment where they normally work a lot, such as Microsoft Visual Studio. If you are a person who likes keyboard shortcuts, you may well find customizing Toad for your preferences and fingers' memory to be worthwhile.

Startup Windows/Screens

One of the most basic customizations that almost every Toad user wants to define is what screens automatically open upon a new database connection, and whether that screen is permitted just once per database connection and/or once per Toad instance running. Note that this topic was only very superficially covered in the prior chapter—here we'll once again dig into all the fun details.

By default Toad auto opens just an Editor screen whenever you establish a new database connection. However, as we learned in the prior chapter, both the Editor and Schema Browser are the two most used screens, and we'd like to have them both launch on a new database connection. Furthermore, maybe your preference is to have the Schema Browser display in the foreground (that is, up front) with the SQL Editor in the background. Thus, as before, you'll launch the Options screen by either clicking the 🖳 icon on the main window toolbar or choosing Main Menu → View → Toad Options, and then navigating to the left-hand tree view entry for Windows, as shown in Figure 2.11. Note the right side display. The column Auto Open is checked for the Editor (as well as the Schema Browser, which is not in view). The Auto-open Bring to Front option is a drop-down list that will display all the auto open checked screens, and you merely select the one you want to be up front. In this case that is the Schema Browser. Now on any new database connection, Toad will open the SQL Editor and Schema Browser, with the latter up front. You can select as many windows as you like to auto open; just note that you only get to select which one is the topmost.

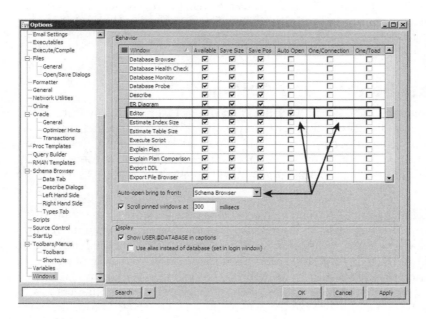

FIGURE 2.11   Customizing auto open windows

Also note that the more windows you set to auto open on a new database connection, the longer that process will take and the more system memory Toad will consume. Therefore, choose wisely. Setting more than, say, four to six windows to auto open might easily get out of hand, especially if you tend to connect to many databases while running Toad.

Because many Toad users remain in Toad for hours, days, or even weeks at a time (no kidding), the setting here can be a major detractor from your perceived Toad performance. We've seen users auto open six screens per connection with as many as ten connections per run, resulting in 60 screens in memory. You can't be in 60 places at once, so this would be quite suboptimal.

Lastly, note in Figure 2.11 the two highlighted columns at the far-right side for One/Connection and One/Toad for permitting only one running copy of a screen per database connection or one per instance of Toad running. These can be quite useful. For example, you might quite naturally want to open multiple Editor windows for a database connection to work on different types of queries. However, limit yourself to one Database Monitor window because by its very nature you can only benefit from one instance of it running for any given database—plus the screen's built-in queries are fairly expensive. As for the One/Toad option, its usage depends on your preferences. In general, windows that are not tied to a database connection and for which you really only need one to effectively perform all your work, such as the Automation Designer, Toad Advisor, and FTP Utility, are good candidates for this feature.

Startup Files, Scripts, and Actions

Sometimes when you start up Toad you'll want certain things to automatically just happen as part of the product launching. For example, maybe when you launch Toad you want the Connection screen to pop up, or for Toad to play its "ribbit" sound, or for some file to auto open within an Editor, or for some SQL command or script to automatically run. As you become a more advanced Toad user you will quickly find the need for such things.

As before, you launch the Options screen by either clicking the [icon] icon on the main window toolbar or by choosing Main Menu ➔ View ➔ Toad Options, and then navigating to the left-hand tree view entry for Startup, as shown in Figure 2.12. Note the four box highlighted options on the right-hand side. Most Toad users choose to disable playing the WAV file (that is, "ribbit") and for the Connection (that is, login) screen to auto launch (because you really cannot do database work if you're not connected). The other choices require a little more imagination. For example, you might want to INSERT a row of data into a logging table that says Toad connected at this date and time for this user so that you have a record of Toad usage. You really are limited here only by your imagination. We purposefully skipped covering actions here because they are covered in Chapter 8, "Getting Started with Toad Automation" (they require a complete description before setting this option will make sense).

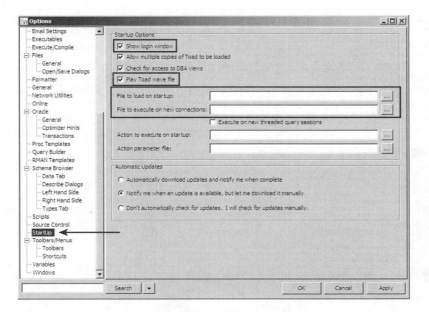

FIGURE 2.12   Common Toad startup options

Advanced Toad Customizations

If you've been paying attention to all the other prior mentions and figures for the Toad Options window, you've already started to imagine that there appear to be hundreds if not possibly even thousands of settings—and you would be correct. But don't let that scare you. Most defaults will suffice until you think to yourself, "I wish feature X worked a little differently." Then it will be time to come back to the Options screen to see whether it's possible, because much like the old Prego spaghetti TV commercials, "It's in there." However, many people routinely call support or post to the Toad web forum requests for a new feature that almost always is already in the Options. So you should just assume Toad can do what you want via Options until you absolutely find out or prove it cannot. I can honestly say that in my more than 15 years' experience, I've seen only a few new feature requests that were not already in the product and controllable via Options.

So how do you find the needle in the Options haystack? It's actually quite easy. Let's assume you wonder how Toad handles NULL values—which in the database world are always a special case. However, you have no idea where in the Options screen that setting might exist. The way to find a new or unknown option is a simple four-step process as shown in Figure 2.13:

1. Enter text for the likely name or concept in the Options screen Search box.

2. Click the Search button.

3. Double-click on items found and displayed below the Search box.

4. Toad automatically navigates to the proper left-hand tree view category and flashes a blinking circle on the right-hand side over the option setting.

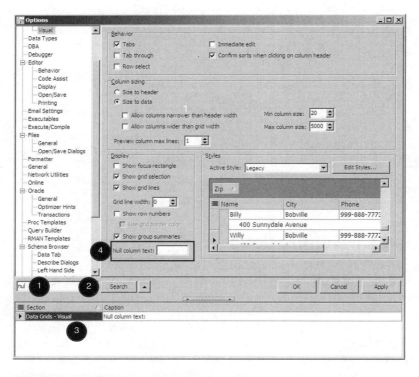

FIGURE 2.13   Finding new or unknown options

However, you cannot find nor learn every useful option by using such a hunt-and-peck method. So a good rule of advice is to focus on some key areas that you know are important, get them right, and then gradually learn more as your Toad experience broadens. You already know from this chapter and the prior one that the Editor and Schema Browser are the two most used screens and that they both contain data grids. That alone is sufficient information to direct your initial Options learning. Look at the box highlighted areas in Figure 2.14, and take 10–15 minutes to learn and set the options for these three key areas. If you are not sure what a particular option is for, simply select it (that is, mouse click on it) and press the F1 key—which launches Toad's help contextually for the item. Thus there's no need to go to the Main Menu → Help → Contents and then start blindly looking around for information on a topic. In fact, remember the F1 key, because it works this way almost anywhere within Toad.

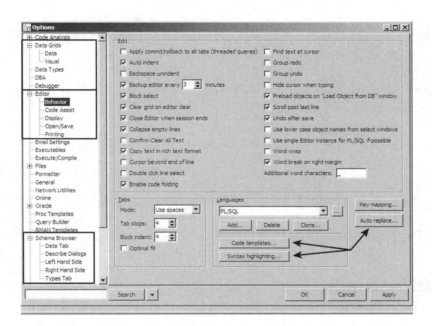

FIGURE 2.14   Initial options to focus on

Simply too many Toad options exist to cover them all, especially since on some Options categories buttons on the right-hand side of the screen launch pop-up windows with even more settings like those highlighted by arrows in Figure 2.14. In fact just clicking the Syntax Highlighting button in Figure 2.14 will result in the pop-up window shown in Figure 2.15—which all by itself has eight more tabs' worth of complex settings to define. In fact so many options exist that no one person probably knows them all at this point. Thus it's no exaggeration to say that there are literally thousands of options settings that you will have to learn over a long period of time. Just keep chipping away at them by learning new ones as your needs evolve.

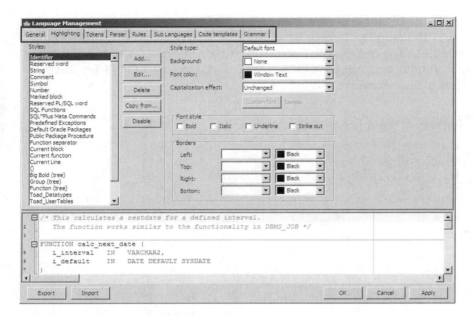

FIGURE 2.15   Options screen pop-ups for yet more options

Sharing Toad Settings

One of the most common Toad user questions (after both basic connectivity and configuration) is how to get the same options or settings (and thus behavior) as a buddy whose Toad works differently (that is, better) than one's own. Another common reason is that a team working together on a common project might like to share settings for consistency and standardization.

Beginning with Toad 12.5 the process to share all your settings is trivially easy: You simply choose Main Menu → Utilities → Copy User Settings, which launches the Copy User Settings window, as shown in Figure 2.16. In fact this screen offers three useful functionalities:

▶ You can copy your settings from a prior install of Toad. So if you have Toad 11.6 installed with all your settings chosen and then install Toad 12.0 but choose not to automatically copy over your settings, you can point to the old Toad install and copy over your settings to the new Toad install.

▶ You can zip up your settings and then give them to others via email, flash drive, or network share.

▶ You can quickly and easily reset all your settings back to the Toad defaults. This can be handy if you change a whole bunch of settings that you were not 100% sure about and end up with Toad not behaving as you like.

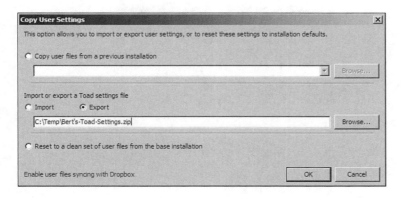

FIGURE 2.16   Sharing your user settings (that is, options)

Summary

This chapter provided a fast-track introduction for customizing Toad to substantially enhance your productivity. Toad's defaults are quite good and permit many users to hit the ground running; nonetheless a little time and effort to make Toad work your way is well worth the time invested. We started with simply organizing all of your database connections because most database work requires a connection, making this both a mandatory and recurring task. Next we examined customizing toolbars, menus, and keyboard shortcuts such that Toad looks, feels, and works the way you like. Then we covered automatic startup screens, files, and SQL commands or scripts that can automate certain critical tasks such as logging all Toad activity. Finally, we covered Toad's numerous options and how to locate them, learn them over time, and share them with other Toad users. In short this chapter armed you with all the key tools to increase your Toad effectiveness and efficiency, and thus your productivity, because for many users the justification for purchasing Toad was exactly that.

CHAPTER 3
Working with SQL

IN THIS CHAPTER

► Editor Window
► SQL Editor Output Area
► Object Describe
► Toad Insights
► Code Snippets
► SQL Recall
► Auto Replace
► Query Builder

This chapter covers various aspects of the SQL Editor window, such as

► Various modes to compile and execute code

► Using Toad history for past SQL

► Enhancing the interface to best fit your needs

► Using little-known items within the SQL Editor

► Code templates

► Building SQL without typing

Editor Window

Dell Software has a single editor now for all types of code, including SQL and PL/SQL. This editor is the main interface to Toad and enables the execution of SQL and SQL scripts, viewing data, saving data into various formats, and more. The SQL is saved in a history. Toad saves on keystrokes in a variety of ways; you can develop working SQL with a minimal amount of key entry. Toad also makes it easy for you to rerun recent work (using the Rerun menu button; see Figure 3.1).

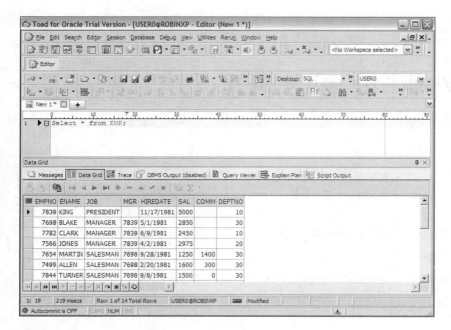

FIGURE 3.1   Toad SQL Editor panel

The SQL Editor is the main interface to Toad. Simply type in a SQL statement and click the green triangle execute button ▶. You can also press F9. This sends the SQL statement that the cursor is on (or the highlighted SQL) to the Oracle database. If the query is successful, then the data or success of the statement will be returned and displayed.

The Editor button 📄 makes opening additional Editor windows possible. This version of Toad enables you to open additional tabs in the Editor window. Simply right-click the tab just above the selected statement and select SQL or PL/SQL tab type. This opens another Editor window using the same database connection. Use the Editor button in the top-left row of buttons to open another Editor window, perhaps using a different connect string.

NOTE

Hover the mouse over any button to see a brief description of what it does.

TIP

You typically have three ways to do most any function in Toad:

▶ Menu item

▶ Keystroke

▶ Function key

Activating a menu item shows whether there is a button (it will appear) and any keystrokes that you can also use to activate the feature.

The top toolbar (refer to Figure 3.1), called the standard toolbar, provides access to various Toad browsers, features, commit/rollback, and initiating additional connections. Right-click on any of these top toolbars and you can select the ones you wish to have visible. By closing the ones you don't use, Toad can perhaps have a larger Editor window. The window toolbar shows the active Toad windows. There are also toolbars for team coding, desktops, connection, jump search, and workspaces. You can change the color border per your needs. Dan uses red borders for SYS and SYSTEM accounts, and then a different color for each different Oracle database to which he connects. The next toolbar enables you to open code from the file system or from the database and also offers access to other features. You can right-click on these toolbars to show or hide the ones you don't work with. The bottom toolbar has the Execute, Execute as Script, Clear, and Halt buttons. The Execute button ▶ will run all code in the Editor window. You can also just put the cursor on a SQL statement (if there are multiple SQL statements in the Editor window) and click this button. Toad will just execute the one SQL statement. Some people highlight the SQL they wish to execute. After execution, the Data Grid output tab will be populated. This technique works fine as well. The Execute as a script button ▶ runs the contents of the Editor window as if it were using a SQL*Plus character-mode interface. There is a separate Script Output tab for the result of this type of execution.

The Halt button ⏹ stops the current SQL execution. It will un-gray as SQL is executing in Toad. This feature is also dependent upon Toad Options ➔ Oracle ➔ Transactions Run in Threads selected.

The Clear button (see Figure 3.2 at the cursor position) clears the contents of the SQL Editor window. One of the authors likes to simply open a new tab (right-click the tab, and select New Tab) and put each individual unit of work in its own tab. Use the + next to the existing open tab to open others. These tabs are associated with a single connection to the Oracle database. This approach makes it easy to rerun prior SQL statements, particularly when testing. This technique is also useful for PL/SQL code such as packages. Putting the package specifications in one tab and the package body in another tab keeps the two separate. The package body won't compile correctly if any issue exists with the specifications, as shown in Figure 3.3. Dan likes to work with package specifications and the body in separate tabs for this reason. This is a good technique to follow. Toad automatically puts the package spec and body in separate tabs when opening a package either from a file or from the database. This feature is controlled by Toad Options ➔ Editor ➔ Open/Save Packages/Types settings. You can choose this behavior or turn this feature off.

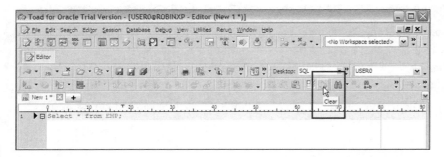

FIGURE 3.2   Clear button

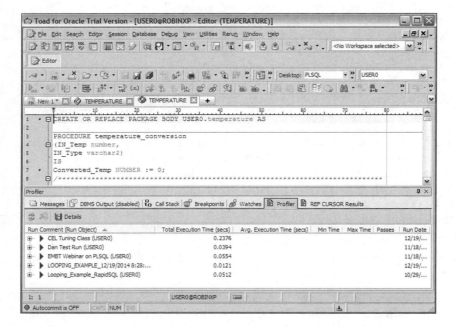

FIGURE 3.3   Toad with separate tabs for the package specification and body

TIP

You can also initiate multiple logins instead of using multiple tabs. Multiple logins can make moving data/objects between instances of Oracle a snap. Multiple tabs share the same database connection.

The toolbars are easy to configure. Right-click one to see the pop-up menu shown in Figure 3.4.

FIGURE 3.4   Configuring the toolbars

Notice the menu enables you to turn on and off the various toolbars. You can also configure the individual toolbars from here. You can delete unused buttons you find cluttering the toolbars, move buttons around, and add additional buttons. Figure 3.5 shows the toolbar configuration menu. The Toolbars tab enables you to turn toolbars on or off. The Commands tab enables you to add or delete buttons from each particular area of Toad. Drag and drop to move the buttons, remove the buttons, or add additional buttons. The Options tab enables you to turn on or off the mouse hover tips, change the size of the icons, and adjust how Toad stores your executed commands.

FIGURE 3.5   Configuring the toolbar buttons

Notice in Figure 3.4 that you can easily reset these options back to the Toad defaults.

TIP

One of the authors typically closes the Windows menu, and the Team Coding and Connections toolbars to give additional space to the editor windows.

SQL Editor Output Area

The data grid has a tool palette that enables the user to scroll up or down the returned rows, add rows, and delete rows (see Figure 3.6). Notice the light at the cursor along the bottom of the SQL Editor screen (see the cursor position in Figure 3.7). If this is red, then the data in this data grid cannot be changed and the commit/rollback/add/delete rows buttons will be grayed out. If the pseudo column ROWID was selected in the SQL, then this light will be green and the commit/rollback/add/delete rows palette will not be grayed out and the data can be changed.

FIGURE 3.6   Data Tool palette

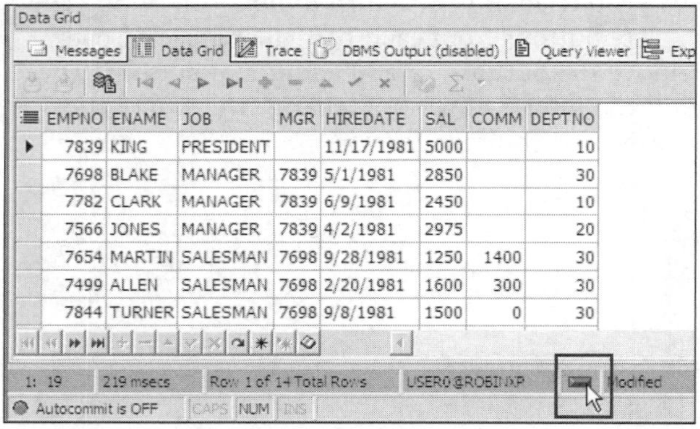

	EMPNO	ENAME	JOB	MGR	HIREDATE	SAL	COMM	DEPTNO
▶	7839	KING	PRESIDENT		11/17/1981	5000		10
	7698	BLAKE	MANAGER	7839	5/1/1981	2850		30
	7782	CLARK	MANAGER	7839	6/9/1981	2450		10
	7566	JONES	MANAGER	7839	4/2/1981	2975		20
	7654	MARTIN	SALESMAN	7698	9/28/1981	1250	1400	30
	7499	ALLEN	SALESMAN	7698	2/20/1981	1600	300	30
	7844	TURNER	SALESMAN	7698	9/8/1981	1500	0	30

1: 19   219 msecs   Row 1 of 14 Total Rows   USER0@ROBIN XP   Modified

Autocommit is OFF   CAPS NUM INS

FIGURE 3.7   Toad data grid

> **WARNING**
>
> Toad only retrieves 500 rows at a time. In Toad11+, moving the scroll bar retrieves the next 500 rows. In older Toad versions, if you move the data scroll bar on the right-hand side, Toad will retrieve all the remaining rows. Be careful!

Many output tabs are available in Toad. These tabs usually automatically display when a request occurs for the data contained to be displayed, such as when you execute the PL/SQL profiler. In that case the Profiler tab should automatically appear. Figure 3.8 shows this list.

FIGURE 3.8   Available output tabs

You can easily display or hide these tabs. Right-click the tab line to see all the tabs available. Simply adjust per your needs. You can also right-click the editor panel and select Desktop from that pop-up menu to get the same list.

The Breakpoints, Call Stack, and Watches tabs are all associated with the PL/SQL Debugger (covered in Chapter 6, "Working with PL/SQL"). The Data Grid tab is associated with any SQL select statement execution. Data grids appear throughout Toad, and the options that are available for this data grid are also available for any data grid. The DBMS Output tab shows any DBMS_OUTPUT.Put_Line output from a PL/SQL routine. The Explain Plan tab (discussed later this chapter and again in Chapter 10, "Toad as a SQL Tuning Tool") shows the SQL execution plan; it also has many display options. To populate this tab, click the Explain Plan button 🖩. The Messages tab shows any output from the executed SQL, including error messages (its real value). The Navigator tab displays the Navigator panel to the left of the Editor window. The Profiler tab is associated with the PL/SQL Profiler discussed in Chapter 6. The Query Viewer tab shows SQL and PL/SQL that was executed in the SQL window and some interesting statistics such as how long it took to execute. This information is useful for either rerunning that exact same SQL or when doing performance tuning (to easily compare one SQL execution with another). The REF CURSOR Results tab is also associated with PL/SQL execution. The Script Output tab shows character-mode output when the Run as Script button is clicked for execution. Team Coding illustrates others' participation in coding of particular PL/SQL code and is covered in Chapter 7, "Miscellaneous Tools." The Trace tab enables SQL statistics and/ or SQL Trace files to be generated and displayed for this particular SQL statement. Notice that you can enable both Auto Trace and SQL Trace from this tab (see Figure 3.9). The

Trace tab is discussed in detail in Chapter 10. The remaining items on this menu deal with these tabs themselves—which ones appear when Toad starts up, where they appear—and this includes saving the changes for the next time Toad is started, as well as restoring the default settings from when Toad was originally installed.

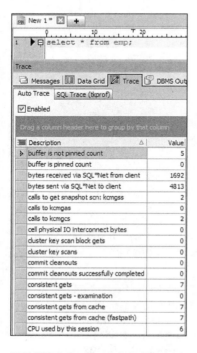

FIGURE 3.9   Toad Auto Trace

Clicking the Explain Plan button on the lower-left SQL Editor toolbar shows the Oracle explain plan for the SQL just executed. Right-clicking in this window enables the display to be adjusted.

The Auto Trace tab provides a variety of SQL runtime statistics. You can enable this feature using the check box or right-click in the editor window and select Auto Trace to enable, and then re-execute the SQL to populate the Auto Trace panel. Notice that you can also run a SQL trace on this particular SQL from the SQL Trace sub-tab. This feature needs the ALTER SESSION privilege; SQL trace is covered in detail in Chapter 10. Toad will run the SQL trace and either bring up the output using the TKProf Wizard or the Trace File browser, depending on which feature of Toad you have purchased.

NOTE

The Auto Trace, SQL Trace, and Explain Plan tabs are covered in detail in Chapter 10.

Object Describe

The F4, or Describe Object button, is one of the most versatile features of Toad. Simply put the cursor on a function, table, or other object in the editor window and press the F4 key, and detail about the object appears. The F4 or Describe window is useful for displaying object information and table information including data, syntax, and statistics. You can also access this screen by entering DESC <object *name*> in the SQL Editor.

Figure 3.10 shows a Describe Objects panel. You can call one up by pressing F4 with the cursor on the EMP table in the editor window. Notice the tabs across the center of the screen. Using those tabs you can easily access the other related objects, constraints, statistics, code, privileges, and more.

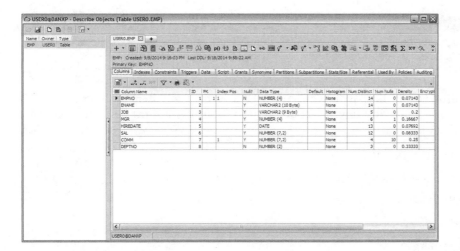

FIGURE 3.10   Describe Objects panel

You can drag and drop column names on the Columns tab onto the SQL window and show other information such as available indexes, constraints, triggers, and so on from this interface as well. This section covers the more important tabs individually.

TIP

You can drag and drop columns displayed in the Columns tab into the SQL window—SQL coding without typing!

The location of the Describe Objects panel can be adjusted. Figure 3.11 shows the buttons that control how the panel appears on the screen.

FIGURE 3.11   EMP Table Describe Objects panel buttons

NOTE

Toad 11 and newer put a new tab in this Describe Objects panel for each additional object being described. Older Toads open a new Describe Objects panel for each.

Buttons across the top of this panel (see Figure 3.12) control many items surrounding the object. Use the mouse and hover over any button to display a short description of its function. These buttons include:

▶ Add objects to this object

▶ Add to project manager (discussed later in this book)

▶ Alter/analyze/audit

▶ Compare

▶ Create another similar

▶ Create a script

▶ Show in various diagrammers

▶ Generate SQL (generates a select/insert/update/delete and puts it on the clipboard)

▶ Count/truncate

FIGURE 3.12   EMP Table Describe Tab buttons

WARNING

Toad is *not* one of those tools in which you should just click the button to see what it does. For example, if you have permissions to delete rows, the Truncate button will delete *all* the rows! Be careful out there!

The Script tab, shown in Figure 3.13, creates a script that could be saved and used to re-create the object. You can copy this script into a file and use it when creating a test environment for your application. Figure 3.14 shows the options available when you click the Options button on this script panel. Notice the adjustments you can make to the scripts. You can include the data, include drop statements, exclude schema owners (useful when setting up tables/objects for other users), and make other adjustments. Figure 3.15 illustrates the other content that you can include in the script output as well.

TIP

The author finds the ability to create scripts from this Scripts tab incredibly useful when creating a test environment for an application change.

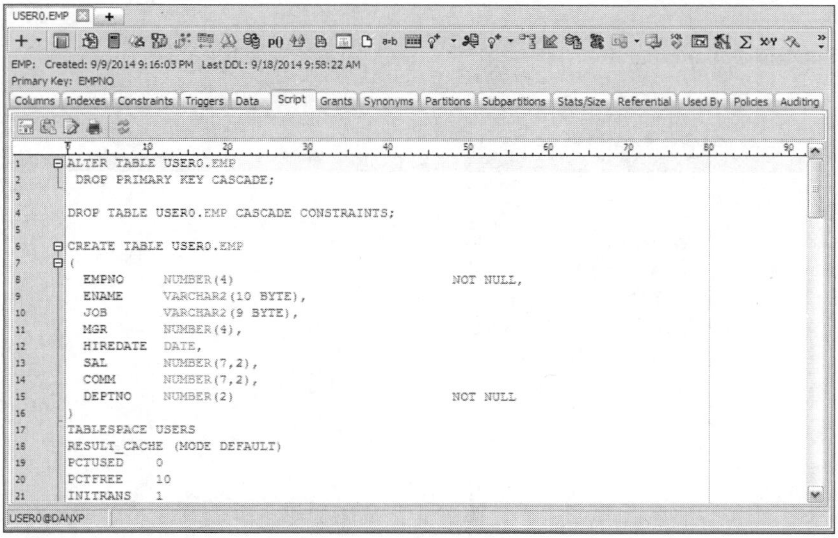

FIGURE 3.13   EMP Table Describe Object panel showing Script tab

FIGURE 3.14   Script Tab Options panel

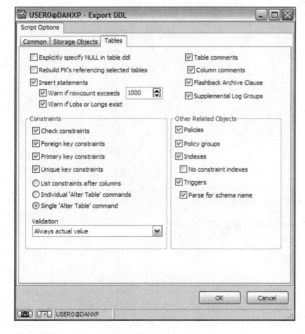

FIGURE 3.15   Script Tab Tables Option tab

The Export DDL button (shown in Figure 3.16) enables easy DDL syntax generation. Notice all the options available for optional syntax in the panel in Figure 3.17.

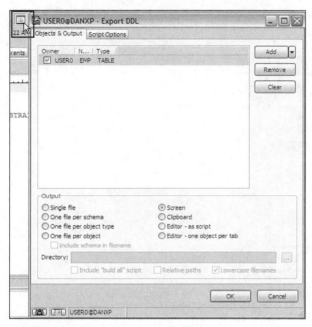

FIGURE 3.16   Export DDL panel

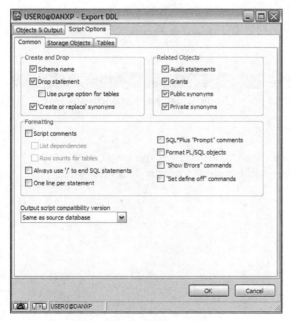

FIGURE 3.17   Export DDL Options panel

Figure 3.18 shows another data grid but just for the object selected. You can see the same navigation and data control buttons as discussed earlier for the SQL Editor Data Grid tab. Many features are common to all data grids and these are covered in detail in Chapter 5, "Working with Data."

EMPNO	ENAME	JOB	MGR	HIREDATE	SAL	COMM	DEPTNO
7839	KING	PRESIDENT		11/17/1981	5000		10
7698	BLAKE	MANAGER	7839	5/1/1981	2850		30
7782	CLARK	MANAGER	7839	6/9/1981	2450		10
7566	JONES	MANAGER	7839	4/2/1981	2975		20
7654	MARTIN	SALESMAN	7698	9/28/1981	1250	1400	30
7499	ALLEN	SALESMAN	7698	2/20/1981	1600	300	30
7844	TURNER	SALESMAN	7698	9/8/1981	1500	0	30
7900	JAMES	CLERK	7698	12/3/1981	950		30
7521	WARD	SALESMAN	7698	2/22/1981	1250	500	30
7902	FORD	ANALYST	7566	12/3/1981	3000		20
7369	SMITH	CLERK	7902	12/17/1980	800		20
7788	SCOTT	ANALYST	7566	12/9/1982	3000		20
7876	ADAMS	CLERK	7788	1/12/1983	1100		20
7934	MILLER	CLERK	7782	1/23/1982	1300		10

Row 1 of 14 total rows

USER0@ROBINXP

FIGURE 3.18   Data Grid panel

TIP

Be careful with large amounts of data on this panel. Use the Esc key to cancel any long-running data retrieval.

Clicking the Generate Statement button (see Figure 3.19) enables the easy creation of an Insert, Update, or Select statement from the visible columns of this data grid. Make your selection and then *paste* into the SQL Editor.

Generate Insert Statement
Generate Merge Statement
Generate Update Statement
Generate Select Statement

FIGURE 3.19   Generate Statement panel

Toad Insights

Toad provides easy creation of SQL. The previously mentioned Describe Objects panel enables you to drag and drop columns out of any table object into the SQL Editor. You can also enter the table name (or table alias) with a single period, the table name, another period, and partial leading column spelling, and Toad will pop up a box containing your table object columns and column attributes. Figure 3.20 shows a table with just a single period.

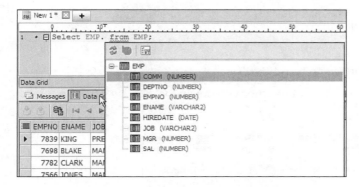

FIGURE 3.20   Toad Insights pop-up panel

You can double-click a column in this pop-up window, or multiple select using the mouse and either the Shift (list of items) or Ctrl buttons (specific items in the list) and then press the Enter or Return key to add the items to your code at the current cursor position. Notice in Figure 3.21, three columns were selected, and Toad qualified each with the table name! If you are utilizing table aliases, Toad remembers these and will qualify your code correctly.

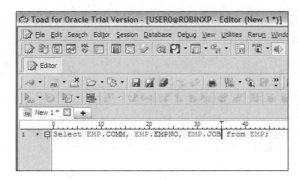

FIGURE 3.21   SQL Editor after using Insights

Notice earlier in Figure 3.20 that the items appearing in the Insights panel are in alphabetical order. One of the authors prefers the order as they appear in the object. Notice the Options button on the Insights panel. You can also access this area via the Configure Toad Options button on the top toolbar.

Figure 3.22 shows the Toad Insights configuration options. Notice that you can define the objects that this feature works on along the top. The center part of this screen allows you to

▶ Turn off the feature

▶ Cache the results (default)

▶ Display as text

▶ Sort the list (the author prefers to turn this off)

▶ Delay the popup (handy for those of us who type slowly...)

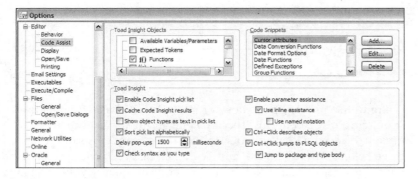

FIGURE 3.22   Insights Configuration panel

You can see some other items (discussed in Chapter 6) such as the Enable parameter assistance (sometimes the author turns this off as it can slow down PL/SQL coding), and some other built-in keystroke assistance.

Code Snippets

Toad contains bits of code called code snippets. These snippets contain most of the SQL functions, date formats, hints, and other bits of SQL and PL/SQL code that are of interest to the Oracle developer. Toad configuration options make it possible for additional items to be added or existing items to be changed.

To see the Code Snippets panel choose View → Code Snippets. The panel then appears and auto hides along the right side of Toad (see Figure 3.23). The push pin button can make the panel remain visible on your desktop.

FIGURE 3.23   Code Snippets panel

You simply drag and drop the code pieces from this panel to your code.

Figure 3.24 shows the various categories for the snippets. There are snippets for date formatting, various function templates for almost anything, and even SQL Optimizer hints (discussed some in Chapter 10).

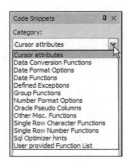

FIGURE 3.24   Code Snippets code categories

These snippets are configurable as well. Click the Configure Toad Options button (or access via the menu using View → Toad Options) and visit the Editor → Code Assistant panel as shown in Figure 3.25. This panel enables you to either clean up the categories you will never use, or better yet, add your own custom code snippets that you can easily add to your code via drag and drop.

FIGURE 3.25   Configuring code snippets

SQL Recall

Toad saves all the work that was done in any of the editor windows.

ALT+Up Arrow and Alt+Down Arrow walk through this storage area. Choose View → SQL Recall or press F8 (see Figure 3.26) to open the interface shown in Figure 3.27.

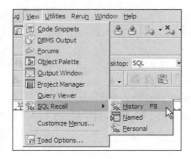

FIGURE 3.26   Accessing SQL Recall

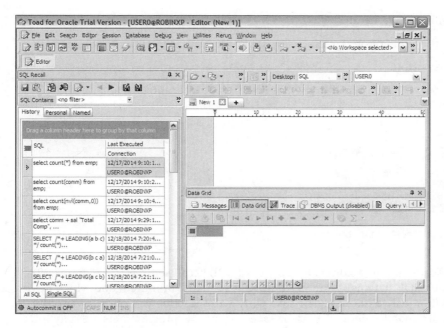

FIGURE 3.27   SQL Recall panel

Notice that the SQL Recall panel shows up as an autohide panel on the left side of Toad.

You simply double-click a SQL statement in this panel and Toad will open a new tab and put the SQL in it.

TIP

One of the authors uses this SQL Recall during SQL tuning. If a prior SQL statement worked better, then it is easy to find and revisit.

This version of Toad enables the SQL to be moved to the Personal tab or the Named tab. Simply click the Edit Selection button in the SQL Recall window, and then select the Personal or Named option from the Type drop-down menu.

The buttons on the top of this panel (see Figure 3.28) enable you to do the following:

▶ Save selected SQL to a file

▶ Copy selected SQL to the clipboard

▶ Edit the selected SQL (allows for the SQL to be added to the Personal or Named tabs, which makes finding SQL easier, perhaps)

▶ Delete from the SQL Recall

▶ Load into the SQL Editor (Append, New Tab, or Replace into current tab)

▶ Navigation buttons

▶ Export/Import all the SQL (useful when updating Toad or moving to a new computer)

FIGURE 3.28   SQL Recall panel buttons

The Configure Toad Option ➜ Editor ➜ Code Assist SQL Recall settings (see Figure 3.29) control how many SQL statements are saved (max is virtually unlimited) and which SQL will be saved (all, or just valid ones). The Save Only Valid Statements option saves only the successful SQL, enabling more SQL to be saved. Typically, programmers are only interested in the SQL statements that didn't have syntax errors.

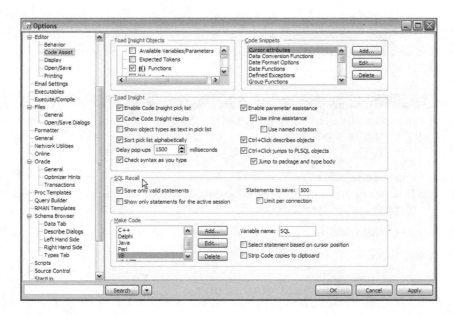

FIGURE 3.29   SQL Recall options

Auto Replace

Auto replace is like a spell checker; in fact, this feature actually does correct some spelling errors as well as correct obsolete code. This feature is activated via the space bar. It takes the last item entered since the prior space bar and compares it to a list. If the text is found in the list, the auto replace item is automatically substituted.

This feature is nice for long column names perhaps (although Toad Insights is a better mechanism for this), but it is used more for commonly entered items such as sf for SELECT * FROM or pl for DBMS_OUTPUT.PUTLINE( );.

Chapter 6 discusses a way to use existing code templates and how to add your own.

In an editor window, type in "teh" and when you press the space bar, it will be corrected quickly to "the." The space bar activates the check. If an item is in the Auto Replace panel, it is substituted.

To remove some auto correct items or to add your own (a good place to add any coding shortcut!), choose View → Toad Options, visit Editor → Behavior, and click the Auto Replace button on the lower-right part of the Behavior panel.

> **NOTE**
>
> Notice all the items that you can control in an editor window from this Behavior panel.

> **TIP**
>
> Dan uses this feature to code his own coding shortcuts.

This button opens the dialog in Figure 3.30. Notice the "teh" in the left side and the "the" in the right column.

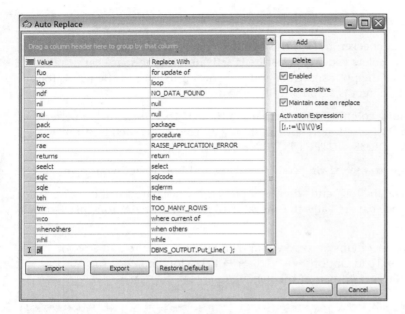

FIGURE 3.30   Adding an Auto Replace correct item

To add your own code assistants, click the Add button and fill in the grid as shown in Figure 3.30. One of the authors uses DBMS_OUTPUT.Put_Line frequently, so he wants a pl shortcut for it. Figure 3.31 shows the output when pl is entered and the space bar is tapped.

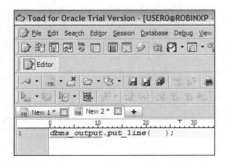

FIGURE 3.31   Auto Replace used for coding shortcuts

Query Builder

Toad has a nice Query Builder feature. This feature enables SQL code to be built using mouse operations. This feature is excellent for power users, analysts, and managers using Toad to create reports and access data but who have little knowledge of the SQL language.

The Query Modeler button is on the standard toolbar (the top menu bar, see Figure 3.32). You can also access it via Database ➔ Report ➔ Query Builder, and the button also appears on the ER Diagrammer panel.

FIGURE 3.32   Query Builder button

The object palette appears on the right (if it doesn't automatically appear, click View ➔ Object Palette). The various items that can be included in a select statement appear on the left. Figure 3.33 shows the canvas with both the EMP table and the DEPT table. These were added using either a double-click operation on each in the object palette or a drag and drop mouse operation from the object palette to the canvas. Notice how Toad built the SQL in the bottom Generated Query tab. As you click on the column names, Query Builder will adjust the SQL! The query can be executed from here, saved, and even moved to a tab in the SQL Editor!

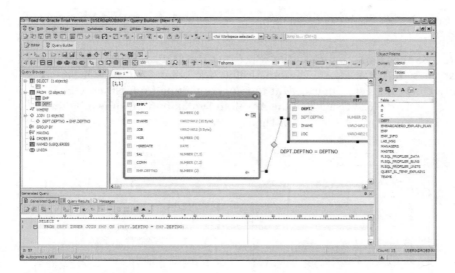

FIGURE 3.33   Query Builder in action

To add WHERE, GROUP BY, HAVING, UNION, and the other clauses, simply double-click the syntax item of interest and use mouse operations to draw in the options you desire. Figure 3.34 shows the Where Conditions clause panel, accessed by double-clicking the Where in the left Query Builder panel (titled Query Browser). Buttons on the toolbar control and bring up these same wizards. You can also build WHERE clauses by simply dragging a column of interest from the canvas object and drop it on the WHERE clause. This feature works for the other items in the left panel as well. If the operation is a valid request, a wizard will appear to finish the syntax.

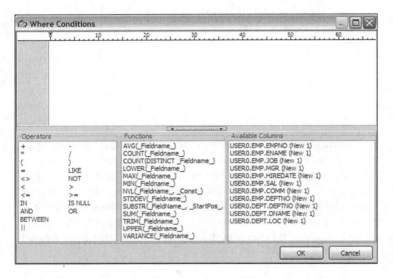

FIGURE 3.34   Query Builder using the Where item

Notice in Figure 3.35 that some columns were selected in the EMP and DEPT tables in the canvas and that the syntax was adjusted automatically. Also notice that the SQL syntax is using ANSI joins. Query Builder is an excellent tool for converting from either ANSI SQL to standard Oracle SQL or vice versa! Click the Ansi Join Syntax button, shown by the cursor in Figure 3.35, and you get the SQL in Figure 3.36!

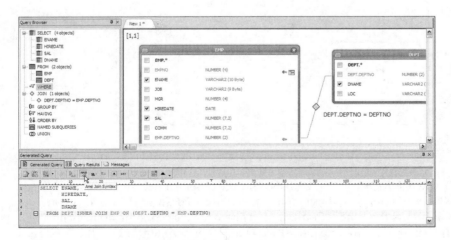

FIGURE 3.35   Query Builder ANSI SQL

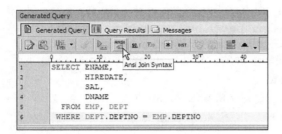

FIGURE 3.36   Query Builder Oracle SQL

Figure 3.37 shows the Generated Query panel control buttons. The first two buttons enable the generated SQL to be copied to either the editor (a new tab) or to the clipboard. The SQL Optimize button is a purchased feature of Toad (it enables the SQL to be automatically tuned). The Execute Query button will run the SQL from the Query Builder interface and populate the other two tabs present. The Add Table name button enables all the columns to be qualified. The next two buttons make it possible for either an * or the distinct clause to be added to the generated SQL.

FIGURE 3.37   Generated Query Panel control buttons

The Update Diagram and Update SQL can be useful buttons. You can make changes to the SQL via typing or you can paste a SQL statement into this generated SQL area and click the Update Diagram button, and the diagram in the canvas will be updated. Likewise, you can make changes to the diagram in the canvas and click the Update SQL button, and the changes will be made to your generated SQL. The Ansi button is a toggle; it will rewrite your SQL using ANSI join syntax if clicked. The Add Schema Name to Tables and Add Table Names to Column buttons are also toggle buttons. If clicked down, the SQL text will be adjusted accordingly. The final two buttons (Run Query in Threads and Allow Modify Query Results) pertain to how you would like to execute the SQL and possibly have the ability to change results from within the Query Builder environment.

You can add your own subqueries and calculations. There are right-click options under each object on the canvas, different options when right-clicking the object header on the canvas, and others. Calculations are easy to add by either

▶ Right-clicking the select line on the left Query Builder panel and selecting Add New Expression Column as shown in Figure 3.38.

▶ Adjusting the text in the Generated Query and clicking the Update Diagram button.

Options for each of the other items appear in this left panel as well. Just right-click and check out the various options. Right-clicking the columns on the canvas enables column aliases to be added. Right-clicking the table name enables an alias to be defined. Remember that a button on the Generated Query panel can add the table name or alias to all the columns in the SQL (a good idea).

There isn't any SQL that cannot be built using Query Builder. Figure 3.38 shows a calculated column, sal * 1.1, being added to the query.

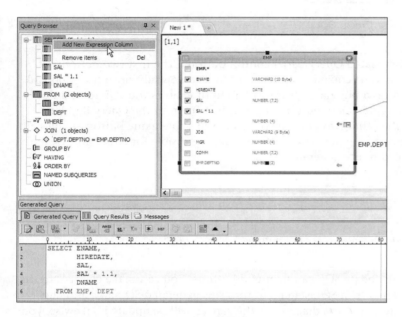

FIGURE 3.38   Adding calculations using Query Builder

Summary

This chapter covered various aspects of the main SQL Editor window. It is easy to build SQL, using the describe function and code snippets. You can enhance Toad for your own coding style using Auto Replace. Toad remembers the SQL that it has worked with. This chapter also covered the Query Builder, a useful tool for those new to Oracle but who have a need to access data within the Oracle RDBMS.

CHAPTER 4

Schema Browser

IN THIS CHAPTER

▶ Configuring the Schema Browser

▶ Creating and Editing Objects

▶ Printing Data Using FastReport

▶ Using the Reports Manager

The Schema Browser is a useful interface to the various database objects. It is similar to the Describe Objects panel discussed in Chapter 3, "Working with SQL," except that with this interface, you can see and easily click on any object.

> **TIP**
>
> Dan usually opens both an Editor window and a Schema Browser window and uses the Window ➔ Tile Vertical option to display both panels at the same time within Toad.

Configuring the Schema Browser

The Schema Browser is a way to see the objects you have available. This configurable window has information useful to database administrators as well as developers. Sometimes developers have to do some of their own admin work within a test or development environment. Toad and this Schema Browser window are useful tools for both kinds of users.

Figure 4.1 shows the Schema Browser. You can open more than one Schema Browser. Choosing Database ➔ Schema Browser also opens the Schema Browser. A reason for opening more than one Schema Browser could be if the user were connected to more than one Oracle instance. The Schema Browser button (upper left-most, second button) can open additional Schema Browser windows.

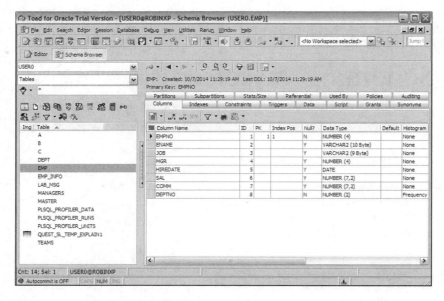

FIGURE 4.1   Schema Browser window

The Schema Browser is easy to configure by using the drop-down menu shown in Figure 4.2. Notice that this Toad is configured for the drop-down object display in the far-left panel in Figure 4.1. Figure 4.3 shows the tabbed single row of tabs and Figure 4.4 shows the tree view (which is similar to what you might find in other tools).

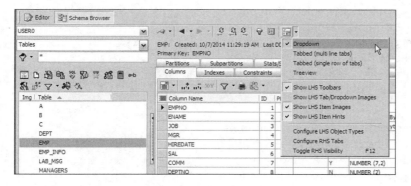

FIGURE 4.2   Object display drop-down menu

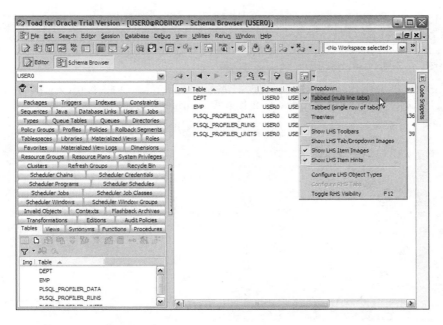

FIGURE 4.3   Object display tabbed display

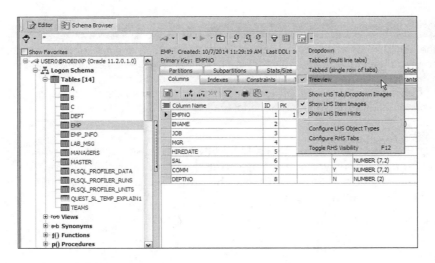

FIGURE 4.4   Object display tree view

The two tabbed options have an additional feature (as shown in Figure 4.5) where you can hide the object information within each tab from display if this information is not of value to you.

You can right-click on the tabs, or you can use the options drop-down menu (see Figure 4.4) and select Configure LHS Object Types. Notice the buttons on the lower-left part of the Configure Browser Tabs tab—one for putting the tabs in alphabetical order and another to restore the Toad original settings.

In Figure 4.4, LHS stands for left-hand side of the Schema Browser, and RHS is the right-hand side of the browser. This Schema Browser is highly configurable for the type of person using Toad.

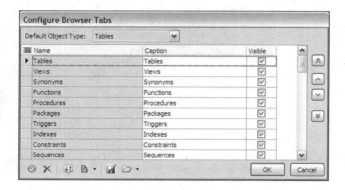

FIGURE 4.5   Configuring object display

NOTE

Dan asked for the ability to reset various aspects of Toad back to their original settings, based on the lab environment he used to use for his on-site training. He has a good working relationship with the Toad team. The Toad team has included buttons like the Restore Defaults button throughout the tool. The ToadWorld.com site has a page for users to make recommended updates and new features to Toad.

Toad enables any of the object names on the left to be filtered. This is really handy when there are hundreds of objects displayed and the objects desired have a specific pattern. Notice in Figure 4.6 that the filter is set to EMP*. Use the * for a global search character and press Return or Enter to activate the filter.

FIGURE 4.6   Filtering objects

Toad enables adding and maintaining all the various object types in the Oracle RDBMS. Each tab or object type has specific buttons for that function. These buttons enable the user to create a similar object, maintain the object, and so on. Each object type has specific tasks that apply to it.

NOTE

This chapter focuses on the table objects.

WARNING

The buttons on each of these object tabs will provide Oracle functionality only if the user has permissions at the Oracle database level to do so. Toad is NOT one of those tools where you click the button to see what it does! You can get into trouble very quickly if you have lots of permissions and you are not careful.

The Schema Browser enables objects to be selected and grouped together on a single tab. Right-click in the LHS and select Add to SB Favorites List. The first time you do this, there will not be any folders. Click Add Folder to add one. Favorite Folders are a way of organizing commonly accessed items. Select a folder to add the selected item and it will be there for future reference. Figure 4.7 shows the EMP table being added to a Favorite folder.

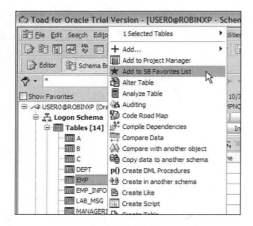

FIGURE 4.7   Using the Favorites List

In Figure 4.7, you can also add objects to the project manager. Project manager also enables this grouping of objects and works across the Toad tool. Chapter 7, "Miscellaneous Tools," covers the project manager in detail.

To view your favorites, use the tree view and select the Show Favorites box. This opens a box and makes visible all the folders currently created (see Figure 4.8).

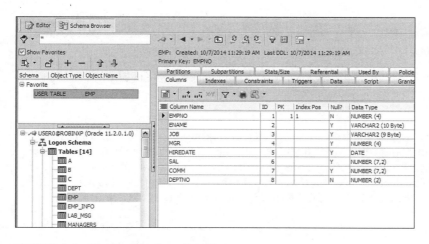

FIGURE 4.8   Viewing the Favorites List

Buttons on each of these tabs enable the creation and maintenance of the object referenced in the tab. For example, the Tables tab (refer to Figures 4.1 through 4.3, or 4.6) has buttons that enable Toad to

▶ create a script 🔲

▶ create a new table 🔲

▶ alter a table 🔲

▶ export data 🔲

▶ load into the Query Builder 🔲

▶ load into the Code Road Map 🔲

▶ view/change permissions 🔲

▶ add constraints 🔲

▶ compute statistics 🔲

▶ create a synonym 🔲

▶ rebuild the table 🔲

▶ compile dependencies 🔲

▶ filter the tables in this view 🔲

▶ drop the table 🔲

▶ truncate the data in the table 🔲

Toad will not allow any activity that the user ID does not have Oracle permissions to perform. Like with all other buttons in Toad, simply hover the cursor over the button for a simple description of what the button does.

The buttons in Figure 4.9 show the current database connections 🔲, present the SQL Browser history with a drop-down menu to access individual items 🔲, refresh the list on the left, refresh just the current list on the left, refresh the list on the right 🔲, clear all filters 🔲, show the browser legend 🔲, and show the Schema Browser options 🔲.

FIGURE 4.9   Schema Browser control buttons

Creating and Editing Objects

Toad makes it possible to create and edit any object, and in several cases, copy from other existing objects. Toad has quite a few administrative functions that fall into this category (editing of objects) and which are covered later in this book.

This chapter reviews creating and editing tables, indexes, and users.

> **NOTE**
>
> The menu item Database ➔ Create starts wizards to create just about any object in Oracle.

> **NOTE**
>
> The connected Toad user needs the Create Table privileges to create tables and indexes. The Toad user needs the correct database permissions to be able to execute any syntax generated by Toad.

The Schema Browser enables easy access to the wizards that can create any database object. Use the Create Table button on the LHS on the Tables tab (see Figure 4.10) to start the Create Table wizard. Because it was started from the Schema Browser, the current schema user is plugged in. Notice Toad is current to Oracle12 with the virtual default column values. The data types are selected from the visual drop-down menu. You can maintain these items (and delete them if there are way too many for your needs) using Main Menu ➔ View ➔ Toad Options ➔ Data Types (see Figure 4.11).

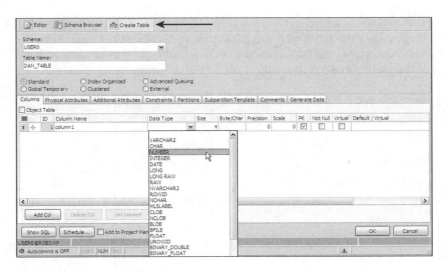

FIGURE 4.10   Create Table wizard

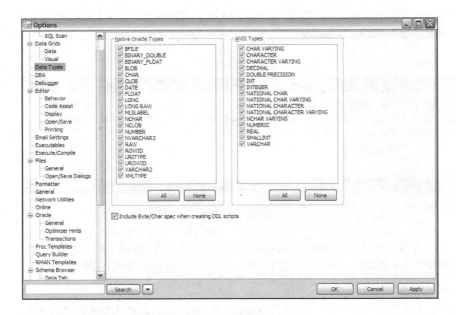

FIGURE 4.11   Toad Options → Data Types panel

Figure 4.12 shows some columns added to the new table. Notice the various tabs (including Generate Data to populate the table with test data) that are available to control literally every aspect of this object. Notice this table object covers all table types available for the latest version of the Oracle RDBMS that this version of Toad supports.

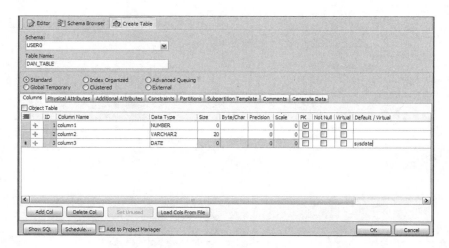

FIGURE 4.12   Create Table wizard in action

NOTE

Keeping your Toad product current is rather important. Older Toad products do not have the current Oracle RDBMS syntax, and you may be missing important performance syntax that is available but not to your old version of Toad.

WARNING

When you click the OK button, Toad will execute the syntax generated!

You can choose Show SQL and schedule this object to create at a different time. Figure 4.13 shows the Show SQL button output. Notice the syntax is correct. This is also a nice way to learn the newer syntax for the latest Oracle RDBMS features.

TIP

The author likes to use these wizards to create the SQL syntax, and then he clicks on the Show SQL button and copies/pastes that syntax into a script he is building to create/refresh his test environment.

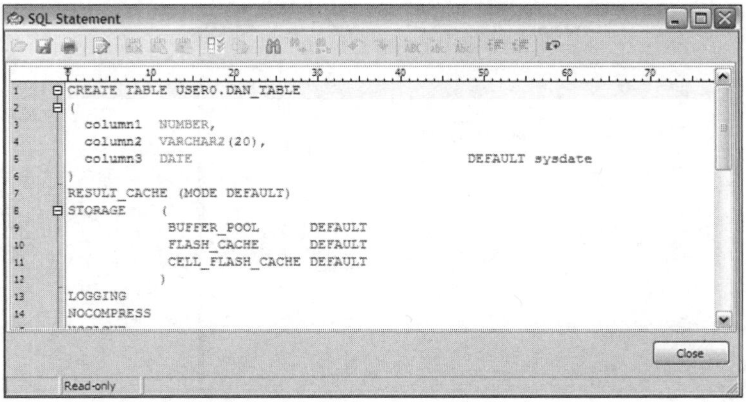

FIGURE 4.13   Show SQL button output

Printing Data Using FastReport

Toad makes possible the simple printing of the data grid. Right-click on any data grid and select Print, as shown in Figure 4.14. You can see in the Main Menu → View → Toad Options → Editor → Printing pane (see Figure 4.15) that you can set fonts, headings, footings, and more. Toad formats and prints the data that is selected from the parameters and columns that appear in the data grid. Chapter 5, "Working with Data," discusses more about formatting and selecting data in these data grids.

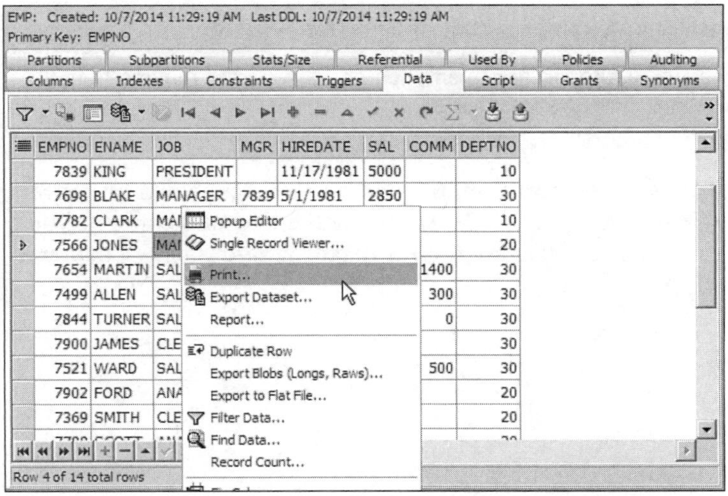

FIGURE 4.14   Printing from a data grid

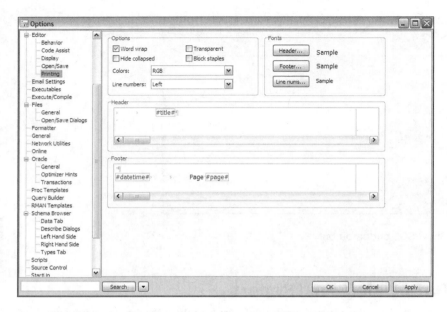

FIGURE 4.15   Configure Toad Options → Editor → Printing panel

Toad contains a product called FastReport that serves as a primer on using FastReport from within the Toad environment. Please note that FastReport is a full-featured report writer and its output can be embedded in Toad's Reports Manager (covered next in this chapter in the section "Using the Reports Manager").

TIP

You can download the complete FastReport documentation and a separate runtime from the Internet. Google "FastReport" for more information.

Right-click on any data grid and select Report from the pop-up menu as shown in Figure 4.16. This starts the Report wizard (see Figure 4.17). Arranging the data and columns you want in the report in the data grid before starting the FastReport wizard is best. Chapter 5 covers formatting data grid output.

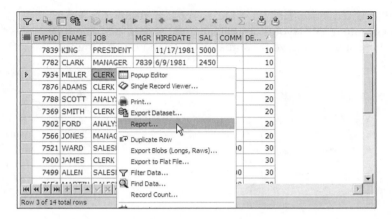

FIGURE 4.16   Data grid output menu

FIGURE 4.17   Report wizard

NOTE

The data is sorted in DEPTNO sequence. This allows for the Groups to be illustrated.

This wizard has four tabs that control the fields, groups, layout, and style of the report. Select the columns you desire for your report (see Figure 4.18). Notice that you can either select and move the columns in the order they are to appear on the reports, or you can highlight the selected items in the right side and use the up/down arrows to move the columns around.

Because the data is in DEPTNO sequence, let's illustrate doing data groups (see Figure 4.19). The Style tab enables basic report layouts, and Figure 4.20 shows the basic styles available. You can create these styles using your company's logo and other common formatting features.

FIGURE 4.18   Report wizard Fields selection panel

FIGURE 4.19   Report wizard Groups panel

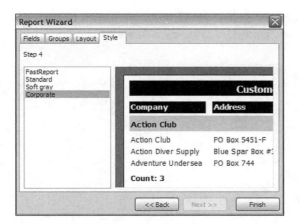

FIGURE 4.20   Report wizard Style panel

Figure 4.21 shows the output of the wizard. This is where the FastReport documentation would be helpful. If you have a working knowledge of report writers, many of these items should be familiar to you.

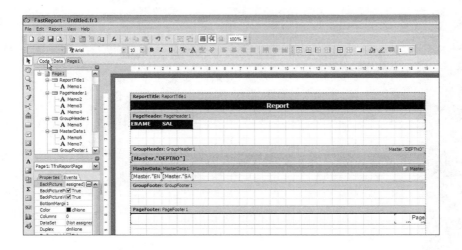

FIGURE 4.21   Report wizard output

On the far upper left, click on the Code tab, and then click the green run script button on the page that appears (see Figure 4.22) to run your report. Figure 4.23 shows the output.

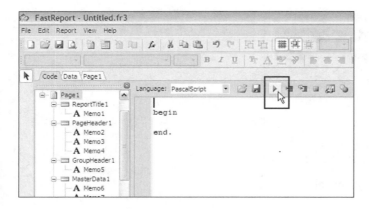

FIGURE 4.22   FastReport Code tab

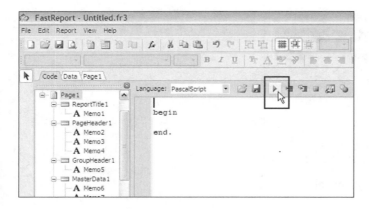

FIGURE 4.23   FastReport finished report

Close the Print Preview window, and then save your new report using the Save button. Figure 4.24 shows the resulting dialog. Notice the report is being named EMP_Report.fr3. The next part of this chapter shows how to add this report to the Toad Reports Manager.

FIGURE 4.24   Saving the finished report

Using the Reports Manager

In the last section you created a report using the FastReport wizard. Follow these simple steps to add the new report to the Toad Reports Manager:

1. Start the Reports Manager by choosing Database ➔ Report ➔ Reports Manager (see Figure 4.25).

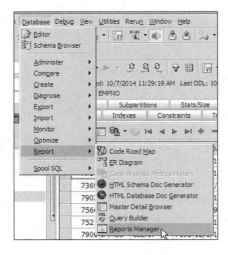

FIGURE 4.25   Toad Reports Manager

The Toad Reports Manager already contains a variety of reports (see the left side of Figure 4.26). Take a minute and review all the useful information available. You can easily copy the SQL out of this area for use in your other scripts and so on.

Notice the toolbar buttons. These buttons enable the following:

▶ Change database connection

▶ Save or export any or all report definitions

▶ Two Import buttons for all report definitions (useful to save your newly added reports, move between new PCs, and so on)

▶ Copy and Rename buttons

▶ Start the Reports wizard

▶ Execute any report (green button)

▶ Print selected reports

▶ Create a command-line script for any of the reports (convenient if you are going to use your own production scheduler to run reports)

▶ Schedule

▶ Create new Report Categories

▶ Delete report

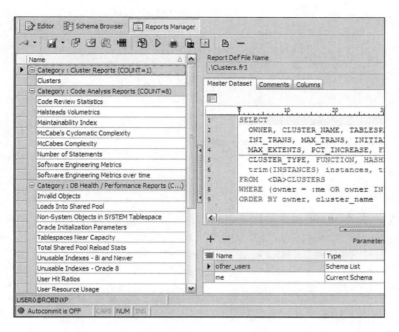

FIGURE 4.26   Toad Reports Manager

2. To add your new FastReport from the prior section, click the New Reports button and make a category called My Reports (see Figure 4.27).

3. Highlight this new category (or select the category you want to add the new report to) and then add your report name when the Rename Report/Change Category dialog box appears (see Figure 4.28). You can right-click on the categories on the left, as shown in Figure 4.29, to get the same options.

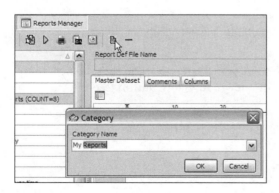

FIGURE 4.27   Create a new Reports category

FIGURE 4.28   Rename Report/Change Category dialog box

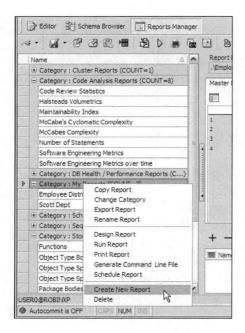

FIGURE 4.29   Right-click menu items for naming reports and changing categories

4. Return to the data grid from which you built your FastReport. Capture the SQL that was passed to the Report Builder using the View/Edit Query button (see the cursor in Figure 4.30).

5. Copy this SQL and press Ctrl+V to paste it into the new report's Master Dataset panel (see Figure 4.31).

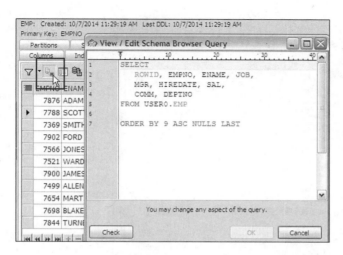

FIGURE 4.30   View/Edit Query button on a Schema Browser data grid

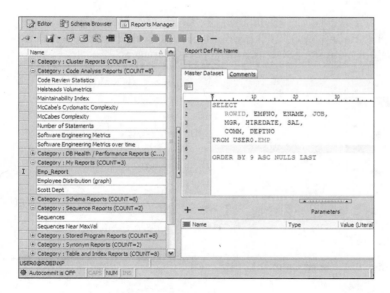

FIGURE 4.31   Master Dataset panel

6. Open the report previously developed using FastReport (see Figure 4.32).

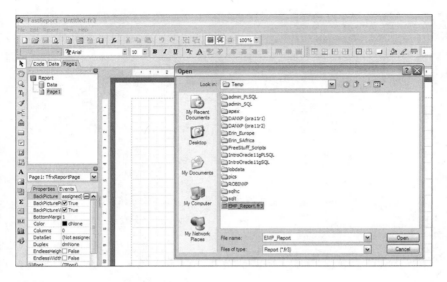

FIGURE 4.32   FastReport interface

7. Close the FastReport interface. Notice, as shown in Figure 4.33, that your report definition now appears along with your SQL in your Reports Manager.

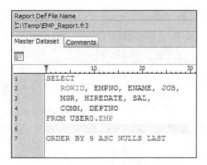

FIGURE 4.33   Completed Master Dataset panel

This report can now be run, scheduled, and modified just like any other report stored in Reports Manager.

TIP

You can easily add your own scripts to this Reports Manager by simply following the first four steps and pasting in your SQL. You can easily execute or schedule any report in this environment out of Toad.

Summary

This chapter covered the Schema Browser, a more comprehensive environment for adding and maintaining your application objects. This chapter also covered the printing of data and using the FastReport report writer that comes with Toad. The chapter concluded with an overview of the Toad Reports Manager and adding the FastReport you created to the Toad Reports Manager.

4

CHAPTER 5

Working with Data

IN THIS CHAPTER

▶ Reviewing Data Grid Options

▶ Save Data in Various Formats

▶ Master Detail Browser

▶ ER Diagrammer

▶ HTML Documentation Generator

This chapter illustrates the various options of the data grids. These data grids appear all over in Toad. Prior chapters have shown these in the describe panel and the Schema Browser. This chapter shows more data grids that contain related data (perfect to save for application test data) and how to save the data into various formats. Toad supports saving data in several common Microsoft Office formats as well. The Entity Relationship Diagrammer (ERD) shows the relationship of various application tables, and the HTML documentation generator is the perfect solution to take to meetings to discuss application data and various aspects of the application database setup.

Reviewing Data Grid Options

The data grids that appear in a describe panel (see Figure 5.1) and the Schema Browser (associated with a table object) have these common capabilities:

▶ Show/Hide columns from the display 🗒

▶ Filter or Sort the table data
  (except for the SQL Editor) 🔽

▶ View/Edit Query (except for the SQL Editor) 🔍

▶ Show Detail Dataset 🖼

▶ Export Dataset 📑

▶ Cancel Query Execution or Fetch 🚫

▶ Rowset navigation buttons (begin, end, next, and previous) ⧏ ◂ ▸ ⧐

▶ Add/Delete rows ⊞ ⊟

▶ Edit Record ▲

▶ Post Edit/Cancel Edit ✔ ✖

▶ Refresh Dataset ⟳

▶ Calculate selected cells (standard aggregate functions) Σ ▾

▶ Commit/Rollback ⬆ ⬇

▶ Additional buttons along the bottom of the dataset:

Bookmark navigation ✳ ✳

Single record viewer (convenient way to edit/change data) ◈

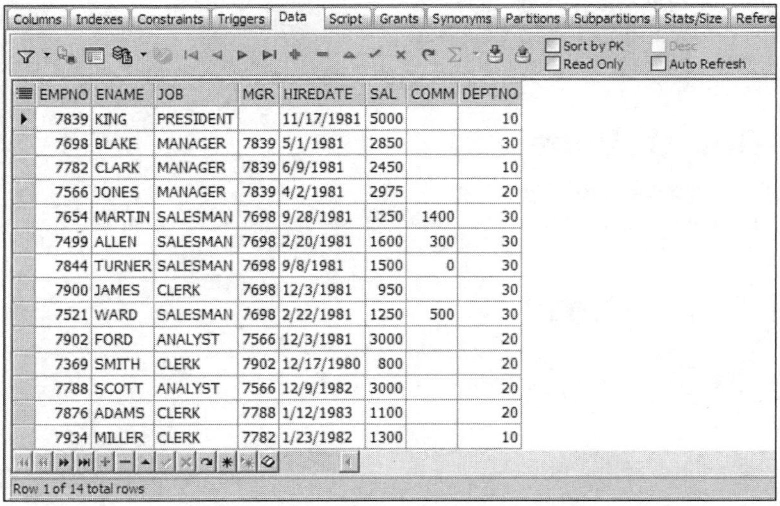

EMPNO	ENAME	JOB	MGR	HIREDATE	SAL	COMM	DEPTNO
7839	KING	PRESIDENT		11/17/1981	5000		10
7698	BLAKE	MANAGER	7839	5/1/1981	2850		30
7782	CLARK	MANAGER	7839	6/9/1981	2450		10
7566	JONES	MANAGER	7839	4/2/1981	2975		20
7654	MARTIN	SALESMAN	7698	9/28/1981	1250	1400	30
7499	ALLEN	SALESMAN	7698	2/20/1981	1600	300	30
7844	TURNER	SALESMAN	7698	9/8/1981	1500	0	30
7900	JAMES	CLERK	7698	12/3/1981	950		30
7521	WARD	SALESMAN	7698	2/22/1981	1250	500	30
7902	FORD	ANALYST	7566	12/3/1981	3000		20
7369	SMITH	CLERK	7902	12/17/1980	800		20
7788	SCOTT	ANALYST	7566	12/9/1982	3000		20
7876	ADAMS	CLERK	7788	1/12/1983	1100		20
7934	MILLER	CLERK	7782	1/23/1982	1300		10

Row 1 of 14 total rows

FIGURE 5.1   Data grid

Many of these same options are available via a right-click pop-up menu (see Figure 5.2).

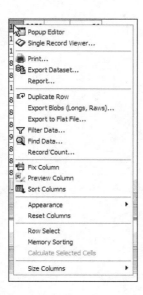

FIGURE 5.2   Data grid pop-up menu

You need proper permissions (privileges) at the Oracle database level to make changes to the data. Toad is not a tool to click the button to see what the function does.

These options usually appear in the same place on each of the grids, but for some of the data grids, such as the ones in the SQL Editor, the driving SQL is in the SQL Editor window. Many of the control buttons for the data grid are along the bottom of the data grid window (see Figure 5.3).

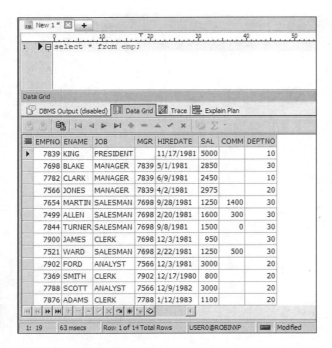

FIGURE 5.3   Editor window data grid

The arrow along the left side of the data grid indicates the current record. This arrow also indicates the row that will be presented in the Single Record viewer. Data can be changed right in this grid. With the proper Oracle permissions, users can change the data in these data grids on the fly, using the commit/rollback buttons to save the data or revert to the data prior to the change. The + and – buttons add a row or delete the current row in the dataset. Again, the commit/rollback buttons will save or reject these changes as well.

> **NOTE**
>
> Click the Configure Toad Options button on the menu bar and then choose Oracle → Transactions, or choose Main Menu → View → Toad Options → Oracle → Transactions to turn the autocommit feature on or off. Notice in Figure 5.4 that the autocommit feature can be turned on/off in the first area (see cursor position), and the last area in this panel dictates how changes will be handled if the data grid is being exited without using the commit or rollback functions.

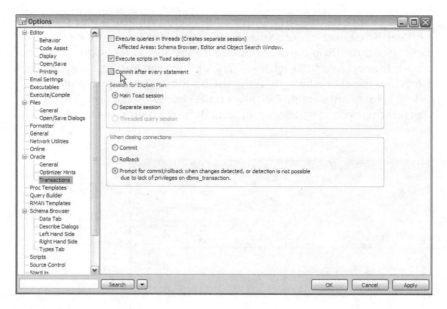

FIGURE 5.4   Toad Options autocommit feature

NOTE

Toad returns 500 rows at a time. A running count along the bottom edge of the data grid shows the current row counts of the data.

You can sort each of the data columns individually by simply clicking on the column header and selecting Ascending or Descending.

The data grid can be refreshed by using the Refresh Data button. Use the data navigation buttons to return to the beginning or the end of the dataset and walk a row at a time through the dataset.

The remaining part of this section discusses the specifics of buttons that require a little more detail.

Filter/Sort the Table Data

The Filter/Sort the Table Data option enables the data to be filtered (where clause) and/or put into a particular order (order by clause for one or more columns). Figure 5.5 shows a filter being added—be sure to click the Add to Filter (And) button shown with the cursor. Figure 5.6 shows a sort being added. Use the center arrows to move the selected columns for sorting to the right-hand side. The up/down arrows in the right side enable you to change the order of the sort columns. Notice the funnel icon in Figure 5.7; when a filter is being applied, the funnel appears red, and when a sort is being applied, a blue triangle appears above the funnel. These sort options will be maintained by Toad until cleared by the user. You can click on the drop-down menu next to the Sort/Filter button to clear the options (clears both the sort and filter settings). The options can also be cleared from within the Table Sort/Filter panel (via buttons along the bottom). These options are maintained by Toad on subsequent data grid displays until cleared by the user. The Add to Filter button is useful when you're sorting or limiting data based on more than one column.

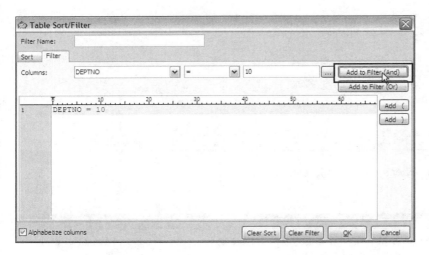

FIGURE 5.5   Filter data

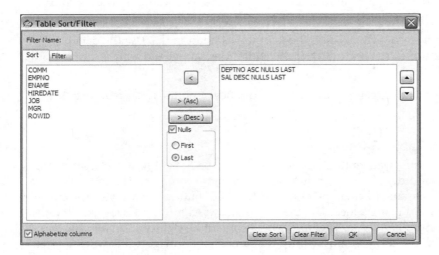

FIGURE 5.6   Sort data

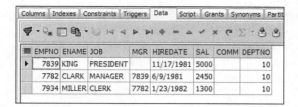

FIGURE 5.7   Sort/Filter indicator

Filtering adds a `where` clause to the SQL used to populate this data grid. This simple wizard enables you to add almost any condition to the data. Notice the View/Edit Schema Browser Query option panel now in Figure 5.8 (the View/Edit Query button is covered in the next section).

Sorting uses a wizard to make multiple field sorting possible. Remember, to sort on just a single column you can just click on the data heading in the data grid.

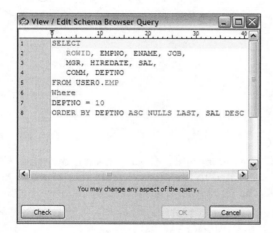

FIGURE 5.8   New syntax in Show Query

View/Edit Query

The View/Edit Query panel shows the current SQL being used to populate the data grid (see Figure 5.8). You can make changes to this SQL and use the check button to make sure your changes are syntactically correct. When you click OK, the data panel will be refreshed via the new SQL. This panel also shows any filters or sorts being applied as well.

TIP

The author has copied and pasted the SQL in this panel for use in other areas of Toad and Oracle applications.

Show/Hide Columns

Figure 5.9 shows the Show/Hide Columns drop-down menu. This useful feature is for getting the data grid into the order and appearance needed for the final output of the data. Use the View/Edit Query button to show the SQL used to create the current data grid. The Export Dataset button and report button will use the data and columns that appear in the data grid and in the order that they appear in the data grid. This feature is one way to remove unwanted columns from the output, no matter if the output is Export Data, Report Printing, and so on.

You can drag and drop the columns by clicking and dragging the header to the location in the data grid that you desire.

The Show/Hide Columns button also enables ROWID and, depending on the data grid, ROWNUM to appear in the output.

FIGURE 5.9   Show/Hide Columns drop-down menu

Show Detail Dataset

The Toad team has sprinkled the Master Detail Browser around in Toad. This button opens an additional data grid for the data of any object related to the primary table data being displayed. The data in the detail dataset follows the referential relationship defined by the existing primary/foreign key constraints.

Notice in Figure 5.10 that the DEPT table is the primary data grid, and when you click the Show Detail Dataset button, the EMP table data appears for the current row in the primary set.

TIP

The author uses the Show Detail Dataset button, along with Export Dataset, to save related test data for testing.

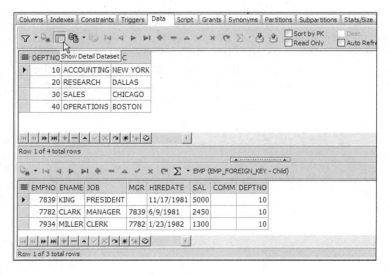

FIGURE 5.10   DEPT/EMP detail datasets

Calculate Selected Cells

The Calculate Selected Cells feature enables you to apply the SQL aggregate functions (count/min/max/avg/sum) to the selected items in a number column. Notice in Figure 5.11 that the SAL numbers are highlighted, the Calculate Selected Cells button was pressed, and the totals appear across the bottom of the data grid.

The Calculate Selected Cells drop-down menu enables you to select some or all of the aggregate functions.

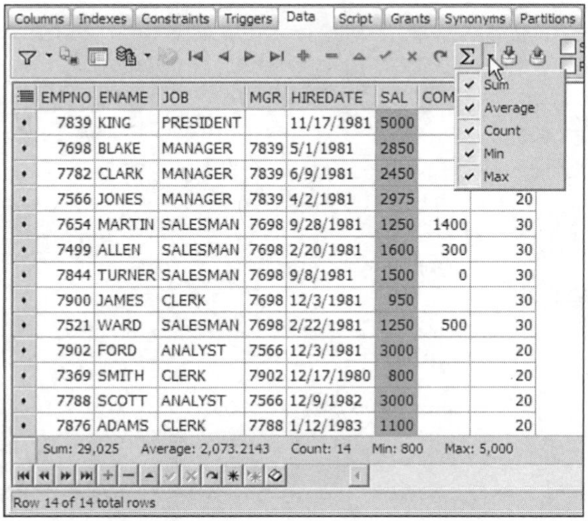

FIGURE 5.11   Calculate Selected Cells in action

Export Dataset

The Export Dataset button starts the Export Dataset wizard (see Figure 5.12). You can also access this option via a right-click on the data grid. The data and columns that appear in the data grid will be exported to one of a number of available formats. The order of the data and any applied filters will also be followed. In other words, you can use the View/Edit Query button to display the SQL that Toad will pass to this wizard.

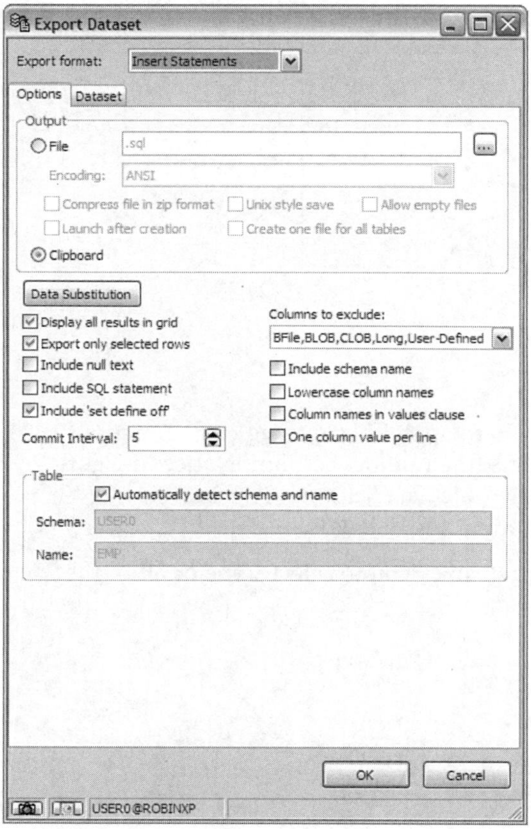

FIGURE 5.12   Export Dataset wizard

You can save data in the following formats:

▶ Access Database File

▶ Delimited Text

▶ Excel File

▶ Excel Instance

▶ Fixed Field Spacing

- ▶ HTML Table

- ▶ Insert Statements

- ▶ Merge Statements

- ▶ ODBC Database

- ▶ SQL Loader

- ▶ XML (plain)

- ▶ XML (with XSL)

These options share some common features, but each choice also has settings unique to it. For example, the Excel Instance option opens a new workbook in an open Excel file. Most of the options enable you to save the data in a file or paste it to the clipboard.

Specific options such as having commit points for the Insert Statement option, including or excluding headings in an Excel file output, and so on are also available.

Figure 5.12 shows the Options tab. The Dataset tab shows the query used to process the data into the selected format. The buttons on the bottom enable you to create and/or schedule an action, as well as the connection string used for the data access.

TIP

The author uses the Insert Statement options, saves the data to the clipboard, and then pastes it into his test data script. He typically has a commit added after 100 rows (by using the Commit Intervals option).

Refresh Dataset

The Refresh Dataset button ⟳ refreshes or reruns the query to repopulate the data grid. This feature is useful to run after some changes have been made to the data. You can automate it by using the Toad Options button on the menu bar or by choosing Main Menu → View → Toad Options → Data Grids → Data and making the selections as shown in Figure 5.13.

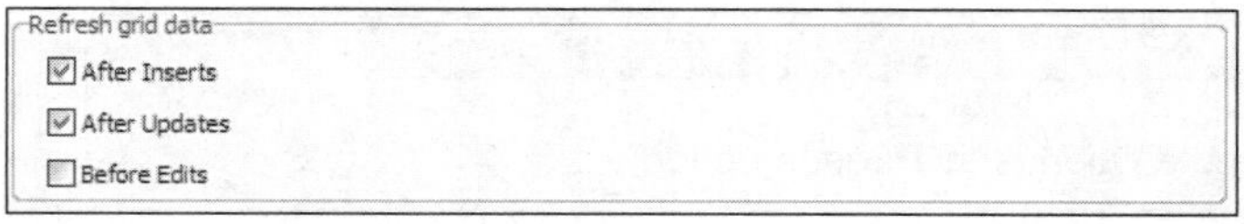

FIGURE 5.13   Toad Options auto refresh options

Cancel Query Execution or Fetch

The Cancel Query Execution or Fetch button enables a long-running SQL query to be interrupted and control returned to Toad. To be able to cancel queries, you must select the Execute Queries in Threads option by choosing Main Menu → View → Toad Options → Oracle → Transactions, as shown in Figure 5.14.

> **NOTE**
>
> The Execute Queries in Threads feature should already be enabled by default with any Toad10+ installation.

> **NOTE**
>
> The Transactions panel also controls the commit/rollback features when exiting Toad, the autocommit feature (shown here as disabled) discussed earlier, and which connection to use when running items in the Editor window when the Run as Script button is selected.

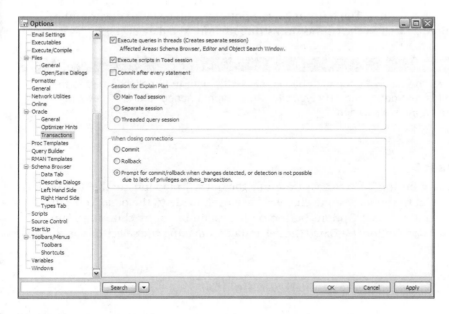

FIGURE 5.14   Toad Options Execute Queries in Threads option

Add/Delete Rows

The Add and Delete buttons ⊞ ⊟ appear in most data grids (all except for the Editor window) and also appear with the navigation, edit, and bookmark buttons across the bottom of the data grid. The + button opens an empty row in the data grid and the - button deletes the current row in the data grid. If the Commit After Every Statement feature is enabled, the changes are immediately written to the database (see Figure 5.14).

TIP

The Add and Delete buttons are a handy way to manipulate data for a report or for dataset export. Make sure the autocommit feature is not enabled, make your changes, save your data, and then roll back the changes.

Row Set Navigation Buttons

The row set navigation buttons ▸◂▸▸ enable the user to walk up and down the row set and quickly navigate to the first row and the last row if so desired. These buttons also appear across the bottom of the data grid.

Edit Row Set Control Buttons

The Edit Row Set Control buttons ▣ enable the row set to be edited and changes to be posted to the data grid window. Remember, the Commit and Rollback buttons control when the changed rows are saved to the database. These Edit Row Set buttons also appear across the bottom of the data grid.

Commit/Rollback

The Commit and Rollback buttons ▣ ▣ are important to use if the Commit After Every Statement option is not enabled (see Figure 5.14). The commit records the changes to the database. The rollback undoes any changes back to the prior commit. The Refresh button might be used after a rollback to restore the data grid to the data as it is stored in the database.

Bookmark Navigation

Any rows can be bookmarked so users can easily locate them while analyzing the row set. The * button along the bottom places a bookmark at the current row (where the arrow is on the left column), and the Go to Bookmark button will display the current bookmarked rows. The user can select which row to jump to.

Single Record Viewer

The Single Record Viewer button is also along the bottom of the data grid and appears as an open book. Clicking it brings the current row into a nice panel showing all the data, giving more options for date field manipulation, and so on (see Figure 5.15).

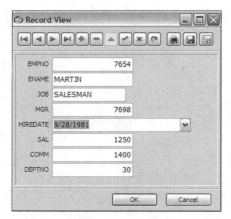

FIGURE 5.15   Single Record Viewer

Save Data in Various Formats

This section expands on the previous section "Export Dataset." You use the same button (Export Dataset) to access the save options, and Toad remembers the last Export Format selected.

The Access Database File format option creates a file of the data from the data grid for use with Microsoft Access.

Figure 5.16 shows the Access Database File options.

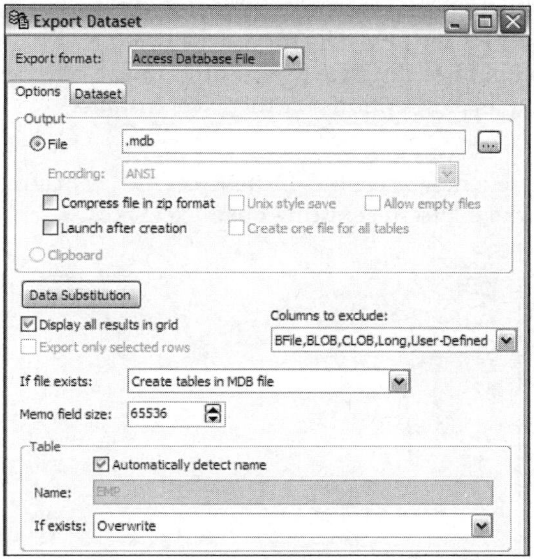

FIGURE 5.16   Export Dataset Access Database File Options panel

The Delimited Text format option enables the data grid data to be formatted in about any way for use with other products' data loaders. Figure 5.17 illustrates the various options for creating text files out of the data grid data. Notice that headings can be included or excluded, character strings can be quoted, and more.

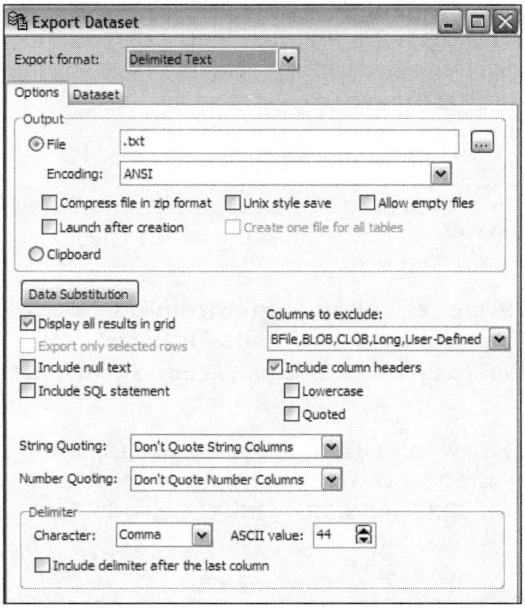

FIGURE 5.17   Export Dataset Delimited File Options panel

Excel File and Excel Instance options are similar in that they work with Microsoft Excel files and workbooks. Figure 5.18 shows the options for Excel File format. Notice the control over how date fields appear, if the column headings are to appear, how the cells are to be formatted, and more. There are just a few less options for the Excel Instance format option.

The Excel File and Excel Instance options create a new Excel file. If the Excel file is already open, the Excel Instance will add another workbook to the existing open Excel file.

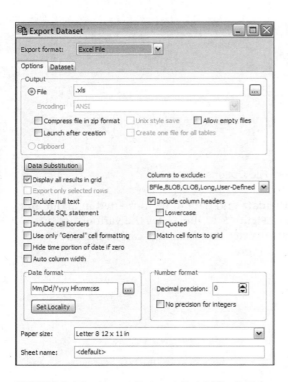

FIGURE 5.18   Export Dataset Excel File Options panel

The Fixed Field Spacing option (see Figure 5.19) creates a file of fixed-length fields, based on the database attributes for each column. This feature is similar to the Delimited Text option. Notice that the output can be put into the clipboard to be pasted into another file or program.

The format options HTML Table, XML, and XML (with XSL) are similar in that Toad will export the data and insert the proper tags in with the text. Figure 5.20 shows the dataset export options for the HTML; the options for the XML and XML (with XLS) are similar.

FIGURE 5.19   Export Dataset Fixed Field Spacing Options panel

FIGURE 5.20   Export Dataset HTML Table Options panel

The Insert Statements format option was covered earlier in this chapter and is without a doubt the author's favorite Export Dataset option. The Merge Statements format options are very similar (see Figure 5.21) to it. Both formats enable the schema owner to appear in with the generated syntax, as well as the generated syntax to be directly written to a file (perhaps useful when used on larger volumes of data) or put into the clipboard for pasting into other files/applications.

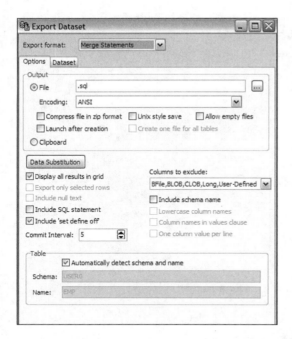

FIGURE 5.21   Export Dataset Merge Statements Options panel

The ODBC Database format option writes data directly into another data store using an existing ODBC connection (see Figure 5.22).

FIGURE 5.22   Export Dataset ODBC Database Options panel

The final option in the Export Dataset menu is the SQL Loader option (see Figure 5.23). Notice the Options panel enables you to define the type of loader operations. This option creates the necessary data loader script to quickly load the data back into an Oracle table.

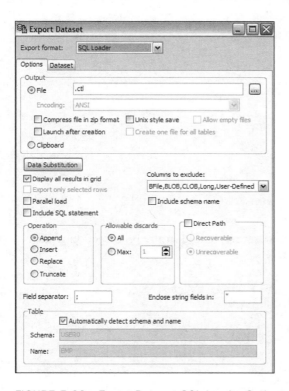

FIGURE 5.23   Export Dataset SQL Loader Options panel

Master Detail Browser

You access the Toad Master Detail Browser by choosing Database → Report → Master Detail Browser as shown in Figure 5.24. A Master Detail Browser button also appears on the top toolbar (you can see the button image in the drop-down menu).

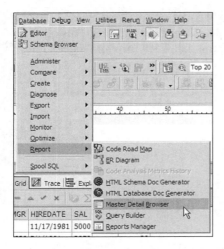

FIGURE 5.24   Accessing the Master Detail Browser

This interface is similar to the Show Detail Dataset referenced in the prior section. Figure 5.25 shows the Master Detail Browser interface.

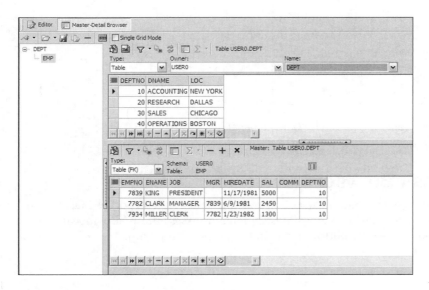

FIGURE 5.25   The Master Detail Browser

Select the parent table in the Type, Owner, and Name options and, as with Show Detail Dataset, use the Add detail under this dataset button to find the related data stores to this identified data object.

This browser interface is handy for those users who need to see related data quickly and easily. IT professionals will like this feature for finding related data for testing perhaps. Right-click on any of the data items and select Export Dataset to save the data in the desired format for further examination, testing, or moving.

The same data grid options appear here as were discussed in the "Reviewing Data Grid Options" section at the beginning of this chapter. There are a few new buttons such as Generate Dataset that will start Toad FastReports (covered in Chapter 4, "Schema Browser") and pass in the datasets present in this browser.

You can save this master/detail relationship and then open it again at a later time.

The Refresh button refreshes all the data grids that appear in this interface.

ER Diagrammer

Toad contains an Entity Relationship (ER) Diagrammer that is useful for visualizing application table and other objects' relationships.

TIP

The author uses the ER Diagram feature when he's assigned a new project. He extracts the objects in his current assignment, prints them, and posts them in plain sight for quick reference.

You access the ER Diagrammer by choosing Database → Report → ER Diagram; see Figure 5.26.

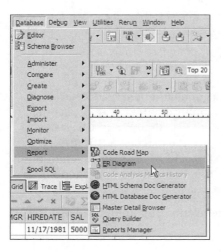

FIGURE 5.26   Accessing the ER Diagrammer

This feature works in conjunction with the Object Palette (choose View ➔ Object Palette).

Using the diagrammer is easy; just drag and drop your table objects from the Object Palette and drop them onto the canvas, the center part of the diagrammer interface, as shown in Figure 5.27. Notice that as you drop objects onto the canvas, if there is a database relationship established, it will also be painted in. In Figure 5.27, a one-to-many relationship exists between the DEPT table and the EMP table—one row in the DEPT table is related to one or more (many) rows in the EMP table, as depicted by the direction of the row's foot connector.

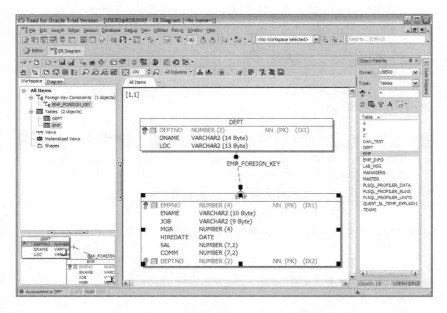

FIGURE 5.27   ER Diagrammer showing DEPT and EMP tables

There are buttons to create a new diagram, save this diagram, and then load it back into this interface ⬚⬚-⬚⬚. Notice the buttons to generate a graphical output ⬚⬚⬚, pass the output to other features of Toad such as the Query Builder ⬚ (discussed in Chapter 3, "Working with SQL"), and so on. There are buttons to give the diagram a title ⬚, make the objects larger or smaller ⬚⬚⬚, generate data ⬚, and generate data definition language (DDL) ⬚ (to recreate the Oracle syntax used to recreate these objects and their relationships).

If you double-click on any of the objects, including the relationship lines, Toad opens a describe panel for that object.

HTML Documentation Generator

The HTML Documentation Generator is a handy schema or database documentation generator within Toad. You can easily move the output over to any laptop and take it to meetings to quickly answer technical questions about application and/or database content. You can also easily add output to web pages for end user usage.

> **TIP**
>
> The author has used the HTML Documentation Generator feature to create the detailed information in web page format and taken this information to meetings.

To access the HTML Documentation Generator, choose Database ➔ Report ➔ HTML Schema Doc Generator (see Figure 5.28).

> **NOTE**
>
> Notice the very next item in this menu tree is the HTML Database Doc Generator. This feature documents ALL the schemas and DBA features of any database. DBAs might find this information useful. The author might use this feature to create HTML documents to post on an internal website for offsite reference.

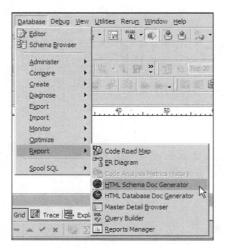

FIGURE 5.28   Accessing the HTML Schema Doc Generator

The main interface is shown in Figure 5.29. Notice you can select more than one schema account. The triangular (green) button will generate the output. After generation, Toad will ask whether you want to see the generated HTML output. If you reply Yes, Toad starts your default browser and loads the HTML file.

> **NOTE**
>
> The Summary.html file is the starting point for the output for this generated report. Look for it in the folder that the output was sent to.

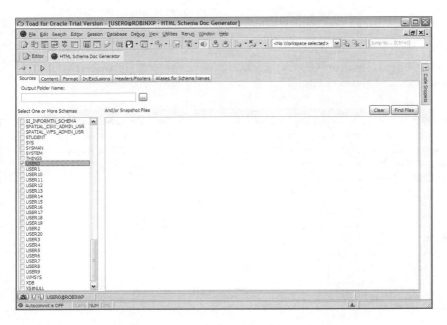

FIGURE 5.29   HTML Schema Doc Generator main interface

The Content tab, shown in Figure 5.30, lists the types of objects that you can include or exclude from the output.

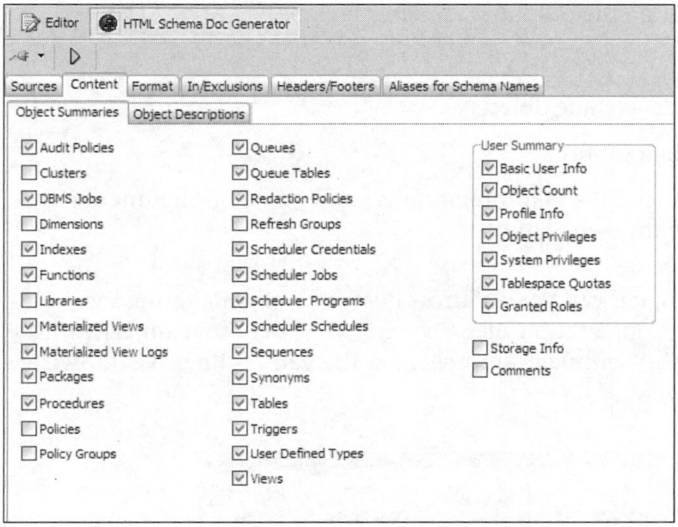

FIGURE 5.30   Content tab

The content tab has a sub-tab of Object Descriptions where the content for each object type can be further qualified; see Figure 5.31.

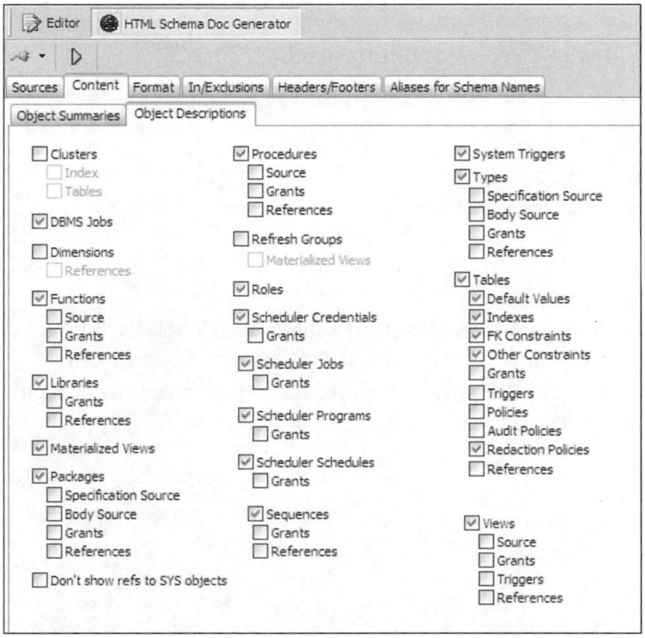

FIGURE 5.31   Object Descriptions tab

The other tabs to format and define the output parameters include:

▶ Format (colors/fonts)

▶ In/Exclusion (group include/exclude objects)

▶ Header/Footer (labels in the output)

▶ Alias for Schema Names (useful if the information is going to be on the Internet perhaps—to hide real account ownership)

When all the criteria are selected, click the green arrow button on the main interface to execute the generation of the documentation files. Figure 5.32 shows the main HTML document output. Everything is hyperlinked—just click on the various links based on the content you selected earlier.

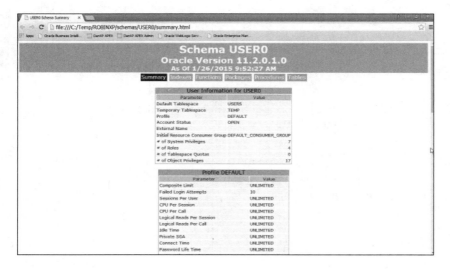

FIGURE 5.32   HTML output

The output is created in the folder indicated on the main interface page. There will be a folder that starts with the Database name that contains the HTML output for anything Toad generated (see Figure 5.33). Copy this folder and its contents to take the output to a web location or to put onto a laptop to take to a meeting.

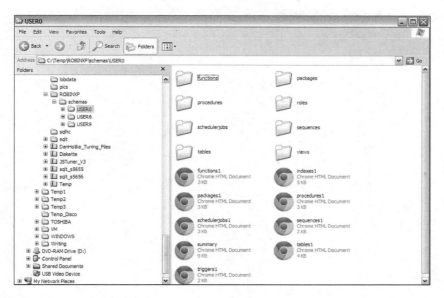

FIGURE 5.33   HTML output name and location

Summary

This chapter covered various options with the data grids. Toad contains useful functions to also see the data relationships, access data in a related format, and to document all table/data relationships.

CHAPTER 6

Working with PL/SQL

IN THIS CHAPTER:

▶ Using the Editor

▶ Using Code Templates

▶ Project Manager

▶ Using Code Snippets

▶ Code Shortcuts

▶ Code Analysis

▶ Using the Debugger

▶ Using the PL/SQL Profiler

There is no PL/SQL-specific editor in Toad. This chapter covers some PL/SQL specifics when working with the main Toad Editor. The templates (along with the Auto Replace, discussed in Chapter 3, "Working with SQL," as a way to create your own shortcuts) are nice features and can easily be adapted to your code and coding style. This chapter covers the Project Manager, a nice way of organizing database objects by project. The Code Snippets are covered in detail as well again in Chapter 10, "Toad as a SQL Tuning Tool." This chapter concludes with a walk-through of both the Debugger and the Profiler.

Using the Editor

The Editor is used to develop procedures, functions, and packages. This is not a course on PL/SQL but a course on using the various Toad interfaces. This chapter introduces you to more code templates (called snippets), code substitution (kind of like Auto Replace but a bit more fancy), and the PL/SQL Debugger.

You can bring code in from the file system 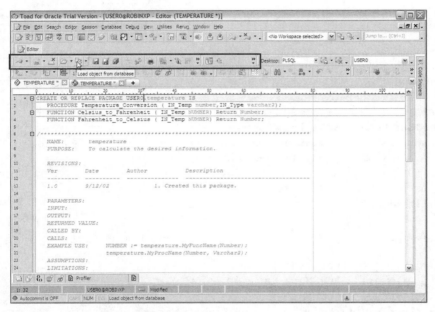 or load from the database ![icon]. Notice the row of buttons where the cursor is in Figure 6.1. You can open files from your workstation's file system or load existing PL/SQL code from the connected Oracle database. The buttons to the right of where the cursor is enable you to save the current tab or all the tabs back to the filename that they were loaded from. If the tabs were not loaded from a file, you will be prompted to supply filenames when saving the output to workstation files.

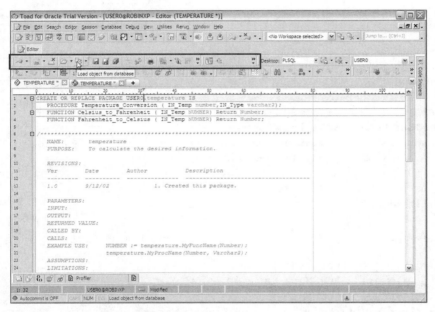

FIGURE 6.1   Toad Editor with PL/SQL code

NOTE

When you open a package, Toad automatically opens both the package spec and the package body in separate tabs.

If you choose View → Toad Options → Editor → Open/Save, you see an option to Load Spec/Body as Pair and Separate Tabs (both are the default settings).

Figure 6.2 shows the Load Database Object wizard. Adjust the schema owner if needed; you can also use the Object Type drop-down menu to show only specific objects. You can either double-click on an object in the window or highlight it and click the OK button. This loads the PL/SQL code into a new tab for the current connection in the Editor window.

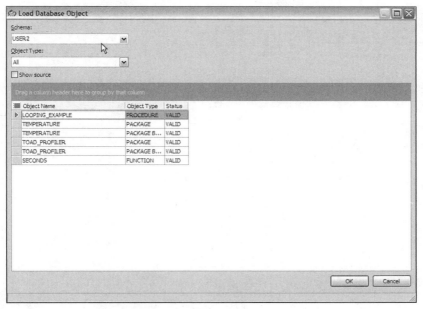

FIGURE 6.2   Load Database Object wizard

NOTE

Notice in Figure 6.2 that Toad remembers the last schema name that was used to run the wizard. This could potentially lead you to access the wrong code.

You can also load PL/SQL code from the Schema Browser (discussed in Chapter 4, "Schema Browser"). Right-click on the Procedure, Function, or Package tab and select Load into Editor from the drop-down menu.

Figure 6.3 shows the Execute/Compile button [image] (or you can press F9) and the Execute PL/SQL button [image] (or press F11). Your code gets automatically saved to the database when you click the green Execute/Compile button, which the cursor is on in Figure 6.3. Remember, the Execute/Compile button runs the statements in the Editor window. The Execute PL/SQL with debugger button will be highlighted when there is executable code to be processed. The button to the right, Set Execution Parameters [image], enables runtime parameters to be set for this PL/SQL module. PL/SQL also enables these options to be entered when you click the Execute PL/SQL button. Figure 6.4 shows the Set Parameters and Execute Options screen after the Execute PL/SQL button has been clicked, and Figure 6.5 shows the output and messages from a PL/SQL execution.

FIGURE 6.3   Execute buttons

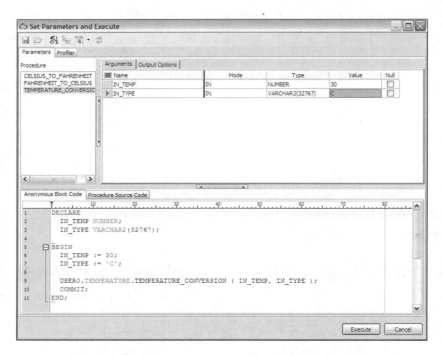

FIGURE 6.4   Set Parameters and Execute options panel

NOTE

Notice in Figure 6.5 that Toad will open the appropriate output tabs. In this panel, Toad noticed that PL/SQL was being executed and maybe debugged, so the Debugger output tabs were displayed. The PL/SQL Debugger is covered later in this chapter.

TIP

Use the F2 keystroke to toggle the Editor to full screen mode and autohide the output tabs across the bottom. This feature gives you more room to work with the code. Moving the mouse to the bottom of the Editor panel pops up the tabs. Pressing F2 again puts the output tabs in plain display. You can also use the pushpin in the heading of these output tabs to display or autohide the output tabs.

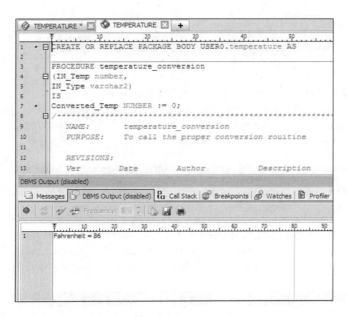

FIGURE 6.5   Successful PL/SQL execution

The Editor has some neat attributes that are useful when you're working with PL/SQL. Figure 6.6 illustrates some of these.

```
39
40  •  ⊟ BEGIN
41
42  •  ⊟ IF    IN_Type = 'C'
43       THEN
44  •        Converted_Temp := TEMPERATURE.Celsius_to_Fahrenheit(IN_Temp);
45
46  •        DBMS_OUTPUT.PUT_LINE('Fahrenheit = ' || Converted_Temp);
47  •        RETURN;
48  •      ELSIF In_Type = 'F'
49       THEN
50  •        Converted_temp := TEMPERATURE.Fahrenheit_to_Celsius(IN_Temp);
51  •        DBMS_OUTPUT.PUT_LINE('Celsius = ' || Converted_Temp);
52  •        RETURN;
53  •      END IF;
54  •  ⊟ DBMS_OUTPUT.PUT_LINE('Bad Temperature Conversion Code: ' ||
55              IN_Type);
56  •      RETURN;
57
58  •  ⊟ END temperature_conversion;
59
60
```

FIGURE 6.6   PL/SQL Editor features

First, notice that the BEGIN and the END labels are both highlighted (lines 40 and 58 in Figure 6.6), as is the IF and the IF in the END IF (lines 42 and 53 in Figure 6.6). Toad highlights the beginning and ending of routines such as the entire module, IF, loops, and case statements. Notice on line 51 that if you click one parenthesis, the other matching parenthesis also bolds and highlights. If there is no matching parenthesis, the unmatched parenthesis becomes highlighted and turns red.

Code Folding is also a useful tool. Notice the - in the gutter at line 42. This enables that entire IF statement to be condensed. If the code is condensed, a + sign will appear in the gutter. Hovering the mouse pointer over the condensed code pops up a bubble displaying the code. This feature is nice when you're working with larger objects.

TIP

If you highlight any text, Toad will highlight all similar text.

The Action toolbar also has many related coding features on it. Press Shift+F4, or right-click and choose Action Console to see this menu of options (see Figure 6.7). You can save code from here and perform a number of related tasks such as compile, execute, and save.

NOTE

The Code Analysis feature does a code review and uses industry standard methodologies to give a rating of difficulty and sophistication of the PL/SQL routine. Programmers should run and record the output of this analysis both before and after making changes to any PL/SQL code.

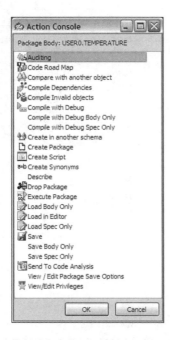

FIGURE 6.7   Auto Action menu

Toad can format your PL/SQL and SQL code. Right-click in the Editor window and select Formatting Tools. Figure 6.8 shows the formatting options.

- ▶ **Format**—Formats the code (everything on a single line) and indents nested code
- ▶ **Format Case Only**—Formats the code but does not indent nested code
- ▶ **Profile Code**—Gives a nice statistical summary of PL/SQL code
- ▶ **Formatter Options**—Enables indenting and colors to be defined

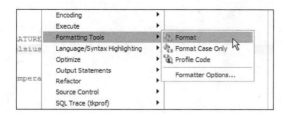

FIGURE 6.8   Code formatting

Using Code Templates

Toad comes with many useful code templates. These templates range from nested IF-THEN-ELSE logic to cursor loop examples. These templates also can contain substitution variables.

Ctrl+spacebar opens the templates pop-up menu (see Figure 6.9). Dozens of templates are available; take a few minutes to explore the code that comes with Toad. Figure 6.10 shows the template and any substitution variables. The Cursor Loop template has one substitution variable—notice that EMP will be substituted into the code when you click the OK button. Figure 6.11 shows the code after substitution. The vertical bar in the template code indicates where the cursor will be placed as well. These templates can contain more than one substitution variable.

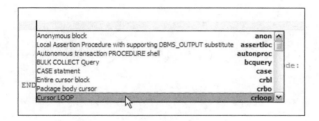

FIGURE 6.9   Signaling code templates

Variables
&&c1
Type:
Direction:
Substitution
Value
Literal
Environment Variable
EMP
OPEN &&c1;
LOOP
FETCH &&c1. INTO ;
EXIT WHEN &&c1%NOTFOUND;
END LOOP;
CLOSE &&c1;
OK
Cancel

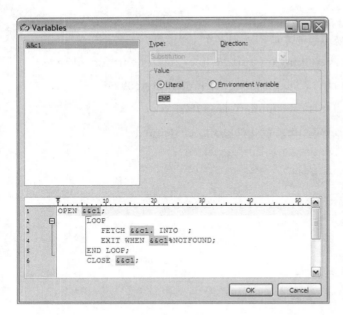

FIGURE 6.10 Code template substitution variables

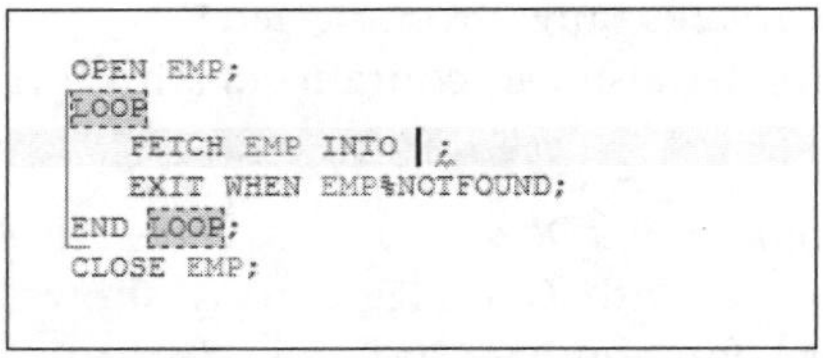

OPEN EMP;
LOOP
FETCH EMP INTO ;
EXIT WHEN EMP%NOTFOUND;
END LOOP;
CLOSE EMP;

FIGURE 6.11 Code template implemented in PL/SQL code

From the Toad Options panel choose Editor ➔ Behavior to modify the templates or add your own (see Figure 6.12).

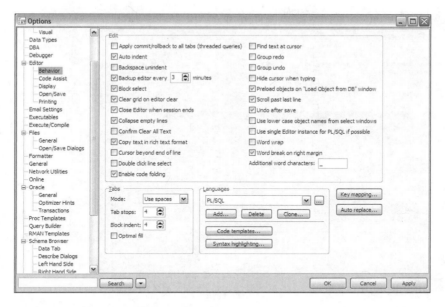

FIGURE 6.12   Code template options

The author will build the template PL for the code DBMS_OUTPUT.Put_Line and put the cursor in the appropriate place. To do this, go to the Toad Options panel (refer to Figure 6.12) and click on Code Templates near the bottom of this panel. Figure 6.13 shows the CRLOOP template code. Notice that the code is both formatted and contains the substitution variables. Notice that the vertical bar is placed where the cursor will be located when the template is used.

TIP

You can make just about any commonly used code into a template.

TIP

You can also signal these templates by entering their short name followed by Ctrl+spacebar.

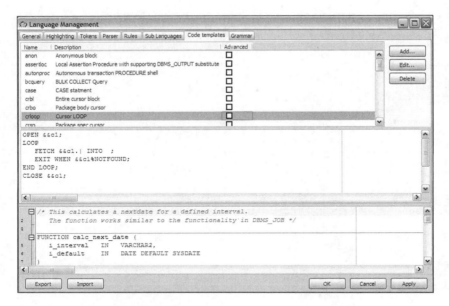

FIGURE 6.13   Code template CRLOOP

To build your own code template, click the Add button on the Code Templates tab and fill out the resulting dialog box as shown in Figure 6.14. This opens a new line in the Code Templates tab where you can then add the text of the template. The text can be quite sizeable. Click OK to accept the changes. Notice the DBMS_OUTPUT syntax and the position of the vertical bar in Figure 6.15. Figure 6.16 shows the code template in use. You can access this information by typing PL, followed by the Ctrl+spacebar key sequence.

NOTE

This is about as close as Oracle gets to a copy library.

NOTE

The shortcut text is not case sensitive.

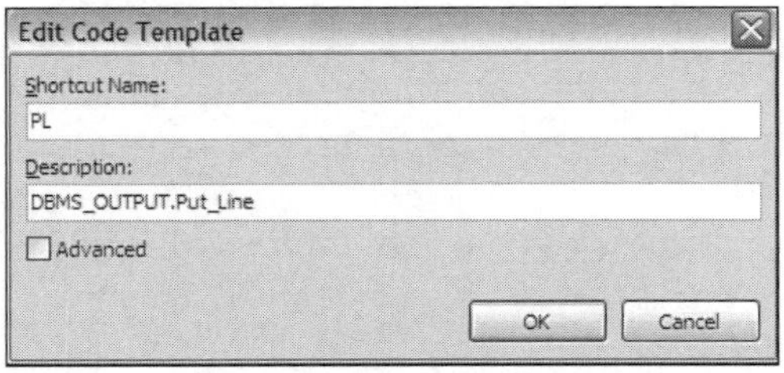

FIGURE 6.14   Adding a new code template

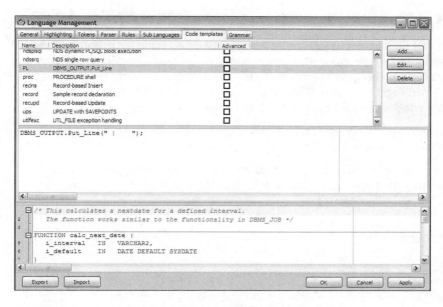

FIGURE 6.15   Adding a new code template, continued

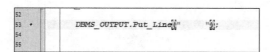

FIGURE 6.16   Using the new code template

Figure 6.17 shows additional code templates for other Toad-supported languages. Explore per your needs at your company.

FIGURE 6.17   Code templates for other programming languages

Project Manager

Toad Project Manager allows for objects to be organized and accessed by a project. This allows for various objects to be grouped together and given a name; that is, a project name. Large applications can have thousands of objects and these objects can now be organized or grouped together within Toad. Right-click on an object in the Schema Browser navigator window and select Add to Project Manager.

The Project Manager is probably best maintained from the Schema Browser, although objects can be added to folders within it from about anywhere.

Figure 6.18 shows the Project Manager button along the top (see cursor position) and the autohide type window that appears on the left. Project Manager can also be opened using Main Menu → View → Project Manager.

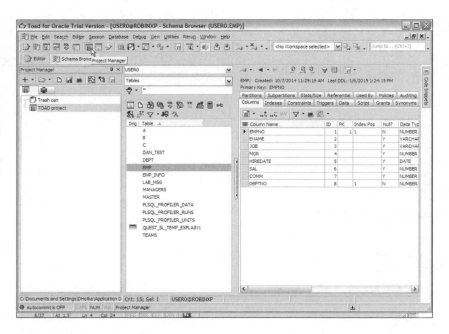

FIGURE 6.18   Project Manager interface

Figure 6.19 shows the drop-down menu from the Add Items button. Notice all the various objects that can be organized under one area.

FIGURE 6.19   Adding objects to the project folders

Create a folder (using the Make New Folder button) or use an existing folder using this same drop-down menu, then drag and drop or use the Add Items button to add tables or other database and related objects to track. This feature really makes it easy to view just the objects being utilized for a particular project.

Notice the buttons on the Project Manager window toolbar. These buttons enable you to save the project information outside of Toad—to either share with other people on the project team or reuse if you are getting a new workstation.

Using Code Snippets

Toad code snippets are short drag-and-drop SQL and PL/SQL assistants. This feature autohides along the right-hand side of Toad and you start it by choosing View → Code Snippets. You can pin the interface open so it doesn't autohide.

The Cursor Attributes panel is open in Figure 6.20. When working with cursors, you can drag and drop these items into your code to save typing and prevent typos.

FIGURE 6.20   Code Snippets autohide panel

Explore the drop-down menu in Code Snippets (see Figure 6.21). Notice it has all kinds of code assistants.

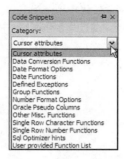

FIGURE 6.21   Code Snippets categories

You can adjust or even add your own snippets! Use View →Toad Options → Code Behavior and see the Code Snippets in the upper-right corner of this panel (see Figure 6.22). After you add your own snippets to Toad, you can then add them to code via drag and drop.

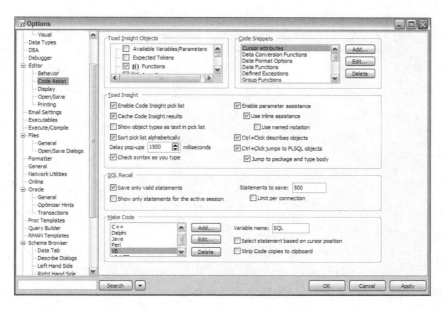

FIGURE 6.22   Code Snippets options

Code Shortcuts

Keyboard shortcuts are one of the features that make Toad so powerful and easy to use. Toad comes with a host of predefined shortcuts. These shortcuts save keystrokes and mouse actions and perform a variety of tasks such as issuing a "describe" on the current highlighted object, or find (find next, find previous, and so on). You can see whether there is a keyboard shortcut by reviewing menu bar items. The menu bar shows the Toad feature and whether it has a button and/or keyboard keystroke associated with it to activate the feature. This section highlights all the shortcuts available for most versions of Toad. Figure 6.23 shows the menu bar keyboard and button options. Table 6.1 and Table 6.2 provide handy cross-references for most of the Editor shortcuts. Table 6.1 shows the shortcuts arranged by keystroke, and Table 6.2 shows the shortcuts arranged by description.

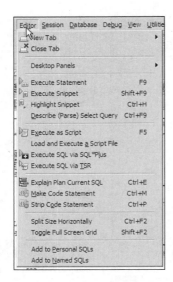

FIGURE 6.23   Identifying keyboard shortcuts via the toolbar menu

TABLE 6.1   Editor Shortcuts by Keystroke

Shortcut	Description
F1	Windows help file
F2	Toggle output window
F3	Find next occurrence
Shift+F3	Find previous occurrence
F4	Describe table, view, procedure, function
F5	Set or delete breakpoint
Shift+F7	Trace into while debugging
Shift+F8	Step over while debugging
F9	Compile
Ctrl+F9	Set code execution parameters
Shift+F9	Execute current source without debugging
F10 or Right-click	Pop up menu
F11	Execute current source with debugging
F12	Execute current source to cursor with debugging
Ctrl+F12	External Editor, pass contents
Ctrl+A	Select all text
Ctrl+Alt+B	Display breakpoint window
Ctrl+C	Copy
Ctrl+D	Display procedure parameters

Shortcut	Description
Ctl+Alt+D	Display Debugger in DBMS output window
Ctrl+F	Find text
Ctrl+G	Go to line
Ctrl+L	Convert text to lowercase
Ctrl+M	Make code statement
Ctrl+N	Recall named SQL statement
Ctrl+O	Open a text file
Ctrl+P	Strip code statement
Ctrl+R	Find and replace
Ctrl+S	Save file
Shift+Ctrl+S	Save file as
Ctrl+Alt+S	Display call stack window
Ctrl+T	Columns dropdown
Shift+Ctrl+R	Alias replacement
Shift+Ctrl+T	Columns dropdown no alias
Ctrl+spacebar	Code templates
Ctrl+U	Converts text to uppercase
Ctrl+V	Paste
Ctrl+Alt+W	Display Debugger watches window
Ctrl+X	Cut
Ctrl+Z	Undo last change
Ctrl+.	Display pop-up list of matching table names
Shift+Ctrl+Z	Redo last undo
Ctrl+Tab	Cycle through the collection of MDI child windows

TABLE 6.2   Editor Shortcuts by Description

Description	Shortcut
Alias replacement	Shift+Ctrl+R
Code templates	Ctrl+spacebar
Columns dropdown	Ctrl+T
Columns dropdown no alias	Shift+Ctrl+T
Compile	F9
Convert text to lowercase	Ctrl+L
Convert text to uppercase	Ctrl+U
Copy	Ctrl+C
Cut	Ctrl+X

Description	Shortcut
Cycles through the collection of MDI child windows	Ctrl+Tab
Describe table, view, procedure, function, or package	F4
Display breakpoint window	Ctrl+Alt+B
Display call stack window	Ctrl+Alt+S
Display Debugger in DBMS output window	Ctrl+Alt+D
Display Debugger watches window	Ctrl+Alt+W
Display pop-up list of matching table names	Ctrl+.
Display procedure parameters	Ctrl+D
Execute current source to cursor with debugging	F12
Execute current source with debugging	F11
Execute current source without debugging	Shift+F9
External Editor, pass contents	Ctrl+F12
Find and replace	Ctrl+R
Find next occurrence	F3
Find previous occurrence	Shift+F3
Find text	Ctrl+F
Go to line	Ctrl+G
Make code statement	Ctrl+M
Open a text file	Ctrl+O
Paste	Ctrl+V
Pop up menu	F10 or Right-click
Recall named SQL	Ctrl+N
Redo last undo	Shift+Ctrl+Z
Save file	Ctrl+S
Save file as	Shift+Ctrl+S
Select all text	Ctrl+A
Set execution parameters	Ctrl+F9
Set or delete breakpoint	F5
Step over while debugging	Shift+F8
Strip code statement	Ctrl+P
Trace into while debugging	Shift+F7
Toggle output window	F2
Undo last change	Ctrl+Z
Windows help file	F1

Code Analysis

Code Analysis displays a series of industry standard metrics useful for determining the following:

- ▶ Whether code contains errors

- ▶ The level of complexity of both the PL/SQL and any SQL code

- ▶ Whether the routine contains SQL and the type of SQL (such as DML)

- ▶ How many lines of code are in the routine

- ▶ Whether code follows rules

A manager can use this report when assigning staff to a project. These reports can quickly assess the type of code and help the manager decide who (in terms of skill level) would be required.

Programmers should run this analysis to make a baseline status of code they are about to start on and compare it to the same report items after the programming task is complete. This information can be used to help programmers ensure they don't make any mistakes.

This feature can also be used to evaluate software packages based in Oracle code and used as another metric to compare the code across the solutions being considered.

To use this feature choose Database → Diagnose → Code Analysis (see Figure 6.24). With the code analysis buttons on the main toolbar, you can initiate this review for any SQL or PL/SQL routine or for just the SQL or PL/SQL code in the Editor window. Open the procedure, function, or packages for analysis and click the green Run Analysis button (to the left on the main interface) to analyze the selected code. All code in the interface can be analyzed, but the report will be vague on individual object detail. Figure 6.25 shows the main interface and the high-level evaluation. Figure 6.26 shows the rest of the report to the right side of the screen. The Report tab shown in Figure 6.27 gives considerably more detail as to the background and data for each of the rankings. The main interface gives each of the metric rankings.

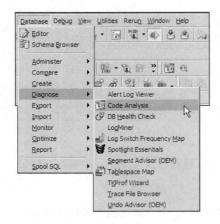

FIGURE 6.24   Starting the Code Analysis interface

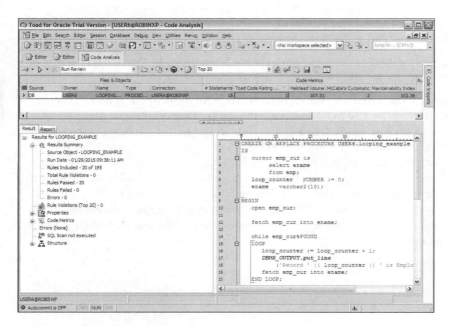

FIGURE 6.25   Code Analysis interface

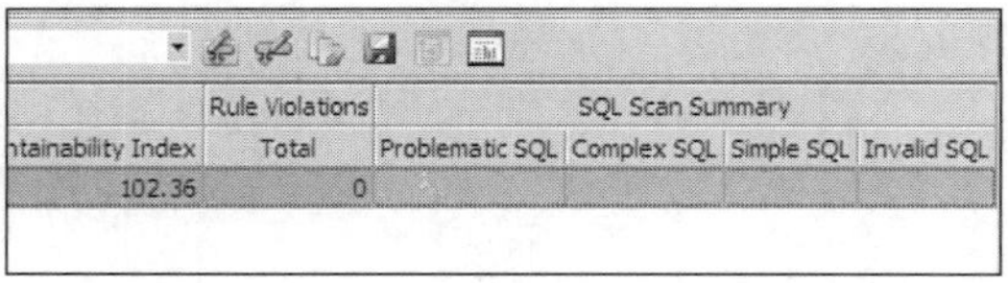

FIGURE 6.26   Remaining Code Analysis interface

TIP

If I were regularly programming, I would definitely attach one of these reports to my completed work. This would show that my code is clean and complies with the rules set up in this area of Toad.

This report (refer to Figures 6.25 and 6.26) shows five main areas across the top of the interface I would like as a manager:

▶ Toad Rating

▶ Halstead Volume—a rating of computational complexity

▶ McCabe's Cyclomatic—a rating of overall program complexity

▶ Maintainability Index—a scale of maintainable code

▶ SQL Scan summary—SQL complexity has four areas:

 ▶ Problematic SQL

 ▶ Complex SQL

 ▶ Simple SQL

 ▶ Invalid SQL

When these reports are run against single program units or single packages, the report contains considerably more detail.

The Report tab (see Figure 6.27) identifies program modules that contain SQL and what that SQL does (that is, SELECT or DML operations).

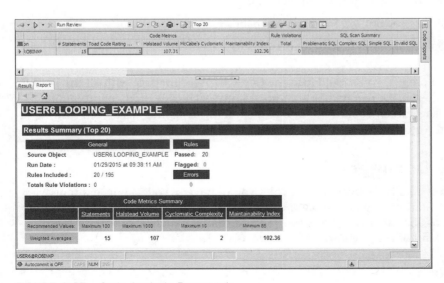

FIGURE 6.27   Code Analysis Report tab

The Toad Code Rating is a scale of 1 to 4 where 1 is the best and 4 is the worst. This is obviously just a simple rating. The rest of the analysis provides far more detail.

The Halstead Volume is calculation/code function complexity. Items considered are any calculation, length of the calculation, flow logic, depth of flow logic, and so on. The Report tab shows all the detail being considered. For example,

▶ 0–1000 indicates code an average programmer should be able to comprehend and maintain.

▶ 1001–3000 means code is more challenging and would take more skills to comprehend and change content.

▶ 3000 indicates that the code is too complex. Redesign this module.

McCabe's Cyclomatic Complexity is a different and simpler metric for identifying program unit complexity:

▶ 1–10 indicates the code is a simple program.

▶ 11–20 means the code is a more complex program.

▶ 21–50 indicates the code is a complex program.

▶ 50+ means the code is an untestable program.

The last item is the Maintainability Index (MI). This metric is meant to reflect how easy or difficult maintaining the code will be. This metric considers the output of both the Halstead and McCabe's complexity scales:

▶ 0–64 means the code is difficult to maintain.

▶ 65–84 indicates code of moderate maintainability.

▶ 85+ indicates code that's easy to maintain.

When you start a project, you should load the Code Analysis interface with all the PL/SQL code involved and run the reports one at a time against each code module (procedure, function, or package) in an application or a programming assignment. You can easily sort the various results by clicking on the heading of each report.

Using the Debugger

Toad contains a symbolic debugger that enables you to traverse code a line at a time, view variable content, start or stop execution of code, step in or out of called PL/SQL routines (such as functions and other called procedures), and change variable content during execution. This kind of code debugging is known as *symbolic debugging*.

Basic Debugging

Toad contains a full-featured symbolic debugger. Toad also enables script debugging using these same debugging techniques. This section covers PL/SQL debugging.

You can debug PL/SQL code while it is executing, change variables on the fly, see the contents of variables and cursors, and stop the execution of code at predetermined points (after so many loops or even after a variable contains a certain value).

Placing the cursor on a line in the code and clicking Run to Cursor will stop the execution of the code when the line with the cursor on it is reached.

> **TIP**
>
> I use the Trace Into (F7 keyboard shortcut) as a next step button. After I get to the section of code I want to monitor closely, I use this button to walk through the code one line at a time. Step Over will not enter into a subroutine. Notice keystroke shortcuts are available for most of the debugging features as well.

> **TIP**
>
> The Looping_Example is part of the download for this book. It uses the EMP table. Install these two objects if you would like to follow along with this working example.

> **NOTE**
>
> Debugging requires some additional database execute privileges to the DEBUG and DEBUG ANY PROCEDURE. I use the following syntax to let anyone run the PL/SQL Debugger:
> ```
> grant debug connect session to public;
> grant debug any procedure to public;
> ```

The debugging toolbar (see Figure 6.28) is useful for controlling the debugging session.

The buttons from left to right include the following:

- ▶ Compile Dependent Objects
- ▶ Execute PL/SQL with Debugger
- ▶ Set Parameters for Use with Debugger
- ▶ Step Over
- ▶ Trace Into
- ▶ Trace Out (grayed out in Figure 6.28)
- ▶ Run to Cursor
- ▶ Toggle Breakpoint

▶ Add Watch

▶ Attach Debugger to External Session

FIGURE 6.28   Debugger toolbar

The code used for debugging is the Looping_Example, as shown in Figure 6.29. The F2 key (toggle full screen) is in use. Having the full editor screen available helps to view the code around the steps being debugged.

The Terminate Execution button (left side of toolbar) will cancel the execution of any PL/SQL routine. This is useful when you have completed your need for the Debugger and you do not desire to let the PL/SQL code complete execution. Perhaps it runs for an hour.

Figure 6.29 shows the Looping_Example ready for debugging along with the Debug drop-down from the main menu. Notice that these menu items match up nicely with the previously mentioned toolbar buttons. Menu items, keystrokes, and buttons enable you to control the debugging session. Also notice that Toad now includes a script debugger. Notice in Figure 6.29 the various keyboard shortcuts for many of the buttons and menu items.

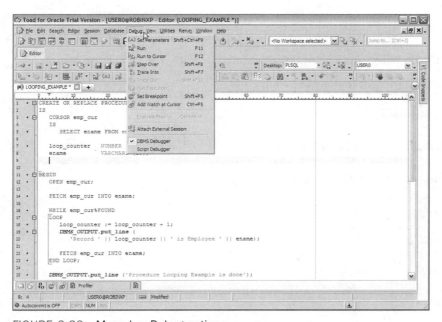

FIGURE 6.29   Menu bar Debug options

Generally, you set some breakpoints within the code by positioning the cursor on the line of code where you want to pause execution and selecting Debug ➜ Set Breakpoint, or pressing Shift+F5. You can also click on one of the little dots in the left gutter.

Toad will also start a debug session if you click the Step Into button (or press Shift+F7). This causes Toad to stop on the first executable line of code. After the debug session has started, you can decide to modify variable content (for items that break the code or that the code struggles with), step through the code one line at a time, or use the Run button to continue to the next breakpoint. If the breakpoint is located within a loop, then the looping code is followed. The advanced debugging features cover conditional breakpoints.

You can also set up watches in Toad, but Toad's newer smart data interface pretty much displays all variables available within the code. The Watches output tab enables you to watch the data change during code execution and to modify any data item you want.

When you get to the code where another PL/SQL routine is called, you can decide whether you want to follow the code into the function or not. If you don't want to go into the routine, simply click the Step Over button. For this example, please just use the Trace Into button.

Watches enable the contents of variables, cursors, and implicit cursors to be displayed. Hover the mouse over a variable when the Debugger has stopped the code to see the contents of the variable. Click on a variable and then choose Debug ➜ Add Watch at Cursor from the main menu (or press Ctrl+F5) to put the watch into the watch tab at the bottom. After this is done, you can watch the variables change during code execution and modify the value as well.

Figure 6.30 shows a breakpoint that is in place at line 18 just inside the LOOP code. These breakpoints show red during setup but turn blue when the Debugger stops at these lines of code. After you add the breakpoint, it appears in the breakpoint tab at the bottom. This tab displays all the breakpoints and enables each breakpoint to be edited, if the desire is to stop the execution after either a specific number of iterations of a loop have been performed or a specific data item appears. When you add these conditions, the breakpoint is then known as a conditional breakpoint.

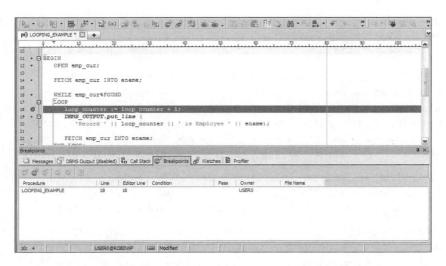

FIGURE 6.30   Breakpoints and the Breakpoint output tab

Click the Execute PL/SQL with Debugger button (or press F11) to run the code for the Debugger. Toad will ask whether you want to compile the code with debug information (see Figure 6.31)—answer Yes to this question. Toad will then compile this code and any code it references with debug information so that the Debugger can display useful information during the debugging process. The standard Set Parameters and Execute panel will then appear. Fill this out accordingly and click Execute at the bottom of this panel. If you used the Trace Into button to start the debugging process, the first line of executable code will turn blue. The program is now in debug mode and you can walk through each line of code, place the mouse cursor at any location, and use the Run to Cursor feature. If the program contains breakpoints and you used the Execute PL/SQL button to start the debugging process, when code execution reaches the breakpoint, that line of code will turn blue and execution waits for your additional input (for instance, clicking the Trace Into button to walk through the code one line at a time). Code can contain many breakpoints; the following section covers how to set and use conditional breakpoints.

The example Looping_Example was executed using the Execute PL/SQL button and a breakpoint was set just inside the LOOP code. Figure 6.32 shows that the code has stopped. This figure also shows the Watches tab, where you can see the contents of the variables. Be sure to enable Smart Watches by selecting this option's check box in this tab. Smart Watches opens a visual for every variable in the program unit.

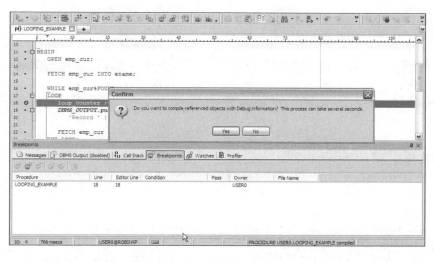

FIGURE 6.31   Compiling objects for debugging

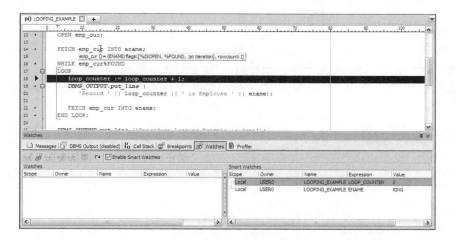

FIGURE 6.32   Debugging the Looping_Example

Notice in Figure 6.32 that the cursor has been positioned over the cursor variable. Toad will show the status of the various cursor attributes. You can move the mouse pointer over any variable to have Toad display its current contents as well, including both ref cursors and implicit cursor data.

The Debugger uses three output tabs:

▶ **Breakpoints**—Enables you to see breakpoints and set breakpoint options

▶ **Watches**—Enables data to be seen and modified

▶ **Call Stack**—Enables visualization of the module relationships during execution

If these tabs are not present, right-click in the Editor window and select them from the Desktop Panels item in this pop-up contextual menu.

TIP

You can organize these output tabs by dragging and dropping them, and easily turn them on or off using the Desktop Panels item (right-click these tabs).

Advanced Debugging Techniques

This section covers changing data on the fly and illustrates the use of conditional breakpoints. This section also shows how to use real-time code debugging (just-in-time debugging).

You can change data items on the fly. For variables for which you want to change the code, after the debugging session has started, click on the variable wherever it appears in the code and click the Add a Watch for Variable at Cursor button. This adds the item to the Watch tab, as shown in Figure 6.33. Notice that you can also add watches on cursors, again seeing the various cursor attributes in the Watch tab.

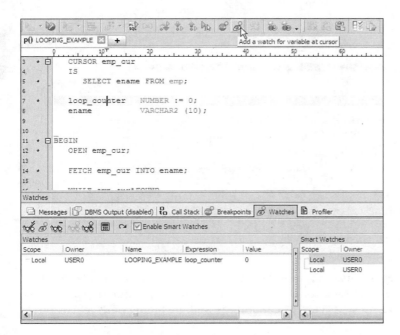

FIGURE 6.33   Add watches on variables

Highlight the variable for which you want to change the data and click the Evaluate/ Modify Watch button (see Figure 6.34) in this section and change the data. Make sure to click Modify in the dialog box that opens, and you will see the data change (see Figure 6.35).

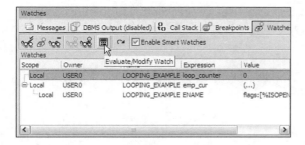

FIGURE 6.34   Modify variable data

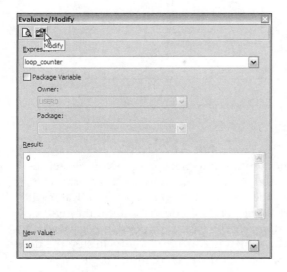

FIGURE 6.35   Changing variable data

The previous section shows how to set breakpoints to stop the code at predetermined lines of code. Toad also allows conditional breakpoints.

The steps to set breakpoint options are as follows:

1. Establish a regular breakpoint where the code is to be stopped.

2. In the Breakpoints tab, highlight the breakpoint to be adjusted, and click the Edit Breakpoint button in this same tab.

3. Notice that a breakpoint can be stopped at a certain variable condition or by the number of passes (such as when placed inside of loops) code execution went past this breakpoint.

To change the attributes of a breakpoint, first establish the breakpoint. In the Breakpoints tab, click on the breakpoint you want to modify (to highlight it) and then click Edit Breakpoint as illustrated in Figure 6.36.

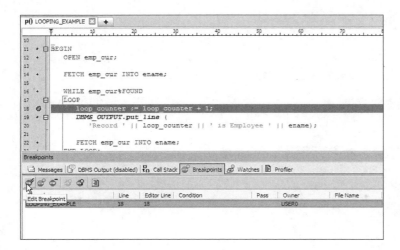

FIGURE 6.36   Setting conditional breakpoints

Notice in Figure 6.37 that you can put a condition into the breakpoint or you can set the pass count. The condition of loop_counter = 10 has been filled in by the Toad user. This type of conditional breakpoint will stop the code execution (the breakpoint indicator will turn blue) when the condition has been met. If the condition doesn't appear during the execution of the code, then the code is not stopped. The Pass Count option is particularly nice when you're working with loops. You can set it, and the breakpoint will stop the flow of execution on, for example, the tenth loop if you set the pass count to 10.

FIGURE 6.37   Conditional breakpoint panel

Figure 6.38 shows the conditional breakpoint using the example Condition shown in Figure 6.37, and Figure 6.39 shows the code stopped when the Pass Count is set to 10. Notice that the loop_counter variable is still set to 9 in Figure 6.39. The code execution stopped on the line of code that increments this counter—that line has not been executed yet.

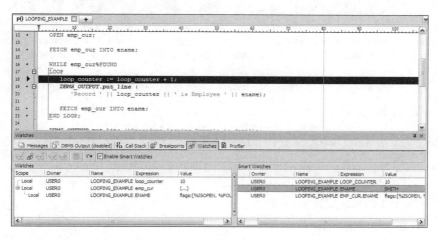

FIGURE 6.38   Conditional breakpoint with Condition set

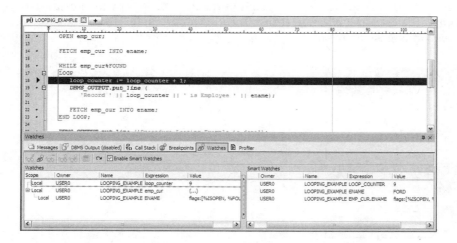

FIGURE 6.39   Conditional breakpoint with Pass Count set

NOTE

Make sure to compile for debug and execute again with each of the previous changes.

> **NOTE**
>
> When you're debugging database trigger code, INSERT INTO, UPDATE...SET, and DELETE trigger code are not available for debug until the variables have been set.

> **TIP**
>
> The Pass Count conditional breakpoint is particularly useful when you're debugging a routine that loops 500 times and has problems exiting the loop. Using the Pass Count option allows debugging to stop automatically for you after, say, 499 iterations of the loop have occurred.

Toad enables code to be debugged from a live transaction environment. This is known as just-in-time (JIT) debugging. The PL/SQL code needs to be in the Editor, compiled with debug information, and you use the Attach Debugger to External Session button.

This kind of debugging requires a bit of setup. In the application from the live environment you need to enter these three commands:

► ALTER SESSION SET PLSQL_DEBUG=TRUE

► id := dbms_debug.initialize('TOAD')

► dbms_debug.debug_on;

Then in Toad, make sure the code to be debugged is in the PL/SQL Editor with a breakpoint set, and enter the same initialization string (Toad in this example) when attaching to an external session (see Figure 6.40).

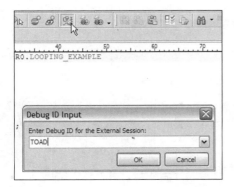

FIGURE 6.40   Just-in-time debugging

After the PL/SQL routine has terminated, be sure to enter **dbms_debug.debug_off;** in the live environment. Otherwise, the next time the application is executed, it will again appear hung while waiting for Toad's debug session to commence.

NOTE

Be sure to enter the DBMS_DEBUG.Debug_off command in the live environment to complete the live debugging session.

Using the PL/SQL Profiler

Profiling PL/SQL enables you to see how long your code took to execute and how long each line of code took to execute. This is important information to have when you're tuning PL/SQL code or a complete set of related routines.

Starting with version 8i, Oracle can track statistics on the execution of SQL, including procedures and functions. Toad interfaces with the DBMS_PROFILE (you will need execute privileges for this package) package, giving you an easy way to track and compare your program statistics. This package then populates three tables in the user's account:

▶ PLSQL_PROFILER_RUNS

▶ PLSQL_PROFILER_UNITS

▶ PLSQL_PROFILER_DATA

Toad prompts you if the required profiling objects do not exist.

Installation is easy. Oracle10g+ has the DBMS_PROFILER package already installed. For databases prior to Oracle10, the DBA staff needs to run the profload.sql script found in the <ORACLE_HOME>/rdbms/admin folder. Toad11 prompts you if the Profiler tables are not created. You can create them manually by running the proftab.sql script found in the <ORACLE_HOME>/rdbms/admin folder. Ask your database administrator for help if you need it.

The Toggle PL/SQL Profiling button (see Figure 6.41) on the Profiler's top toolbar is a toggle. Click it and then execute your code (using the Execute PL/SQL button or the F11 key). When your code has terminated, click the Execute PL/SQL button again to stop profiling. When you start profiling, Toad puts a comment into the PLSQL_PROFILER_ RUNS table of the name of the first procedure and a time stamp. Toad will profile all code called.

FIGURE 6.41   PL/SQL Profiling button

Be careful with the drop-down menu off of this button because it will remove the profiling objects if the user has permissions to do so.

This unit will profile the LOOPING_EXAMPLE procedure. The profiling process will profile any code that is called by the starting program as well.

Open the procedure you want to profile in the Toad Editor and then click on the Toggle PL/SQL Profiling button (refer to Figure 6.41). The button will appear to stay pressed. The profiling process has been started (technically Toad executes DBMS_PROFILER. Start_Profiler). You can also turn on profiling using Main Menu → Session → Toggle PL/SQL Profiling. With the Profiling button pressed, execute the procedure you want to profile using the Execute PL/SQL button or by pressing F11. Figure 6.42 shows the conclusion of executing the LOOPING_EXAMPLE. Notice the mouse cursor is on the Toggle PL/SQL Profiling button. Also notice that the profiling Output tab appears. If this tab is not present, right-click on any of the output area tabs and select Profiler. Click the Profiling button to toggle it off (Toad then executes DBMS_PROFILER.Stop_Profiler and the three Profiler table objects are updated). Make sure the Profiler tab is displayed to show the profiling results.

TIP

The book download contains a PROC_SHELL PL/SQL procedure. Put your function call into this procedure, and then execute the PROC_SHELL procedure to profile your functions.

Figure 6.43 shows the output from the PL/SQL profiling. There will be a line for each item profiled. Opening the line shows any modules that were also executed. You can easily see run times. Opening each module shows the lines of code and how long each took to execute, how many times they were passed in a loop, and more. If you click on a line in the Profiler (for example, a line with a long time), Toad will jump to that line of code in the Editor window.

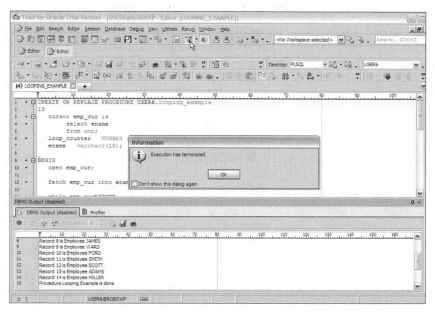

FIGURE 6.42   Executing LOOPING_EXAMPLE while profiling

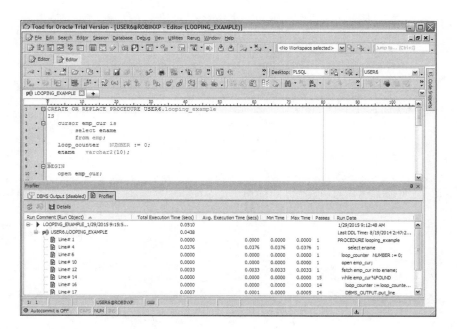

FIGURE 6.43   PL/SQL profiling output

Do you have an older version of Toad? Older than Toad 9? Choose Database → Optimize → Profiler Analysis. Alternatively, you can click Details on the Profiler tab. The resulting display is different than the one you get from the menu options, but the same profiling information is available.

Summary

This chapter illustrated many useful features for working with PL/SQL code. This unit also included information on Code Analysis, the PL/SQL Debugger, and the PL/SQL Profiler.

CHAPTER 7

Miscellaneous Tools

IN THIS CHAPTER

▶ Code Road Map

▶ External Tools

▶ Compare Files

▶ TNS Editor

▶ Script Manager

▶ UNIX Monitor

This book's content has been organized to focus primarily on the major Toad features and/or functionalities that appeal to the most people and that also get used most frequently. However, Toad offers substantially more than what can be crammed into a few chapters and their centralized topics. Thus, this chapter attempts to cover a smattering of unrelated features that don't easily fit into any other chapter's topics, and yet whose functionality is still compelling and worth covering. In baseball parlance this chapter is like the closing pitcher. It attempts to bring together all the outstanding major topics worth reading about and being able to leverage (other than the next chapter's coverage of Toad's new App Designer).

Code Road Map

Have you ever wanted a diagram of some of your PL/SQL objects, so you can visualize their interdependencies among other coded objects or even the tables that they reference? Some people refer to this as *impact analysis,* or what all will be affected by coding or database structural changes. Or maybe you need to attend a code review and need a picture to refer to while assessing code. So how does the new code fit in the overall project and what all does it interact with? Toad offers the Code Road Map for just such purposes. As with the ER Diagram (covered in Chapter 5, "Working with Data"), this feature is not meant to construct mammoth models—rather, it's better for specific and isolated or limited purposes.

To launch the Code Road Map, select Main Menu ➔ Database ➔ Report ➔ Code Road Map. The screen shown in Figure 7.1 appears. Note that this screen launches with nothing displayed in its workspace (that is, empty). You must define what's to be displayed and how—which is fully explained in the following text.

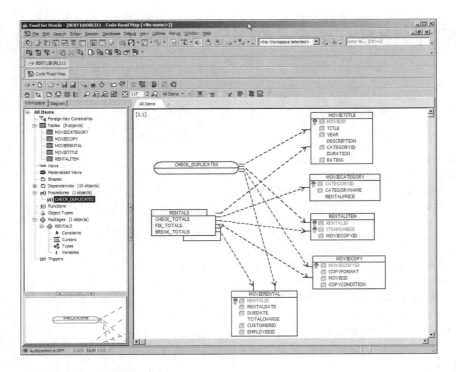

FIGURE 7.1   Code Road Map

Before explaining just how we got the information displayed in Figure 7.1, let's first look at what we see in such a completed screen. On the left-hand side (LHS), Toad displays a panel showing a tree view of the code objects and optional tables in this diagram. When you select an object in this tree-view display, the matching object in the diagram is brought into view and highlighted. So this should be your main quick-navigation tool for these diagrams. Also, the tree-view objects offer all the exact same right-click menu options as the Schema Browser. Thus, you can drop and alter objects, or perform any other Toad action upon those objects directly from inside the Code Road Map. Furthermore, if you use the right-click menu on a diagram object, you'll get all the same options as those in the Schema Browser. So the diagram itself can function as a graphic Schema Browser of sorts if you like.

But how did we get this specific information to display? Unfortunately Toad's Object Palette works for database structural objects, such as tables and views, but not coding objects, such as procedures and packages. So unlike the ER Diagram (covered in Chapter 5), we cannot utilize the Object Palette to incrementally build the model based upon specific selections. We feel that's a major shortcoming or bug—and hope to see it corrected in a future release.

Thus the Code Road Map only offers the automated quick-start method for creating models with a group of related objects already imported. When you click the Add Objects toolbar icon ![icon] (tenth choice from the left on the upper toolbar), then you will see the screens shown in Figure 7.2 (the General tab) and Figure 7.3 (the Options tab).

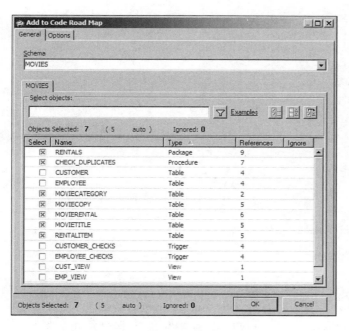

FIGURE 7.2   Code Road Map—General tab

The Code Road Map screen has two tabs that enable you to choose six things that automatically create a complete model for you: the schema, the code object type, the starting code unit, the levels of program interdependencies to automatically traverse, what to display (code only versus both code and tables), and some display options/filters. It's the fourth item that's very powerful, because it tells Toad how many levels of program interdependencies to follow and to include all those objects found. But be careful—if you start at one of your central tables and choose a high level (for example, > 5 with data or > 10 without data), then you might end up with hundreds of items in your Code Road Map. And remember, we stressed that this feature is best for limited-use scenarios. Finally, there's another and interesting way to launch this same Code Road Map pop-up screen. The Schema Browser right-click menu offers a Code Road Map option, which launches the New Code Road Map screen with the schema, object type, and code object already set based upon where you were in the Schema Browser. Again, be careful when selecting the recursion level here as well.

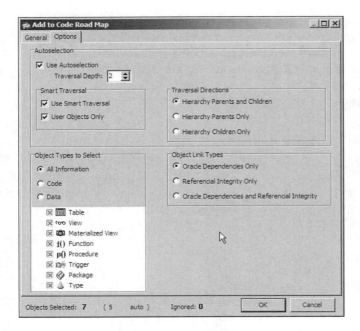

FIGURE 7.3   Code Road Map—Options tab

One final note worth mentioning is that the Code Road Map does a lot more than just follow the Oracle table for code dependencies. The real value here is that Toad also scans the code and finds a plethora of hidden or less obvious dependencies. For example, the Code Road Map includes and handles triggers in its traversal. So if procedure X calls procedure Y, and procedure Y updates table A, which then fires trigger B, which now calls procedure Z, then Toad's Code Road Map will include X, Y, and Z. Many other tools would have missed procedure Z because they don't handle triggers properly. Thus the Code Road Map can eliminate many impact analysis mistakes that get overlooked due to obscure trigger side-effects, which makes Code Road Map very useful.

After you've assembled a Code Road Map diagram that you like, you're going to want to save this work so that you can later reopen the diagram exactly as you have defined it. For that, simply click the floppy disk toolbar icon, which saves the complete current screen definition as a .CRM file. Then later when you start the Code Road Map, you can simply choose to open that pre-built model.

External Tools

There are times while you're in Toad when you need to jump into another program, such as Quest Software's Script Runner or Oracle's SQL Plus. However, you don't want to go out to the Windows Start menu because you would have to repeat information, such as your database connection, user ID, and password. So Toad has an intelligent and customizable program launcher that makes opening other programs clean and simple.

To launch the External Tools Options configuration screen, choose Main Menu → Utilities → External Tools. The screen shown in Figure 7.4 appears. The window is initially empty because Toad by default does not come with any external tools knowledge predefined.

FIGURE 7.4   External Tools—Configuration

To jumpstart the process of defining external tools, Toad offers the Auto Add button, which automatically discovers several key programs you're likely to want to use (if they are installed). When you click this button the screen shown in Figure 7.5 appears. Simply highlight the entries you find useful and click OK. The programs will then show up as available back on the main External Tools screen.

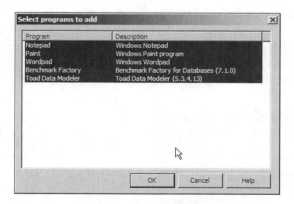

FIGURE 7.5   External Tools—Auto Add

However, you'll want to add your own entries so that you can specify various aspects of the program launch—such as the working directory, Oracle user ID, password, and other parameters. For that you will need to click the Add button, which launches the popup

shown in Figure 7.6. Here we've set it to launch the Oracle SQL*Plus utility in our C:\
Temp directory and to pass in our current connection's Oracle user ID and password.

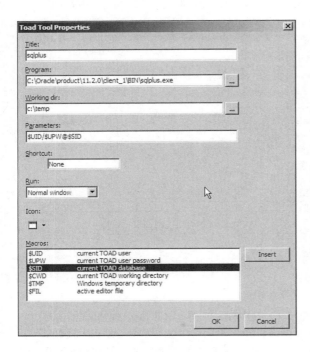

FIGURE 7.6   External Tools—Manual Add

So now anytime and from anywhere in Toad, when I want to launch into Oracle's
SQL*Plus for the same database connection, I simply choose the drop-down menu off the
Toad main toolbar as shown in Figure 7.7. That's all there is to it. Now you might say "So
what?" Toad already offers a similar capability to invoke SQL*Plus from within the Editor.
However, now you get to choose what applications can be easily invoked and how they're
called. Plus, they are now callable from anywhere within Toad.

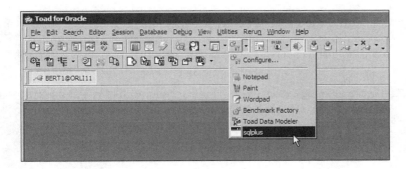

FIGURE 7.7   External Tools—launch an app

Compare Files

One fundamental task that nearly everyone needs to do is to compare text files for differences. Of course, Windows offers the COMP command, and UNIX has diff. But both of these are simply command-line utilities without advanced GUIs or reporting capabilities. So Toad offers the Compare Files utility—an advanced GUI for simplifying all comparison tasks and review.

To launch the Compare Files screen, choose Main Menu → Utilities → Compare Files. After you're prompted to choose both the source and target files for comparison, the screen shown in Figure 7.8 appears.

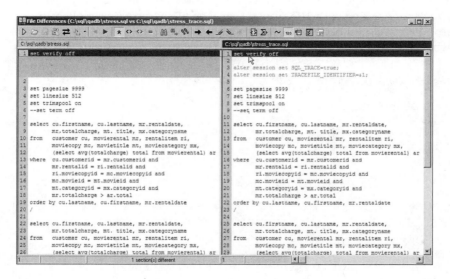

FIGURE 7.8   Compare files—result

The Compare Files screen offers quite a bit of utility, so take time to learn and use all the toolbar icons this screen has to offer. The primary buttons worth knowing include:

- ▶ Switch Sides to interchange the source and target

- ▶ Prior/Next Difference to move backward and forward

- ▶ Just show regular/major differences

- ▶ Just show matching lines

- ▶ Comparison Summary—a pop-up to summarize the overall results

- ▶ Options—a pop-up screen for controlling numerous appearance items

- ▶ File Comparison Rules—a pop-up screen for extensive control of the comparison process (that is, what actually constitutes a difference)

TNS Editor

Any developer or DBA who works with multiple Oracle databases on many different servers will invariably end up at some point with a need to modify their Oracle TNS Names file. Some people will just open the file in a text editor and have at it. Others will use Oracle's Java utilities, Net Manager or Net Configuration Assistant (NETCA), but that requires leaving Toad and its user-friendly and productive GUI. Thus Toad offers the TNSNames Editor screen for making short work of even the most complex TNS Names file (unless the file contains IFILE directives).

To launch the TNSNames Editor screen, choose Main Menu → Utilities → TNS Names Editor. The screen shown in Figure 7.9 appears. You might wonder why it offers a split screen or two panels for working with TNS Names files. The reason is quite simple: very often you'll need to copy entries back and forth between files. That's exactly what the VCR/DVD-type buttons (that is, >, <, >>, and <<) are there between the two sides for.

FIGURE 7.9   TNSNames Editor

Note that the base screen offers some useful toolbar icons that you should know about and use. The green check mark simply performs a rudimentary TNS Names file syntax check for the entire file. The lightning bolt, on the other hand, merely performs a database ping (that is, tnsping) for the selected entry. The New Service and Edit Service (F2) toolbar icons are of the most interest. They both launch the pop-up screen shown in Figure 7.10 that makes defining or updating services straightforward and easy. In fact, this screen very much mimics, in both look and capabilities, Oracle NETCA.

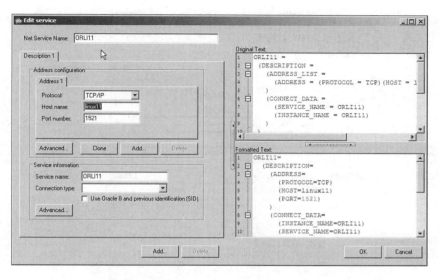

FIGURE 7.10   TNSNames Editor—Edit Service

Script Manager

Over time almost anybody doing serious Oracle work, DBAs and developers alike, will collect numerous SQL scripts. Moreover, there's always those hard-core DBAs and developers who simply prefer SQL scripts to any GUI—period. Wouldn't it be nice if Toad could help you create, organize, manage, and execute your collections of SQL scripts? And for those simply opposed to GUI tools like Toad, such a script library management interface might possibly pique their interest as well. Actually, Toad offers a handy feature to meet these users' needs—it's called the Script Manager.

To launch the Script Manager, choose Main Menu → Utilities → Script Manager. The screen shown in Figure 7.11 appears.

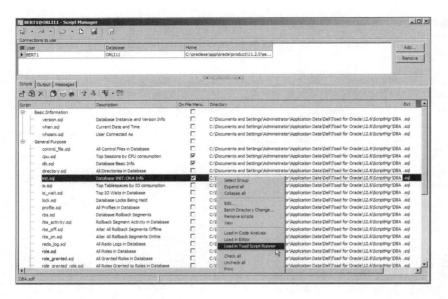

FIGURE 7.11   Script Manager

The Toad Script Manager uses special .SDF files that record the metadata about your script libraries. Toad ships with three highly useful categories of scripts predefined for you: DBA, Schema Objects, and Oracle Data Dictionary. However, you must manually open each category because they are not automatically listed. Of course, you can create additional new categories for your own collections of scripts as well as modify these prebuilt ones. In Figure 7.11 we've chosen to open the DBA library of scripts. Note that the next few paragraphs will first talk about setting up the SQL libraries, which may not seem that exciting. But then we'll show the true power of the Script Manager—which is working with those script libraries after they're defined.

There's quite a bit going on in Figure 7.11, so let's examine it in more detail. Let's start by examining the more important right-click menu options:

▶ Edit opens a pop-up window for modifying the properties (that is, the script category or use, the script description, and its location).

▶ View opens (that is, launches) your external text editor option for the highlighted script.

▶ Load in Editor just sends the script contents to the Toad Editor.

We also need to examine the first five toolbar icons under the Scripts tab. The first and second are simple enough: Add and Edit scripts. These simply open pop-up windows much like the View right-click choice. The third icon (the red X) is simply for removing a script entry from the library. The fourth and fifth icons are what offer some interesting potential. If you multi-select some script entries and then click the fourth icon (Combine

Scripts), Toad will create a new script that you name that simply calls all the selected scripts in the order you selected them. Hence you can select scripts A, B, and C and create a new script called D that calls scripts A then B then C. Don't laugh—many DBAs and developers build scripts incrementally. This enables you to build portions for basic reusability. In fact, any time you multi-select scripts and request an action to be performed, Toad asks whether you want to combine and name them. The fifth and final icon (Schedule Script) simply lets you schedule via your Windows Task Manager.

Finally, in Figure 7.11, what do the scripts with a check mark in the On File Menu column do? That's where the real power of the Script Manager lies and what we alluded to earlier. These checked scripts are known as Quick Scripts. These show up in the main menu toolbar for the Script Manager drop-down menu, as shown in Figure 7.12. Choosing a Quick Script from this drop-down menu causes that script to be loaded into the Editor and then executed as a script (that is, like pressing F5). Thus, now you can run your scripts anytime you need them and from anywhere within Toad. Toad is now serving as nothing more than a script management and execution facility—therefore it should be useful even to those anti-GUI people.

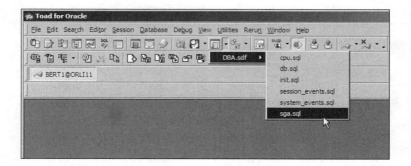

FIGURE 7.12   Script Manager—Quick Scripts

UNIX Monitor

Even though Toad is a Microsoft Windows–based tool, many DBAs and developers have to work with Oracle databases running on UNIX or Linux. In those cases the Toad user might want to monitor not just the database itself, but the operating system hosting it. Therefore, Toad offers a simple but effective UNIX Monitor screen for just that purpose. It's not a great UNIX monitor, but it beats not having one at all.

To launch the UNIX Monitor, choose Main Menu → Database → Monitor → UNIX Monitor. The screen shown in Figure 7.13 appears. However, upon launch this screen will not have a server connection, and hence the graphs will be blank. You must click the connect button to establish a server connection, and then wait for a few refreshes before the graphs will have data.

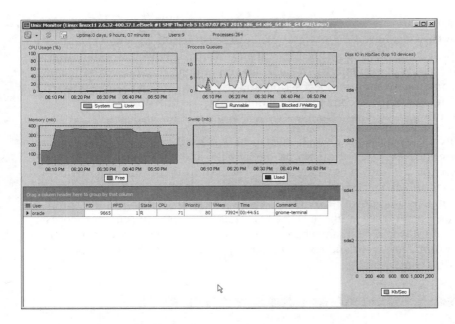

FIGURE 7.13   UNIX Monitor

As you can see in Figure 7.13, the Toad UNIX Monitor displays information for the six most useful metrics for an Oracle database server:

▶ CPU Usage

▶ Process Queue Depth

▶ RAM Memory Used

▶ Swap Space Used

▶ Disk IO by Device

▶ Process Detail List (like a UNIX `ps -ef` command)

Although some DBAs are lucky enough to have access to a full-featured UNIX monitoring tool, many do not. In that case, Toad's UNIX Monitor offers most of the basics one needs for spotting major database performance issues at the operating system level. There are two such issues to look at first. If the database server has insufficient CPU resources, then the CPU Usage chart might consistently hover above the 80% mark and/or the Process Queue Depth chart might consistently display an average of more than four processes deep. If, on the other hand, the database server has insufficient memory resources, then the Memory chart might consistently hover relatively close to the system's total memory and/or the Swap chart might steadfastly display an average of high swap space usage. Of course, in the worst case you might actually see both conditions occurring—and thus you simply need a bigger server.

Summary

Toad has often been likened to a Swiss army knife with numerous types of blades. This chapter covered an eclectic assortment of Toad screens and utilities that are useful, but do not fit neatly into any category covered by other chapters. In fact, many of these screens and utilities negate the need for separate programs to perform that function. For example, the Code Road Map diagrams your code, so you don't need Microsoft Visio or some process modeling tool. And Toad's file compare is sufficient for reviewing PL/SQL and SQL coding differences. In fact, most of these screens and utilities were requests from users like yourself who posted requests to the Toad forum, because they wanted Toad to do everything (except email). They don't want to buy other programs or even leave Toad while doing their database work.

7

CHAPTER 8

Getting Started with Toad Automation

IN THIS CHAPTER

▶ Command Line (Legacy)
▶ Automation Designer (Future)

Toad is first and foremost an Oracle productivity tool—and as we said back in Chapter 2, "Fast Track," productivity is its mantra. Most of this book's content, however, requires a person to launch Toad and perform manual labor or tasks (except for those few screens that offer an option to schedule the final step for execution). Of course, many of you have a need to perform some database tasks on a regular basis, and you don't want to have to do anything in Toad except to instruct it to perform that exact same operation with zero user input. What you're basically asking for is something like a Toad "record" and "playback" macro mode of operation. Furthermore, the playback should be callable via the command line so that you don't have to do anything at all in Toad. Guess what? That capability has been available in Toad for many years now, although it has certainly evolved over time. In this chapter, we'll explain both the older Toad command-line mechanism and the new Toad Automation Designer.

Before reading on, note that the Toad Command Line mode, which has been available for some time, is being gradually (and, in time, completely) replaced by the much more powerful Toad Automation Designer. For this reason, you should embrace the new feature, which debuted in Toad 9.7. A preliminary attempt was made to provide this capability in Toad 9.6 that was called the Action Console, but it quickly evolved into the Automation Designer. Thus, depending on which Toad version you're currently using and the status of the Automation Designer progress to fully provide such capabilities, you might find that you have multiple choices presented under several terminologies. Rest assured, however, that very soon the Automation Designer will be the only method available within Toad.

Command Line (Legacy)

Remember that the Command Line feature is being gradually phased out. Thus, your version of Toad might not entirely match the book's content. Older versions of Toad offer more screens or utilities that can be run via command line, whereas newer versions of Toad have fewer. As of Toad 12.6, the screens or utilities that currently support the command line are:

- ▶ Analyze All Objects

- ▶ Rebuild All Objects

- ▶ Rebuild Multiple Indexes (Legacy)

- ▶ Running a Report (that is, FastReport)

- ▶ Report Manager

The old Toad Command Line feature works fairly simply. When you launch certain screens, they have two icons on their tab and/or toolbar where you control generated output, as shown in Figure 8.1 (in this case, the Email Notification tab of the Rebuild Multiple Objects utility). Load All Settings from File and Save Settings to File will generally (but not always) be in the first two toolbar icon positions wherever they are to be found. When you choose the save icon, it creates a text file that contains all the information that you set for every screen control. In Figure 8.1, we selected from the main menu Database → Optimize → Rebuild Multiple Objects option to rebuild all the tables in the SCOTT schema. If we were to now click the green arrow toolbar button (where available) to execute the task, Toad would execute the required commands and update the display—turning successfully rebuilt data rows green and unsuccessfully rebuilt ones red. If instead we were to now click the red arrow toolbar button (where available) to execute the task, Toad would copy all the required commands to the Windows clipboard. We will not execute this task, however, but rather click the save toolbar icon and ask Toad to create a command-line file called C:\Temp\rebuild_scott.txt.

What does a Toad command-line file look like? It is a human-readable file (well, kind of), and you can set some options in terms of how you make decisions or program for further control. Listing 8.1 shows the simple C:\Temp\rebuild_scott.txt file that was generated for Figure 8.1. Look this entire listing over, but realize there are only two very minor portions that you'll really need to understand and work with—they're covered next. Most of the lines are just screen control settings that reset the screen to the desired state during execution and, therefore, can be safely ignored.

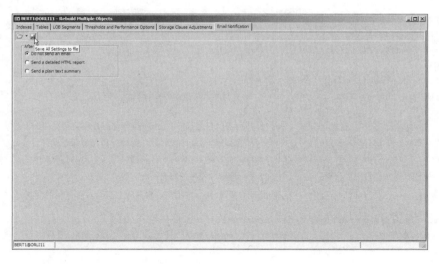

FIGURE 8.1   Save/Load settings

LISTING 8.1   Command-Line Settings File

```
1    #
2    #  You can rebuild multiple indexes or tables from a command line
3    #  using this file with a few modifications.
4    #
5    #  Lines that start with a # are comments.
6    #
7    #  Calling TOAD like this will invoke the rebuild multiple objects screen
8    #  for rebuilding indexes or tables from command line :
9    #
10   #   "C:\Program Files\Dell\Toad for Oracle 12.6\Toad.exe" -c
"BERT1/<nrdOTv8GVSiSvtEpTK2Eow==>@ORLI11" RMO="c:\temp\rebuild_scott.txt"
11   #
12   #  For backward compatibilty, RMI may be used instead of RMO.  Obviously,
13   #  your path to Toad may differ, along with your connect info.
14   #  The file name after "RMO=" is the name of this file.
15   #
16   #  You can also invoke the screen from a command file like this:
17   #
18   #   "C:\Program Files\Dell\Toad for Oracle 12.6\Toad.exe" -c system/manager@mydb
CMDFILE=c:\mycommandfile.txt
19   #
20   #  Where mycommandfile.txt might look like this, doing 2 table/index rebuilds,
then :
21   #  a schema comparison and finally building some html schema documentation.
22   #
```

```
23   #   RMO=c:\rebuild2.txt
24   #   COMP=c:\schemacomp1.txt
25   #   GENHTML=c:\html1.txt
26   #
27   #   To disable the Team Coding login prompt:
28   #   Add "TC=NO" (without the quotes) in the command line string.
29   #
30   #   Uncomment any or all of the following lines for actions to perform
31   #   after the rebuilds.  The file names and other things in quotes are of
32   #   course editable.  Do not put more than one command per line.  Do not leave
33   #   spaces before the commands.   Email settings are taken from 'View' ->
34   #   'Options' -> 'Email Settings'.
35   #
36   #   Note that there is a certain order that these commands should go in,
37   #   as it would not make sense to rebuild indexes/tables before loading them
38   #   to the grid and then checking the ones to rebuild.
39   #
40   # COMMAND SUMMARY:
41   #
42   #   The next group of commands are for loading the index grid or table grid
43   #   ------------------------------------------------------------------------
44   #   LoadUserIndexes('USERA', 'USERB', 'USERC')
45   #   LoadTableIndexes(TABLEOWNER='USERA')(TABLES='TABA', 'TABB','TABC')
46   #   LoadTablespaceIndexes('TABLESPACEA', 'TABLESPACEB')
47   #   LoadUserTables('USERA', 'USERB', 'USERC')
48   #   LoadTablespaceTables('TABLESPACEA', 'TABLESPACEB')
49   #   ImportTablesFromText('c:\MyTextFile.txt')
50   #   ImportTablesFromBinary('c:\MyBinaryFile.bin')
51   #   ImportIndexesFromText('c:\MyTextFile.txt')
52   #   ImportIndexFromBinary('c:\MyBinaryFile.bin')
53   #
54   #
55   #
56   #   The next commands are for reloading information about the currently loaded
57   #   tables or indexes.  You might use one of them after loading tables or indexes
58   #   from a text or binary file to make sure all the information is current.
59   #   --------------------------------------------------------------
60   #   ReloadAllIndexes
61   #   ReloadAllTables
62   #   ReloadAllLobs
63   #
64   #
65   #   The next group of commands are for deciding which ones to rebuild or examine
66   #   --------------------------------------------------------------
67   #   CheckAllIndexes
68   #   CheckAllTables
```

```
69  #  CheckUnusable
70  #  RemoveIndexConsiderationFailures
71  #  RemoveTableConsiderationFailures
72  #
73  #
74  #  The next group of commands are for rebuilding or examining
75  #  the checked indexes or tables
76  #  --------------------------------------------------------------
77  #  ExamineSelectedIndexes
78  #  RebuildRecommendedIndexes
79  #  RebuildSelectedIndexes
80  #  RebuildSelectedTables
81  #
82  #
83  #  The next group of commands are for doing something with the results.
84  #  (there is an on-screen option to send results via email -
85  #    then results will be sent if this option is checked)
86  #  --------------------------------------------------------------
87  #  ExportIndexesToHtml('c:\MyHTMLFile.htm')
88  #  ExportIndexesToExcel('c:\MyExcelFile.xls')
89  #  ExportIndexesToText('c:\MyTextFile.txt')
90  #  ExportIndexesToBinary('c:\MyBinaryFile.bin')
91  #  ExportTablesToHtml('c:\MyHTMLFile.htm')
92  #  ExportTablesToExcel('c:\MyExcelFile.xls')
93  #  ExportTablesToText('c:\MyTextFile.txt')
94  #  ExportTablesToBinary('c:\MyBinaryFile.bin')
95  #
96  #
97  #  The next group of commands are for closing this screen or TOAD after
98  #  the other commands have completed
99  #  --------------------------------------------------------------
100 #  CloseRMO
101 #  CloseTOAD
102 #
103 #
104 #  For backward compatibility, the following functions will work
105 #  and apply to indexes only.
106 #  --------------------------------------------------------------
107 #  ImportFromText('c:\MyTextFile.txt')
108 #  ImportFromBinary('c:\MyBinaryFile.bin')
109 #  ExportToHtml('c:\MyHTMLFile.htm')
110 #  ExportToExcel('c:\MyExcelFile.xls')
111 #  ExportToText('c:\MyTextFile.txt')
112 #  ExportToBinary('c:\MyBinaryFile.bin')
113 #  ReloadAll
114 #  CheckAll
```

```
115 #   CheckUnusable
116 #   RemoveConsiderationFailures
117 #   ExamineSelected
118 #   RebuildRecommended
119 #   RebuildSelectedInds
120 #   CloseRMI
121 #######################################
122 #           Begin Settings
123 #######################################
124 cbLobParts|0
125 RadioGroup1|-1
126 cbHeight|1
127 seHeight|4
128 cbDelRows|1
129 seDelRows|25
130 cbStorageLT|1
131 seStorageLT|25
132 cbStorageGT|1
133 seStorageGT|0
134 RadioGroup2|-1
135 cbSize|0
136 seSize|1
137 cbSizeUnits|MB
138 cbExtents|0
139 seExtents|100
140 cbNologging|0
141 cbRestoreLogging|0
142 cbSAS|0
143 seSAS|10
144 cbSASUnits|MB
145 cbSAS2|0
146 seSAS2|1
147 cbSAS2Units|MB
148 cbComputeStatistics|1
149 cbOnline|0
150 cbParallel|0
151 cbDegree|0
152 seDegree|4
153 cbRestoreNoparallel|0
154 cbNoReload|1
155 cbReload|0
156 cbReloadAll|0
157 cbIndexWithTable|0
158 cbLobsWithTable|0
159 cbCacheLobs|0
160 btnPctAlways|0
```

```
161 sePctAlways|0
162 cbMaxExtents|0
163 eMaxExt|unlimited
164 btnInitialNext|0
165 cbNext|0
166 btnScaleBy|0
167 seScaleBy|25
168 seMinSize|4
169 cbMinSize|KB
170 seMaxSize|200
171 cbMaxSize|MB
172 seSmallThresh|256
173 cbSmallThreshUnits|KB
174 seMediumThresh|5
175 cbMediumThreshUnits|MB
176 seLargeThresh|100
177 cbLargeThreshUnits|MB
178 rgBasedOn|0
179 cbAdjustSizes|0
180 cbForce|0
181 seSmallSize|64
182 cbSmallUnits|KB
183 seMediumSize|512
184 cbMediumUnits|KB
185 seLargeSize|10
186 cbLargeUnits|MB
187 seHugeSize|200
188 cbHugeUnits|MB
189 cbRound|0
190 seRound|2
191 cbAll|0
192 se1Size|1
193 cb1SizeUnits|MB
194 cbChangeSizes|0
195 rbAllTables|0
196 rbSizeTables|0
197 ComboSmallTableTS|Select a Tablespace...
198 ComboMediumTableTS|Select a Tablespace...
199 ComboLargeTableTS|Select a Tablespace...
200 ComboHugeTableTS|Select a Tablespace...
201 ComboAllTableTS|Select a Tablespace...
202 rbAllTabParts|0
203 rbSizeTabParts|0
204 ComboSmallTabPartsTS|Select a Tablespace...
205 ComboMediumTabPartsTS|Select a Tablespace...
206 ComboLargeTabPartsTS|Select a Tablespace...
```

```
207 ComboHugeTabPartsTS|Select a Tablespace...
208 ComboAllTabPartsTS|Select a Tablespace...
209 btnAllIndex|0
210 btnSizeIndex|0
211 ComboAllIndexTS|Select a Tablespace...
212 ComboSmallIndexTS|Select a Tablespace...
213 ComboMediumIndexTS|Select a Tablespace...
214 ComboLargeIndexTS|Select a Tablespace...
215 ComboHugeIndexTS|Select a Tablespace...
216 btnAllIndParts|0
217 btnSizeIndParts|0
218 ComboAllIndPartsTS|Select a Tablespace...
219 ComboSmallIndPartsTS|Select a Tablespace...
220 ComboMediumIndPartsTS|Select a Tablespace...
221 ComboLargeIndPartsTS|Select a Tablespace...
222 ComboHugeIndPartsTS|Select a Tablespace...
223 cbTable|0
224 cbTabParts|0
225 cbIndex|0
226 cbIndParts|0
227 rbAllLobSegments|0
228 rbSizeLobSegments|0
229 ComboAllLobSegmentTS|Select a Tablespace...
230 ComboSmallLobSegmentTS|Select a Tablespace...
231 ComboMediumLobSegmentTS|Select a Tablespace...
232 ComboLargeLobSegmentTS|Select a Tablespace...
233 ComboHugeLobSegmentTS|Select a Tablespace...
234 cbLobSegments|0
235 ComboLobIndexTS|Select a Tablespace...
236 cbLobIndexes|0
237 rgMail|0
```

First, we need to decide how Toad will play back this command file. To run a command-line file, the steps are as follows:

1. The Toad application launches.

2. It opens the requested command file.

3. It calls or opens the screen for that command file.

4. It sets all the screen's controls.

5. It executes that screen (for example, you click the green arrow toolbar icon).

But what should happen after that? Look at the second bolded set of lines in Listing 8.1 (at lines 100 and 101, or about roughly halfway down the listing). The comment describes two commands that you can uncomment: CloseRMO to close the open Rebuild Multiple Object screen and CloseToad to close the Toad application itself. It's been our experience that you'll typically want to uncomment both of these lines, because you'll most often just use the Toad Command Line feature to automate the process of performing a single task.

The second and more important issue is now that we've recorded a screen's settings to a file and possibly edited that file for the desired close action, how do we use it (that is, how do we run Toad and execute the command-line file)? Look again at Listing 8.1. The first bolded set of lines (at lines 23 to 25 and as explained in lines 8 through 18) details the screen-specific command-line parameter to pass to Toad to invoke this command file. We need to run Toad while passing the parameter RMO=, where RMO stands for Rebuild Multiple Objects. We also need to pass a database connection parameter, because this screen requires a database connection. We can accomplish this via the Toad -c param-eter, which provides connection information. The resulting invocation looks like the Windows command-line (.BAT) script shown in Listing 8.2. If we now double-click on this command file from Windows Explorer, Toad will launch, perform this task, shut down, and leave us with the desired output file.

LISTING 8.2   .BAT file Using TOAD Command Line

```
1 SET DB_ID=bert
2 SET DB_PWD=bert
3 SET DB_SID=ORCL
4 "C:\Program Files\Quest Software\Toad for Oracle\toad.exe" -c %DB_ID%/%DB_
PWD%@%DB_SID% rmo="c:\temp\rebuild_scott.txt"
5 EXIT
```

Remember, the Toad Command Line feature is being phased out in favor of the newer and more powerful Toad Automation Designer, so you are likely to see fewer screens with the save and load settings options going forward. Even the screens that now offer this capabil-ity soon will not. Put simply, your collection of command files will be useless someday soon. If you are *not* already using the Toad Command Line, now is probably not the time to start doing so. If you *are* already using the Toad Command Line, now is the time to start changing your process so that you switch to the Toad Automation Designer (covered next—and Toad's future).

Automation Designer (Future)

The old Toad Command Line feature had many problems, most of which are in the process of being corrected by the new Toad Automation Designer. For example, the Toad Command Line suffers from the following shortcomings:

- ▶ It is not consistently offered throughout Toad screens.
- ▶ It can perform only a single screen's tasks or operations.
- ▶ It cannot chain together tasks or operations into streams.
- ▶ It does not provide conditional logic for complex processing.
- ▶ It does not provide loop constructs for complex processing.

Basically, both the feature set and the foundation for Toad Command Line proved to be a dead end. Consequently, something new and more capable was needed. The new Toad Automation Designer meets all these challenges—and many more.

The Automation Designer feature is relatively easy to use. When you launch certain screens, two icons will appear on the lower-left corner of the window, as shown in Figure 8.2. The first icon, the camera, is for Save/Load Window Snapshot. It's the primary interface we examine here. In Figure 8.2, from the main menu we chose Database → Report → HTML Schema Doc Generator to create an HTML report of the SCOTT schema with an HTML index file called C:\Temp\scott.html. If we were to now click the green arrow toolbar button to execute this task, we would find the requested HTML report in the temp directory. However, we will not execute this task, but rather will click the camera icon (Save/Load Window Snapshot) to build our new application.

Clicking the camera icon opens the screen shown in Figure 8.3. What's happening here is that we have started to construct a Toad application. An application has three parts: *App,* which is a collection or grouping of names, *Name* for the specific application name, and *Actions* (that is, operations or tasks) that belong to it. In Command Line parlance, an action is much the same as the command file. It represents the settings selected in a single screen for execution. We can either assign the action to an existing application or create a new application by entering a currently nonexistent application name. Clicking the OK button adds this new action to the chosen application. That's it. No command file is generated, but rather a capability within Toad itself manages the application and its actions.

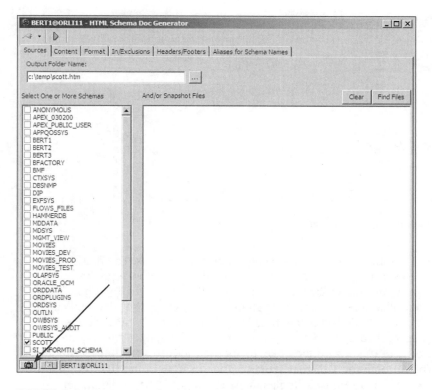

FIGURE 8.2   Automation Designer—Link from Various Source Screens

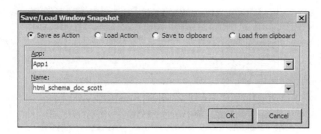

FIGURE 8.3   Automation Designer—Save Snapshot

To launch the Toad Automation Designer, from the main menu select Utilities →
Automation Designer. The screen shown in Figure 8.4 appears. There's a lot going on here,
so let's dissect all the options. After you master this screen, you can actually create all of
your applications and their actions right from it—with no real need to go to each screen
and click the camera icon in the lower-left corner. That means you'll be able to build
applications much more quickly and easily.

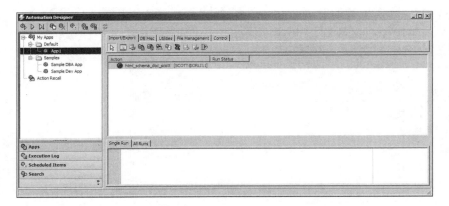

FIGURE 8.4   Automation Designer—main screen

Let's begin with the Automation Designer screen's main toolbar icons. The first three toolbar icons support executing an application (that is, all of its actions), just the action selected, or everything from the selected action in an application to the final one, respectively. The next two toolbar icons are also very straightforward: create a new application or delete one. They are followed by a schedule application icon, which defines the Windows Task Manager scheduled job required to run the Toad application. Figure 8.5 shows what the screens in this wizard look like, including the corresponding Command Line invocation. The Automation Designer syntax is much simpler than the Command Line syntax, because now there is just a single parameter to pass. The -a parameter followed by the application name—that's it. The final two toolbar icons worth mentioning are export the application to and import the application from a file. Basically Toad can save and load application definitions to text files. Note, however, that this capability is not meant to serve as a bridge between the old command-line text files and applications and the Automation Designer.

Can we see what a Toad action really looks like under the covers? You bet—just execute a right-click on an action and choose Copy from the resulting menu. Next, open a text editor and paste in the clipboard contents. You should see text like that produced by our html_schema_doc_scott action in Listing 8.3. But unlike when you are working in Command Line mode, you don't have to edit or even care about the contents of this file. However, a tremendously useful feature is available for cutting and pasting the action contents. You can now easily email or copy them to a flash drive to hand out to your coworkers. This same capability applies to any applications you want to export to text files as well.

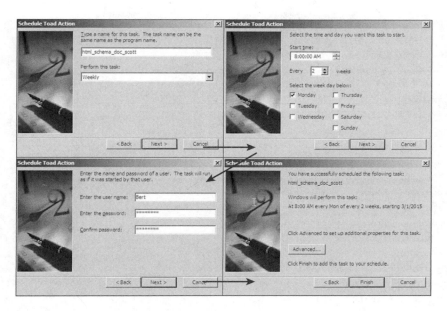

FIGURE 8.5   Automation Designer—Scheduling

Listing 8.3 provides all the Automation Designer code that is generated by this action. Although it might look like a lot of code, this listing is actually far shorter than what the old Toad Command Line mode would have generated; compare Listing 8.3 to Listing 8.1 to prove it to yourself. Yet it accomplishes the same things: It runs the Toad screen or wizard with the chosen settings, but now you don't have to scan that code for command-line parameter name settings or add close commands for either the screen or Toad.

LISTING 8.3   Automation Designer Action Code

```
1    object TarSchemaDoc
2       Enabled = True
3       ID = 43
4       ParentID = 4
5       UserName = 'html_schema_doc_scott'
6       ActionSetID = 0
7       Aliases = 'SourceType'#9'SourceName'#9'Alias'
8       CharacterSet = 'UTF-8'
9       CSS = False
10      DescCluster = False
11      DescClusterIndex = False
12      DescClusterTable = False
13      DescDBMSJob = True
14      DescDimension = False
15      DescDimensionRef = False
```

8

```
16    DescFunction = True
17    DescFunctionGrant = False
18    DescFunctionRef = False
19    DescFunctionSource = False
20    DescLibrary = True
21    DescLibraryGrant = False
22    DescLibraryRef = False
23    DescNoSysRef = False
24    DescPackage = True
25    DescPackageBodySource = False
26    DescPackageGrant = False
27    DescPackageRef = False
28    DescPackageSpecSource = False
29    DescProcedure = True
30    DescProcedureGrant = False
31    DescProcedureRef = False
32    DescProcedureSource = False
33    DescRefreshGroup = False
34    DescRefreshGroupSnapshot = False
35    DescRole = True
36    DescSchedJob = True
37    DescSchedJobGrant = False
38    DescSchedCredential = True
39    DescSchedCredentialGrant = False
40    DescSchedProgram = True
41    DescSchedProgramGrant = False
42    DescSchedSchedule = True
43    DescSchedScheduleGrant = False
44    DescSequence = True
45    DescSequenceGrant = False
46    DescSequenceRef = False
47    DescSnapshot = True
48    DescSystemTrigger = True
49    DescTable = True
50    DescTableDefault = True
51    DescTableFKConstraint = True
52    DescTableGrant = False
53    DescTableIndex = True
54    DescTableOtherConstraint = True
55    DescTablePolicy = False
56    DescTableAuditPolicy = False
57    DescTableRedactionPolicy = True
58    DescTableRef = False
59    DescTableTrigger = False
60    DescType = True
61    DescTypeBodySource = False
```

```
62    DescTypeGrant = False
63    DescTypeRef = False
64    DescTypeSource = False
65    DescView = True
66    DescViewGrant = False
67    DescViewRef = False
68    DescViewSource = False
69    DescViewTrigger = False
70    Footer1Font = '0/0/12/MS Shell Dlg 2/BOLD'
71    Footer2Font = '0/0/12/Tahoma/NORMAL'
72    Footer3Font = '0/0/12/Tahoma/NORMAL'
73    Footer4Font = '0/0/12/Tahoma/NORMAL'
74    Header1Font = '0/0/12/MS Shell Dlg 2/BOLD'
75    Header2Font = '0/0/12/MS Shell Dlg 2/NORMAL'
76    Header3Font = '0/0/12/MS Shell Dlg 2/NORMAL'
77    Header4Font = '0/0/12/MS Shell Dlg 2/NORMAL'
78    IndentHTML = False
79    NavHoverFont = '15780518/16777215/12/MS Shell Dlg 2/NORMAL'
80    NavNormalFont = '15836024/16777215/12/MS Shell Dlg 2/NORMAL'
81    NavSelectedFont = '8388608/16777215/12/MS Shell Dlg 2/NORMAL'
82    OutputFolderName = 'c:\temp\scott.sql'
83    ProcDeps = False
84    rbFilter = False
85    SchemaList.Strings = (
86       'SCOTT')
87    SubTitle1Font = '15836024/16777215/20/MS Shell Dlg 2/BOLD'
88    SubTitle2Font = '15836024/16777215/14/MS Shell Dlg 2/BOLD'
89    SumAuditPolicy = True
90    SumRedactionPolicy = True
91    SumCluster = False
92    SumComment = False
93    SumDBMSJob = True
94    SumDimension = False
95    SumFunction = True
96    SumIndex = True
97    SumLibrary = False
98    SumObjectCount = True
99    SumPackage = True
100   SumPolGroup = False
101   SumPolicy = False
102   SumProcedure = True
103   SumQueue = True
104   SumQueueTable = True
105   SumRefreshGroup = False
106   SumSchedJob = True
107   SumSchedCredential = True
```

```
108    SumSchedProgram = True
109    SumSchedSchedule = True
110    SumSequence = True
111    SumSnapLog = True
112    SumSnapshot = True
113    SumStorage = False
114    SumSynonym = True
115    SumTable = True
116    SumTrigger = True
117    SumType = True
118    SumUserBasic = True
119    SumUserObjPriv = True
120    SumUserProfile = True
121    SumUserQuota = True
122    SumUserRole = True
123    SumUserSysPriv = True
124    SumView = True
125    TableCaptionFont = '15836024/0/12/MS Shell Dlg 2/NORMAL'
126    TableDataFont = '16316664/-16777208/10/MS Shell Dlg 2/NORMAL'
127    TableHeaderFont = '15780518/-16777208/10/MS Shell Dlg 2/NORMAL'
128    TitleFont = '15836024/16777215/24/MS Shell Dlg 2/BOLD'
129    TOCEntries = 100
130    TransparentRows = False
131    UseFooter = False
132    UseHeader = False
133    UseObjectSet = True
134    UseTableExclusionFile = False
135    UseTableInclusionFile = False
136    UseViewExclusionFile = False
137    UseViewInclusionFile = False
138    BackGroundColor = 0
139    BackgroundMode = 0
140    BodyFontColor = 0
141    BodyFontSize = 0
142    FileOption = 0
143    Footer1FontColor = 0
144    Footer1FontSize = 0
145    Footer2FontColor = 0
146    Footer2FontSize = 0
147    Footer3FontColor = 0
148    Footer3FontSize = 0
149    Footer4FontColor = 0
150    Footer4FontSize = 0
151    Header1FontColor = 0
152    Header1FontSize = 0
153    Header2FontColor = 0
```

```
154   Header2FontSize = 0
155   Header3FontColor = 0
156   Header3FontSize = 0
157   Header4FontColor = 0
158   Header4FontSize = 0
159   HeaderColor = 0
160   HoverLinkColor = 0
161  LowercaseTables = False
162   PageBreaksBeforeTables = False
163   RowBackgroundColor = 0
164   SumMViewTable = False
165   TableBorder = 0
166   TableHeaderFontColor = 0
167   TableHeaderFontSize = 0
168   TableRowFontColor = 0
169   TableRowFontSize = 0
170   UnvisitedLinkColor = 0
171   VisitedLinkColor = 0
172   RunData = {
173     545046300A54617252756E44617461000B416374696F6E536574494402FF0249
174     4402FF084661696C4D6F6465070A666D436F6E74696E75650653746174757307
175     096173537563636573730000}
176   Logins = {
177     545046300A544C6F67696E526565637300054974656D730A810100005450463009
178     544C6F67696E526563000B4175746F46636F6E6E6563740805436F6C6F7204FFFF
179     000009436F6E6E656374417306064E4F524D414C11456E637279707074656564061
180     7373776F7264062C31684F4953637575541543435303554B63364E586246524871
181     30594A614E4F3230482F452B41316B57434B773D084661766F72697465080447
182     55494406267B44333734333633442D353341422D344232432D394346342D3231
183     4332454343303074437D0B4C617374436F6E6E656374050000B3F0C44450A4
184     0E40064D6574686F640200064E756D62657202000A4F7261636C65486F6D6506
185     2C433A5C6F7261636C6578655C6170705C6F7261636C655C70726F647563745C
186     31312E322E305C7365727665720850726F746F636F6C0603544E53C50726F74
187     6F636F4E616D65060603544350105265C61746976655506F736974696F6E0203
188     0F53657373696F6E526561644F6E6C79080C5361766550617373776F72640806
189     53657276657206064F524C493131045573657206054245254543100000000}
190  end
```

So far we've covered just the most basic mechanics of creating applications in the Automation Designer, corresponding to the way those tasks were carried out using the old Command Line approach, where the construction process begins from the individual screens. But as we've said, there's a much better way to define actions that is natively available on the Automation Designer screen. Furthermore, this approach nicely answers a very important question: Where within Toad is this feature implemented? Look at Figure 8.6. The first four tabs across the top right-hand side (RHS) of the screen show all the places where the Automation Designer has been implemented. As you can see, the HTML Schema Doc Generator is available and placed under the DB Misc category/tab. What's critical for you to note is that when each Toad screen finally gets Automation Designer support, a notation of its availability will show up somewhere here.

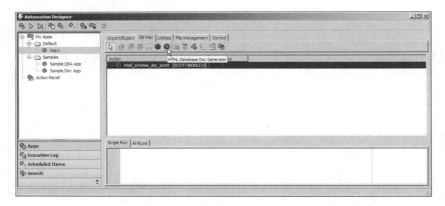

FIGURE 8.6   Automation Designer—Availability

You can simply click on one of these screen toolbar icons to add an action to an application. Also, when you execute a right-click and choose Properties, or when you double-click on an existing or new action, Toad will display the Action Properties pop-up window, as shown in Figure 8.7. Note that this screen is essentially the same one that would appear if you had invoked it via the menu system, although the save snapshot and schedule toolbar icons are no longer visible in the lower-left corner. Toad knows that you're calling the screen from the Automation Designer, so it removes these icons.

At this point, we've covered how to create and manage applications and their actions from within the Automation Designer main screen. Now it's time to add application advanced *programmatic control*—including variables, conditional logic, and looping or iteration constructs—to your arsenal of weapons. That takes us to the fifth and final tab found at the top RHS of the screen, labeled Control, and highlighted in Figure 8.8. Here you'll really be limited only by your imagination and programmatic skills. In our case, we want to perform a TNS ping operation to verify that the database is up and running before we attempt to generate our HTML Schema Doc report. We double-click on the highlighted IF THEN ELSE toolbar icon, and then drag and drop our actions to the specific syntactical portions we desire. Each action returns an action code of pass or fail—so we can place almost any action into any conditional logic expression. Now when we click the Execute Application button, Toad runs everything to completion as expected, as shown in Figure 8.8. Had the TNS ping failed, however, Toad would have skipped over the report creation action.

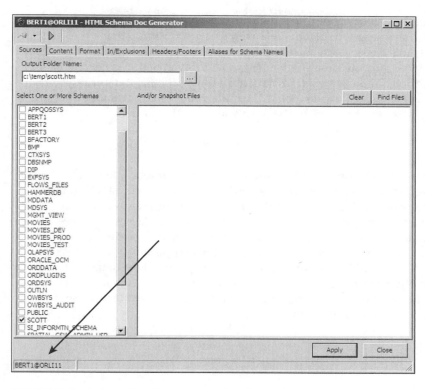

FIGURE 8.7   Automation Designer—Action Properties

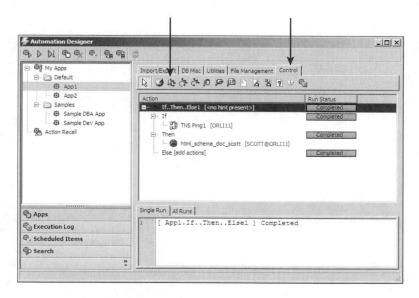

FIGURE 8.8   Automation Designer—Programmatic Control

You should spend time exploring all that the Control tab has to offer. The conditional logic, looping constructs, and variables are relatively straightforward. Three other very powerful constructs make even more wonderful things possible: the file iterator, the folder iterator, and the list iterator. Suppose you wanted to perform an action on every file in a directory (for example, import every Excel file into a table); the file iterator provides exactly this capability. Most real-world jobs will require you to take advantage of one or more of the iterators, so it's best to learn them early and use them often.

Summary

Toad is all about making you more effective and efficient at your job. And it's in terms of this latter aspect—efficiency or productivity—where Toad shines brightest. Of course, for many real-world scenarios, you simply need the capability to both record and play back (very much like macros) what you do in Toad. That way you can automate the execution of those tasks without having to launch and navigate Toad's many menus and screens each and every time you need to perform those tasks. For that purpose, Toad offers two facilities: the older Command Line feature and the newer, powerful Automation Designer. Both make automating repetitive Toad tasks much easier. The Toad Automation Designer is the wave of the future and will soon replace the old Command Line feature, so it's best to use the Automation Designer for all of your current work.

CHAPTER **9**

Database Administration

IN THIS CHAPTER

► Health Check

► Session Browser

► Database Browser

► Simple Export

► Data Pump Export

► Tablespace Management

► Generate Database Script

► Generate Schema Script

► Compare Databases

► Compare Schemas

► Analyze All Objects

► Rebuild Multiple Objects

Although Toad began its life and has historically been regarded as the Tool for Oracle Application Development, it has evolved into so much more over the past few years. Toad has features for data or business analysts, database application developers, more senior or professional database application developers, and so on, up to and including database administrators (DBAs). In fact, informal polls conducted at Toad user group meetings and other Oracle conferences suggest that approximately 40% of Toad users are truly DBAs or routinely perform various and often complex database management tasks. Clearly, Toad has become much more than just a SQL and PL/SQL developers' tool. It is now a legitimate database management offering, often complementing, or sometimes supplanting, tools such as Oracle's Enterprise Manager (OEM) and Embarcadero's DB Artisan.

Regardless of whether your job title includes the three letters *DBA*, you can and should use Toad to perform any database administrative tasks required to support your organization's databases and database applications. For example, some companies hire database consultants and expect them to do everything, whereas other shops segregate developers and DBAs, considering them to be separate job titles. From Toad's perspective, it really does not matter. If you need to do any database administrative tasks, then Toad is the tool of choice. Thus references to the term *DBA* in this book really mean anybody who's doing database administrative tasks, regardless of his or her actual job title. In fact, the DBA moniker was such a highly galvanizing term that the optional Toad DBA Module has been renamed simply the DB Admin Module.

Be aware that many capabilities covered in this chapter are not part of the standard or basic Toad product. To see which Toad options you have bought (that is, which license type you possess), simply choose Main Menu → Help → About. The pop-up dialog will list your Toad bundle and options. Most of the database administrative capabilities discussed in this chapter require the previously mentioned optional DB Admin Module. When in doubt, you can generally check Toad's online help in two places for instant clarification. First, look for help on a given feature (such as the Database Health Check). Note that all such DBA features include the following note just under the help topic headline:

> Note: This Toad feature is only available in the commercial version of Toad with the optional DB Admin Module.

The second, and often best place, to look is the help topic for the DB Admin Module itself, which lists all the DBA-specific screens and/or utilities.

Health Check

There will be numerous times where you either wonder, or get asked, about the relative health of your database. In other words, "Is your database okay?" Although that might seem like a highly subjective question, some guidelines exist by which a database can be statically reviewed and rated. We say *statically*, because the Toad Database Health Check reports on those metrics at a given point in time. It's very much like a physician's report on a person's health. The doctor (that is, Toad) looks at the patient (that is, the database) and measures many key metrics, such as height, weight, temperature, pulse, and blood pressure. These initial observations, plus automatic scanning for numerous other common symptoms, formulate the Toad Database Health Check. Often the resulting report can diagnose what ails your database. It's covered first in this chapter because it should be your first line of defense. A "clean bill of health" from this report is a welcome sanity check to prevent wasting time. Why monitor a database looking for trouble when the basic configuration might be the issue—and an issue that can be fixed upfront?

To launch the Database Health Check, simply choose Main Menu → Database → Diagnose → DB Health Check. The screen shown in Figure 9.1 appears.

The left-hand side (LHS) of the screen lists all of your known databases (with the exception of those defined in IFILE directive files), with the current database connection entry highlighted. You can select multiple items here, but note that such a choice will run the report for each and every selected database, and that could take a long while. Think back to the prior physician metaphor: You're asking for initial consultations with multiple doctors.

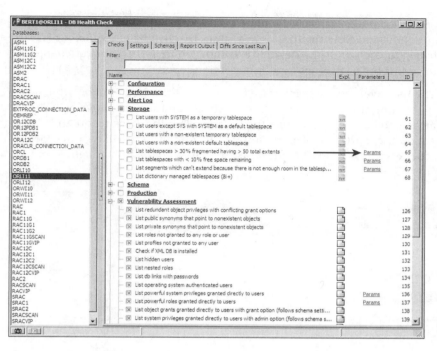

FIGURE 9.1   Database Health Check—More than 100 checks

The remainder of the screen offers five tabs. The first tab, Check, is where you select the database heath checks to perform. More than 100 total individual checks are available, broken down into ten major categories. Again, the more you select, the bigger the report will be and the longer it may take to run. Note that some of these database checks possess, to their immediate right, a "Params" option. For example the highlighted rule in Figure 9.1 lists tablespaces with less than 30% free space remaining. Clicking the Params option opens the pop-up window shown in Figure 9.2, which lets you customize that threshold value. Note that the various checks and their parameters vary, so the pop-up windows are necessarily different.

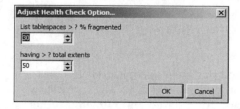

FIGURE 9.2   Database Health Check—Parameter screen

The second tab, Settings, shows Database Health Check specific options with regard to the execution and/or output. Note that there are settings for creating either text or HTML reports to be emailed to you—with the capability to show either just the things changed since the last run or just the bad things (that is, exception report).

The third tab, Schemas, offers a simple interface for filtering the schemas upon which the health checks will be run. After you've selected your checks and schema filters, you simply click the green arrow toolbar icon. That runs the Database Health Check report and displays its output on the fourth tab, Report Output. The output here will be a tree view, with the health check findings or exceptions raised shown in bold and highlighted in red, as shown in Figure 9.3.

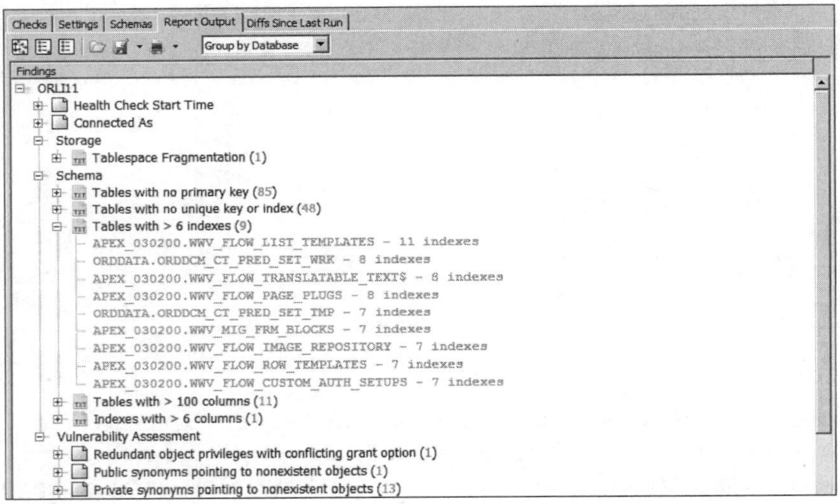

FIGURE 9.3   Database Health Check—report output

The fifth tab, Diffs Since Last Run, is very useful when you are performing iterative health checks. This tab simply displays the same tree-view information as in the Report Output tab, but with one major difference—it shows just those values that differ between run N and N + 1. This feature enables you to perform iterative database health checks, thereby verifying that incremental improvements were in fact effective.

Session Browser

The single most common database administrative task that many people do is to investigate sessions. You might need to look into a session's overall status, its locks, blocking locks, waits, current statement, explain plan, long operation status, and numerous other status or performance metrics. Sometimes this results in sessions having traces initiated or even being killed. In fact, earlier versions of Toad called this facility Trace/Kill. After it was augmented to handle all these scenarios and many others, however, this feature was

renamed Session Browser. It's quite probably one of the most used features of an administrative nature in Toad—and fortunately for many it's part of the standard product (that is,
it does not require the optional DB Admin Module).

To launch the Session Browser, choose Main Menu → Database → Monitor → Session
Browser. The screen shown in Figure 9.4 appears. Note that this screen requires access to
numerous data dictionary V$ views, which generally require extra DBA level privileges.
Also note that by default this screen displays a side-by-side format for sessions; however,
by selecting the Flip Form Layout toolbar icon 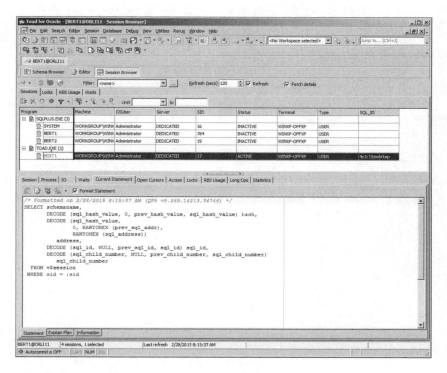 (the eighth button from the left on the
Session tab's toolbar) it switches to a top and bottom format, which often is easier to read.

FIGURE 9.4   Session Browser—main view

The Session Browser presents a very powerful screen both in terms of what it shows and
how it shows it. In fact, it's probably one of the most user-configurable screens in Toad.
You should take a few minutes to review what you can set for this screen, because you
can radically improve its readability and usability for your purposes. That, in turn, can
increase your own productivity when working with sessions.

The top portion of the Session Browser screen shown in Figure 9.4 includes four tabs.
The first tab, Sessions, is the primary focus—that is, the functionality most often used. It
shows all the sessions within your database. If you perform a right-click and click in the
data grid showing the sessions, three key customization options appear. First, you can

decide whether to display the data in a top and bottom panel style versus a side-by-side panel view. Second, you can select which columns to group by in the session's tree view. Third, you can choose which columns to display for each session in that tree view.

The bottom portion of the Session Browser screen shown in Figure 9.4 includes eleven tabs, each of which displays radically different information. Thus you will need to visit each tab and learn what it has to offer. Some tabs provide simple displays of information, whereas others present a series of sub-tabs. Take enough time to learn and master them all.

After you find a session of particular interest, the Sessions tab's session data grid offers you some options on managing them. For example, if you open the right-click menu for a session, you will see that you can kill or trace that session. These options are also available on the toolbar located just beneath the Sessions tab heading. When you choose one of these session management functions, a pop-up parameter setting screen appears, like that shown in Figure 9.5. Even though you might issue a command to trace or kill a session, that action will not actually be carried out until you see the popup and click OK.

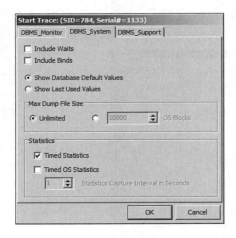

FIGURE 9.5   Session Browser—Start Trace

The second tab (Locks) of the top portion of the Session Browser screen shown in Figure 9.4 is the other most frequently used part of the Session Browser. It lists all sessions that are holding locks or are being blocked by locks. Furthermore, it indicates which types of locks have been implemented and whether they are exclusive. The blocked locks section even shows the SQL statements that are awaiting execution. This information is critical when you try to troubleshoot database lock problems, including the dreaded "dead lock" scenario. On a high-volume transactional system, this tab may take a long time to refresh. That's because these queries are not cheap, and on a busy system their overhead is even worse. Given this fact, be careful when setting any automatic refresh intervals while working with locks.

The fourth tab ("Waits") of the top portion of the Session Browser screen shown in Figure 9.4 also proves useful in many situations. It displays key database wait event information. A major shift has occurred over the past decade to move away from performance metrics such as hit ratios in favor of wait event analysis. The idea is that it's better to know what's holding things up rather than how efficiently an internal operation is performing. An analogy might help to clarify this point. If we needed to know why a trip to the grocery store took too long, which information is more useful: the average miles per hour the car drove during the trip or the fact you stopped for an ice cream cone on the way?

The Waits tab has three sub-tabs: waits during the past minute, waits by session, and waits for the entire system. In Figure 9.6, some wait times are highlighted in blue similar to a Web URL. That simply means that if you double-click on the wait, a pop-up dialog will appear with a description of what the wait means, along with some possible solutions to resolving it.

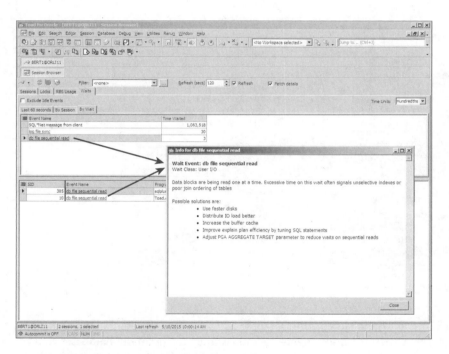

FIGURE 9.6   Session Browser—wait event help

Database Browser

The Database Browser is a relatively new addition to Toad (having debuted with Toad 9.5). It is available in Toad only when you purchase the optional Database Admin Module. The idea behind this browser's development was to create a less cluttered Schema Browser–like interface that would appeal to DBAs, who need a panoramic view of all the database objects, and especially those objects that are not owned by a schema (hence they are truly database-level objects, such as tablespaces, roles, directories, and users). You could argue that all these objects are also available in the Schema Browser and simply show up with no owning schema (for example, PUBLIC). However, as you'll soon see, the Database Browser offers many other options that are not available in the Schema Browser.

You open a Toad Database Browser screen either by clicking the database icon with glasses over it on the toolbar, or by choosing Main Menu → Database → Monitor → Database Browser. The Database Browser window opens, as shown in Figure 9.7.

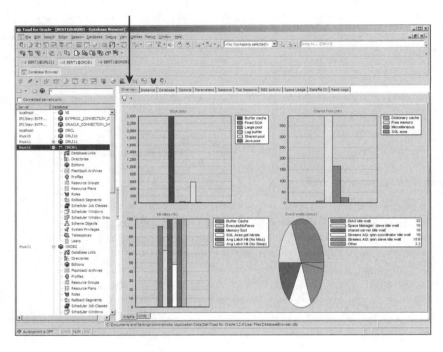

FIGURE 9.7   Database Browser—Overview

The tree view on the left-hand side of the Database Browser screen presents DBAs with a nice, single portal by which to simply navigate and connect to the many databases that they typically manage (with the exception of those defined in IFILE directive files). It's essentially a quick entry to the Toad connection process (without having to open the base connection screen) built directly into the Database Browser.

The tabs that appear on the right-hand side of the screen when you've selected a tree-view node for a specific database display various high-level database performance metrics. The summarized, read-only information presented in these tabs is quite often available elsewhere within Toad with more details and capabilities. For example, the Database Browser's Sessions tab displays a nice summary of what's contained in the Session Browser screen (covered earlier in this chapter) and shown here in Figure 9.8. Note, too, that this tab includes toolbar icons that can send you directly to the session-related screens such as the Session Browser and SGA Trace/Optimization screens. All the tabs offer contextually useful quick launch points to the detailed screens that would be your next logical step.

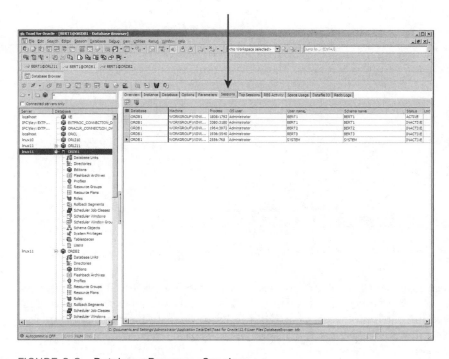

FIGURE 9.8   Database Browser—Sessions

But here's where the Database Browser begins to demonstrate its special and useful features. What if you wanted to know about all the active sessions for all the databases on your server—how would you view all of that information in one spot? To do so, you would either multi-select all the desired databases on the tree view or choose the server node. Now the Toad Database Browser will display the aggregated information for that selected tab, as shown in Figure 9.9.

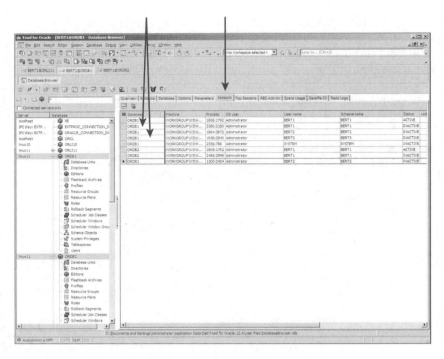

FIGURE 9.9   Database Browser—Sessions multi-select

Note how you can now see all your database sessions across all the selected databases; this is the only place in Toad where you can do any such cross-database analysis and investigation. This aggregation capability works across all the Toad Database Browser tabs—and on some tabs adds even more information. For example, the Space Usage and Datafile IO tabs present a special summary total at the bottom of the tab, as shown in Figure 9.10.

So far, we've covered the most basic items that the Toad Database Browser has to offer. Now it's time to move into the real meat of this function—the really cool stuff that's going to make your database administrative life much easier. One of the chief complaints over the years with Toad has been the seemingly overly complex (or convoluted, depending on whom you ask), ever-growing, and ever-changing list of menu items on the main menu. Basically Toad has become a Swiss Army knife with so many blades to the interface that to choose among them has become overwhelming. Even though (as was pointed out in Chapter 2, "Fast Track") Toad users can customize all the menus and toolbars, users still expressed a desire for some simplification of the workflow (that is, not having to connect, and then navigate the main menu every time they wanted to do something).

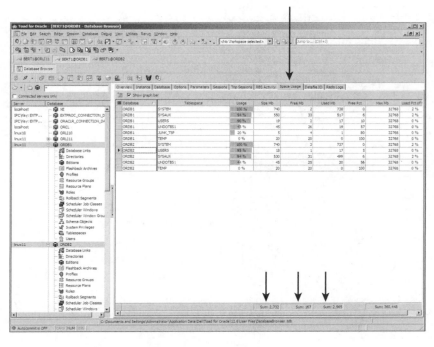

FIGURE 9.10   Database Browser—Space Usage summary

The Database Browser addresses this problem as well. In fact, you should be able to almost forgo the main menu after you begin routinely navigating via the Database Browser. As was mentioned in connection with Figure 9.8, the various tabs offer toolbar icons to send you to the contextually related, full-powered screens—but that's still too cumbersome. The real useful power lies back in the tree view for the database nodes, which offer a right-click providing all the key screens you might need, as shown in Figure 9.11.

Armed with this powerful capability, you should find yourself navigating to the Database area of the main menu much less frequently (if at all). This one time saver alone will pay for itself in short order. But we're not quite done yet—there's one final useful Database Browser capability to examine.

Often while browsing their managed databases, DBAs need to focus on or concentrate on true database objects and their management. The Database Browser addresses this need as well. When you select a database object on the tree view and click on the plus sign (+) as shown in Figure 9.11, the Database Browser displays just a subset of the Schema Browser on the right side for that specific object type. This display is not meant to entirely replace the Schema Browser for DBAs, but rather to augment their 50,000-foot, rapid database viewing and navigation portal with just the basics needed for typical DBA-type object maintenance.

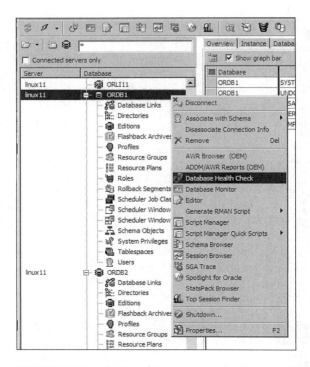

FIGURE 9.11   Database Browser—menu items available

Simple Export

Oracle has historically favored its command-line export utility (that is, EXP) for exporting database objects. This utility can be run on either the database server or a client machine such as your PC, and it creates a proprietary binary file that contains the selected database objects' definitions and data. Using such command-line tools has always been troublesome, however, because you need to be familiar with so many commands. As a result, many people end up having to code the calls to EXP with their Oracle Utilities Manual in hand—and that is not nearly as productively as most of us like to work. Toad offers a wonderful GUI front end to the Oracle utility that can totally eliminate the need for the Oracle manual.

To launch the Export Utility Wizard, choose Main Menu → Database → Export → Export Utility Wizard (note that you must have previously defined the executable and path via Toad Options → Executables on the main menu bar). The screen shown in Figure 9.12 appears.

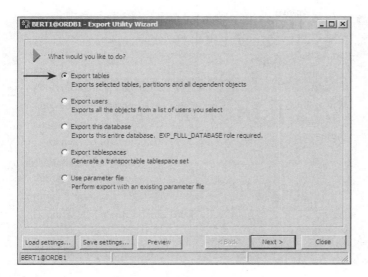

FIGURE 9.12   Export Utility Wizard—Step 1

The export wizard presents a multistep interface; the content of which fully depends on the selections that you make on its screen. For example, we've chosen to perform a user- or schema-level export. Hence the following comments and screen snapshots highlight the process and options for that selection. The other options are not much more complicated, so if you understand this example you'll be more than adequately prepared for the other user cases not presented here.

The second step of the Export Utility Wizard (not shown in a figure) lets you select the schemas to export. On that screen we set the Filter check box to say that the results should display only selection schemas that own objects and should be presented as a simple LHS versus RHS display that shows the schemas available and selected, with buttons available to move them back and forth between panels.

The Export Wizard's third step displays the most common command-line parameters for the Oracle export utility, as shown in Figure 9.13. Of these, the only one that affects what you see on the screen is Number of Rows Between Feedback Dots. When a feedback count is specified, you will see a dot (.) displayed every time that number of rows has been processed.

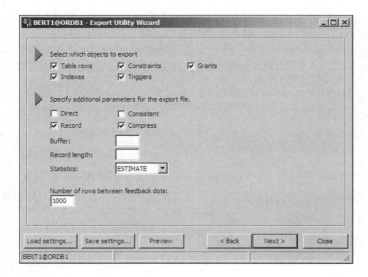

FIGURE 9.13   Export Utility Wizard—Step 3

In the Export Utility Wizard's fourth step (not shown in a figure), you specify the locations for the export's output file, log file, and parameter file. When you first enter a value for just the export file, the other values are filled in by default. Thus, all of these files will, by default, end up in the same directory and with the same name, differing only in terms of their file extensions. For many people, that's good enough.

The export wizard's fifth and final step lets you select how to actually run or execute the export process. As shown in Figure 9.14, you can run it immediately (with or without the feedback being displayed), schedule it to run at a later time using the Microsoft Window's scheduler, or create the export parameter file with all your selections. If you choose to execute the export process now, Toad will display an Export Watch window for monitoring the export utility's execution. This watch window is non-modal, which means you can initiate an export and then go off and do something else within Toad while the process continues in the background.

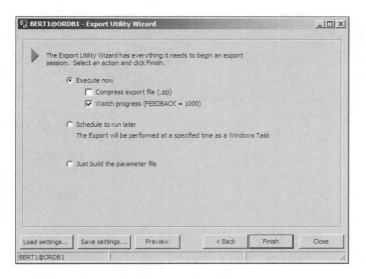

FIGURE 9.14   Export Utility Wizard—Step 5

Data Pump Export

Starting with Oracle 10g, Oracle has offered (and favored) the new Data Pump utility as a general and much-improved replacement for the Oracle Import and Export features. Thus the information in the previous section is probably of more benefit to those people who use Oracle 9i and earlier versions of this application. Nonetheless, you should read the prior section before proceeding with this section on exporting data via the Data Pump, because the Data Pump Export is so similar to the older Export utility that many of the same options, and therefore wizard navigation directions, will apply. Furthermore, Oracle is moving to close that gap and make the two utilities interchangeable in terms of syntax (starting with 11g Release 2), so that knowing one utility will mean knowing the other. However, one key difference exists between the two—namely, Data Pump is purely a database server-side feature. Thus, when Toad initiates a Data Pump export operation, the work is actually performed on the database server. Likewise, the export output file will reside on that same database server. Toad will create and manage that Data Pump Export processing request, but all the activity actually takes place on the server side.

To launch the Data Pump Export wizard, choose Main Menu → Database → Export → Data Pump Export (note that you must have previously defined the executable and path via the main menu's Toad Options → Executables option). The screen shown in Figure 9.15 appears. Note that while it presents the same basic conceptual options as the Export screen shown in Figure 9.12, the screen has been re-engineered from a multi-step wizard into a simpler tabbed design (consistent with all the other tabbed interfaces through Toad). You will see some other, very minor cosmetic differences along the way as well. Some major differences will also be apparent, as the Data Pump offers features and capabilities not found in the older Export utility.

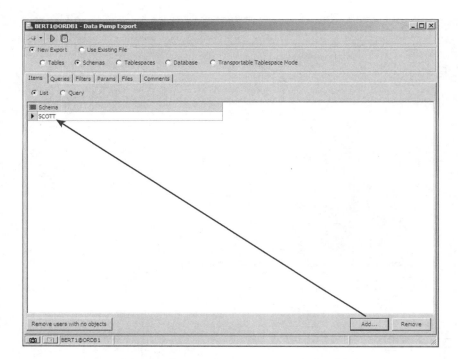

FIGURE 9.15   Data Pump Export—tabbed interface

The Data Pump Export wizard presents a tabbed interface whose content fully depends on the selections you make. For example, we've chosen to perform a user- or schema-level export. Hence the following comments and screen snapshots highlight the process and options for that selection. The other options are not much more complicated, so if you understand this example you'll be more than adequately prepared for the other user cases not presented here.

The first tab of the Data Pump Export Utility wizard lets you select the schemas to export. When you click the Add button, a pop-up screen called the object search (and used elsewhere throughout Toad) will enable you to find all those schemas that match your criteria. After you select them, this pop-up window will close, and the first tab will now contain a row per selected schema.

The second tab offers you the capability to add a data filtering query to the export process. For example, you might add something like "export data for only those customers who reside in the state of Texas and who have active accounts." This type of filter can greatly reduce both the export run time and the export file size.

The third tab enables you to specify some meta-data filters—specifically, which database object types to include or exclude. For example, you could check the options to exclude procedures, functions, package headers, and package bodies. The interface presents an extensive list of all database objects that can be filtered this way.

The Data Pump Export wizard's fourth tab displays all the most common command-line parameters for the Oracle export utility, as shown in Figure 9.16. Note that this tab includes compression (which might require additional Oracle licensing for maximum benefit) and uses transportable options. Plus it also offers the capability to define remap functions to be applied during execution.

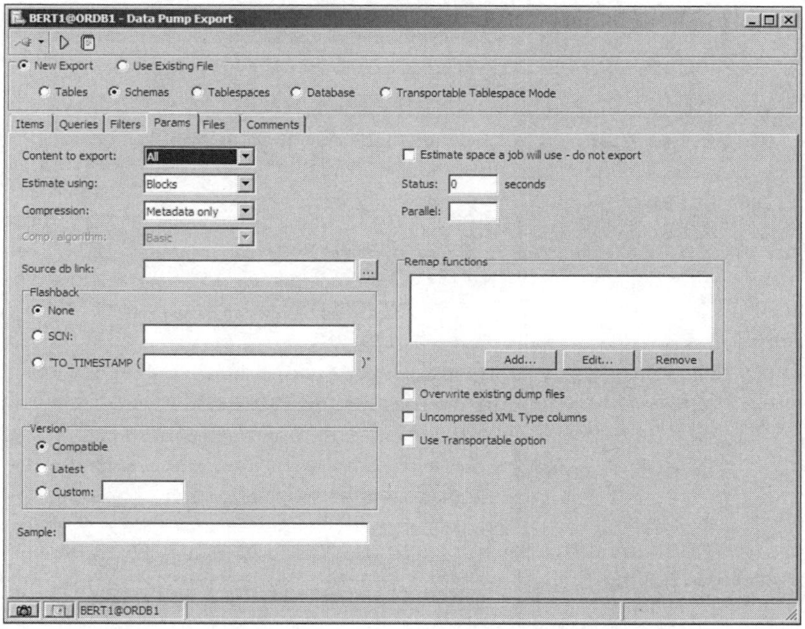

FIGURE 9.16   Data Pump Export—Parameters

In the Data Pump Export Utility wizard's fifth tab, you specify the locations for the export file, log file, and bad records file. When you first enter a value for just the export file, the other values are filled in by default. Thus all of these files will, by default, end up in the same directory and with the same name, differing only in terms of their file extensions. For many people, that's good enough. But there is one major difference here as opposed to the simple export described in the previous section: With the Data Pump, you must specify the name of the Oracle directory object where these files will be located, as shown in Figure 9.17. Also, you have to provide a job name for the export process. This is the database server-side job name that the task will be run under—whether it's run immediately or scheduled for later execution.

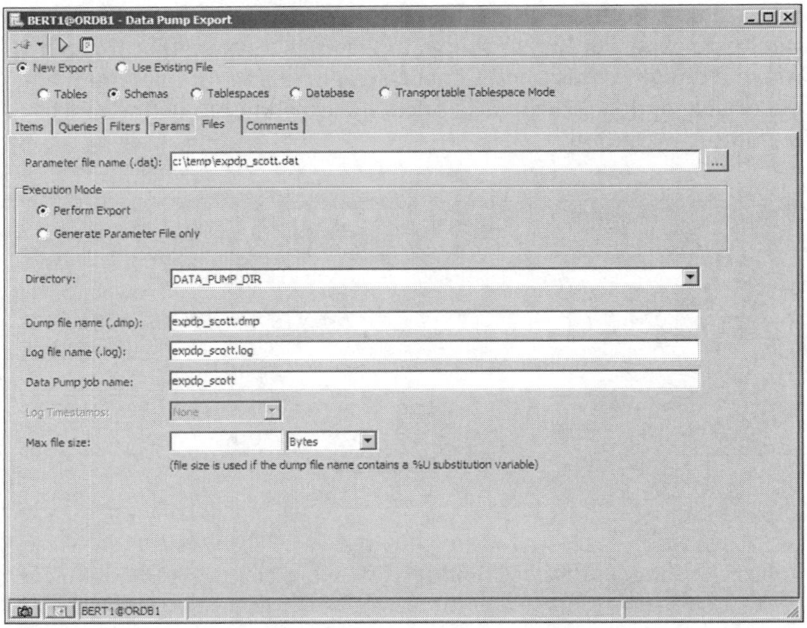

FIGURE 9.17   Data Pump Export—file locations

The Data Pump Export now contains sufficient information for you to actually run or execute the export process by clicking the green right arrow toolbar icon. As shown in Figure 9.18, Toad will display an export watch window for monitoring the Data Pump Export utility's execution and echoed output. This watch window is non-modal, which means you can initiate an export and then go off and do something else within Toad while the process continues in the background.

If and when you schedule Data Pump jobs to run at a later time, or if your Toad session somehow gets disconnected from the Data Pump process while it's running (for example, Toad or Windows crashes), then you can always have Toad reconnect to the prior submitted Data Pump jobs because they run on the database server. Toad provides a simple Data Pump job process monitoring screen so that you can watch the execution of those jobs. To launch the Data Pump Job Manager, choose Main Menu → Database → Import → Data Pump Job Manager. The screen shown in Figure 9.19 appears. With this screen, you can stop or start Data Pump jobs as necessary, as well as reconnect to those jobs that are already running.

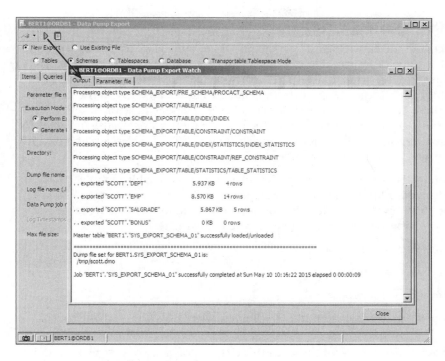

FIGURE 9.18   Data Pump Export—execution

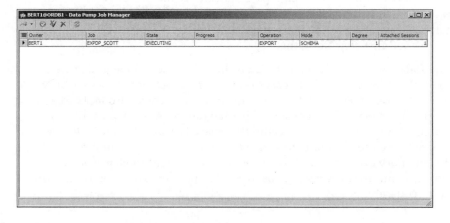

FIGURE 9.19   Data Pump Job Manager

Tablespace Management

Oracle tablespaces are the basic "logical" containers where users place all database objects that require or consume disk space. For example, basic tables and indexes consume disk space, so they must reside within a tablespace. Other database objects such as directories and external tables don't consume space, so they merely require an entry in the data dictionary. For those objects that consume space, a key database management task is to make sure that sufficient room exists for both today's and tomorrow's needs. You want to avoid Oracle error messages such as "cannot allocate extent." Thus tablespace and data file management are key, routine administrative tasks.

Because Toad originally began as a developer's tool and then evolved into more, its tablespace offerings are a little disjointed. We hope to see that inconsistency corrected in the future, but for now there are four locations within Toad for performing tablespace administrative type tasks (which are explained in the following text):

▶ Database Browser → Space Usage

▶ Database Browser → Tablespaces

▶ Schema Browser → Tablespaces

▶ Main Menu → Databases → Administer → Tablespaces

The Toad Database Browser (covered earlier in this chapter) offers two ways to view and work with tablespaces. First, when the LHS focus is on the database instance, the right-hand side (RHS) offers the Space Usage tab. It provides simple "one-stop shopping" for seeing the 50,000-foot overview of your tablespace allocations and current consumptions (see Figure 9.20). Note that in early versions of Toad this tablespace management interface lacked a bar chart representation of the percentage consumed per tablespace. Even with this omission, it's a good first step along the way.

Second, when the Database Browser LHS focus is on the Tablespaces node under the database instance itself, the RHS offers a Tablespaces portion of the Schema Browser (the third way to work with tablespaces). Figure 9.21 shows this interface, which also lacks a bar chart representation of the percentage consumed per tablespace. A bar chart indicating the space consumed per data file for that specific tablespace is available, but you have to visit each tablespace to see the total or cumulative tablespace space consumption picture. Nevertheless, this interface does offer all the right-click options and toolbar icons for numerous tablespace administrative tasks. Thus, this tablespace interface will be one that you'll need to use frequently.

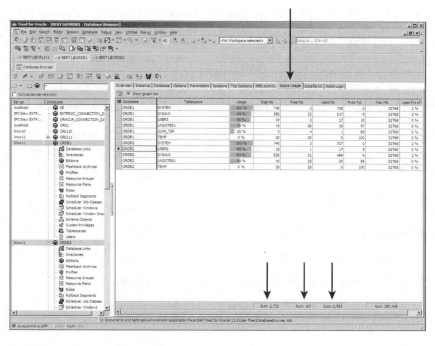

FIGURE 9.20   Database Browser—Space Usage

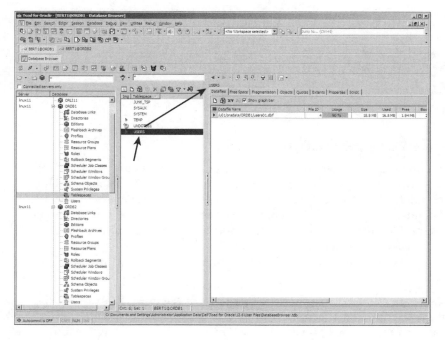

FIGURE 9.21   Database Browser—Tablespaces node

Finally, Toad offers a screen called View Tablespaces that presents much the same 50,000-foot view of tablespace information as the Database Browser Space Usage tab provides. To launch this screen, select Main Menu → Database → Administer → Tablespaces. The screen shown in Figure 9.22 appears. Note that this screen offers three unique features not found in the other three tablespace interfaces: a bar chart representation of the percentage consumed per tablespace, plus the ability to record the history for both the space used over time and the IO bandwidth or load. When you first visit either the Space History or IO History tabs, a pop-up window will remind you to create the server-side tables and database jobs to track this information. You simply connect as the Toad schema and click the Create Space Manager Tables icon on that tab. Of special note is that the Space History tab offers the capability to forecast or predict your space needs. Based on your recent space usage history, it applies proven statistical models to predict your disk space needs over the next user-specified time interval (with 30 days being the default).

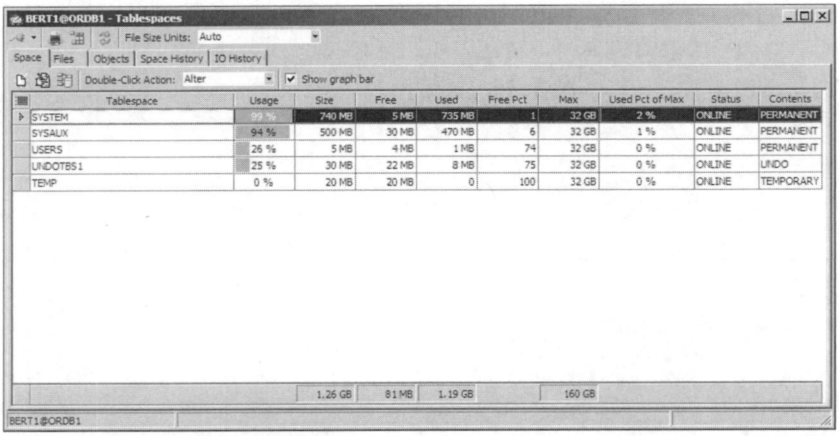

BERT1@ORDB1 - Tablespaces

File Size Units: Auto

Space | Files | Objects | Space History | IO History

Double-Click Action: Alter | ✓ Show graph bar

Tablespace	Usage	Size	Free	Used	Free Pct	Max	Used Pct of Max	Status	Contents
SYSTEM	99 %	740 MB	5 MB	735 MB	1	32 GB	2 %	ONLINE	PERMANENT
SYSAUX	94 %	500 MB	30 MB	470 MB	6	32 GB	1 %	ONLINE	PERMANENT
USERS	26 %	5 MB	4 MB	1 MB	74	32 GB	0 %	ONLINE	PERMANENT
UNDOTBS1	25 %	30 MB	22 MB	8 MB	75	32 GB	0 %	ONLINE	UNDO
TEMP	0 %	20 MB	20 MB	0	100	32 GB	0 %	ONLINE	TEMPORARY
		1.26 GB	81 MB	1.19 GB		160 GB			

BERT1@ORDB1

FIGURE 9.22   View Tablespaces screen

Generate Database Script

On occasion, you might have a need to generate a script for all your database-level objects (that is, those not owned by a schema, but rather required to build the database itself). For example, you might want to create your development and test databases to provide the same basic foundation as your production database server. Thus, you want the same tablespaces, roles, profiles, users, resource plans, resource consumer groups, and so on. Hence, you need an easy way to generate the Data Definition Language (DDL) for that collection of database-level objects. Toad offers the Generate Database Script screen for that purpose.

To launch the Generate Database Script screen, choose Main Menu → Database → Export → Generate Database Script. The screen shown in Figure 9.23 appears. Note that this screen requires access to numerous data dictionary V$ views, which generally require extra DBA level privileges.

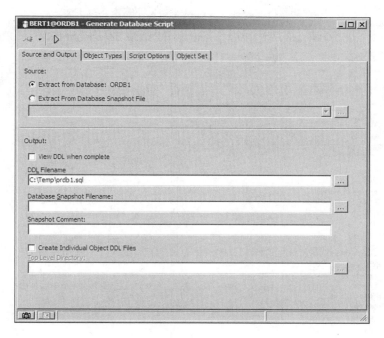

FIGURE 9.23   Generate Database Script—Source and Output

This screen has five tabs; four are present initially, and the fifth is displayed after you click the green arrow (Execute button). The first tab, Source and Output, enables you to specify two critical pieces of information: the source and the output.

Before going any further, we need to explain what a Toad database snapshot (.DEF) file is. Toad can capture an offline copy of your database dictionary and store that metadata in a binary file on your PC. This snapshot file can be used either as a super-fast copy of your data dictionary or as a historical and version control system of sorts for your data dictionary. Toad can process snapshot files hundreds of times faster than even local database data dictionaries. As a consequence, snapshot files are an extremely useful tool for working with large databases when you're doing various compare and generate operations.

Returning to the Generate Database Script screen shown in Figure 9.23, the first tab's options permit you to use either a database connection or a previously captured snapshot file as the source. The target can be a SQL text file, a snapshot file, or both. In our case, we chose to capture both in the C:\Temp directory. The Source and Output table also offers you the option to view the SQL file after it has been generated and an option to create a SQL file per object under a user-specified directory structure.

The second and third tabs, Object Types and Script Options, enable you to choose those database-level objects that will have their DDL generated, plus a few DDL generation syntactical options. The more database-level objects you pick, the longer the run time and the larger the generated script. We skip discussing the fourth tab as it's fairly self-explanatory.

After you click the green arrow (the Execute button), the fifth tab, Object Listing, appears. It presents a tree view showing the object types, their counts, and their object names generated, as shown in Figure 9.24.

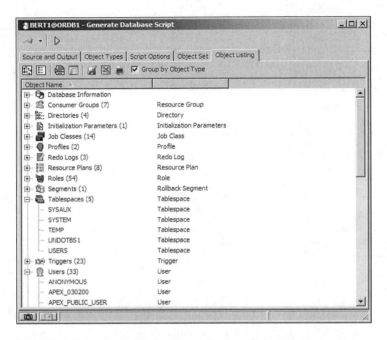

FIGURE 9.24   Generate Database Script—Object Listing

Generate Schema Script

A fairly common database administrative task is to generate a script for all the schema-level database objects (that is, those owned by a schema, and not by the database or PUBLIC). For example, you might want to copy the SCOTT tables, indexes, sequences, views, procedures, functions, and packages from the development environment to the test environment. To do so, you want an easy way to generate the DDL for that collection of schema-level objects. Toad offers the Generate Schema Script screen for that purpose.

To launch the Generate Database Script screen, choose Main Menu → Database → Export → Generate Schema Script. The screen shown in Figure 9.25 appears.

This screen includes six tabs and a pop-up SQL display after you click the green arrow (the Execute button). The first tab, Source and Output, enables you to specify two critical pieces of information: the source and the output.

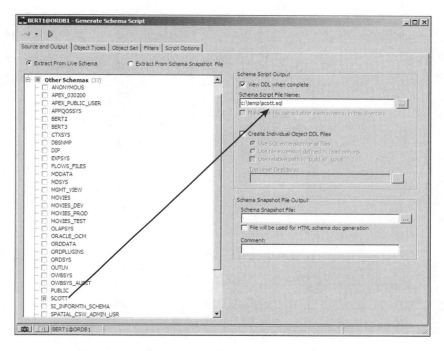

FIGURE 9.25   Generate Schema Script—Source and Output

The Source and Output tab's options permit you to use either a database connection or a previously captured snapshot file as the source. (See the discussion of snapshot files in the preceding section.) When using a database connection, you can select multiple schemas to reverse engineer. The target can be a SQL text file, a snapshot file, or both. In our case, we chose to capture both in the C:\Temp directory. The Source and Output tab also provides the option to view the SQL file after it has been generated, as well as an option to create a SQL file per object under a user-specified directory structure. Note, too, that there is a check box for indicating whether this snapshot file will later be used for Toad HTML Schema Doc report execution, in which case Toad captures some extra information necessary for that purpose.

The second and fifth tabs, Object Types and Script Options, enable you to choose those schema-level objects that will have their DDL generated, plus a few DDL generation syntactical options. The more schema-level objects you pick, the longer the run time and the larger the generated script.

After you click the green arrow (the Execute button) and the processing completes, the pop-up SQL window appears, as shown in Figure 9.26. It includes a comment at the top showing the object types, their counts, and their object names generated. Note that this screen requires access to numerous data dictionary V$ views, which generally require extra DBA level privileges.

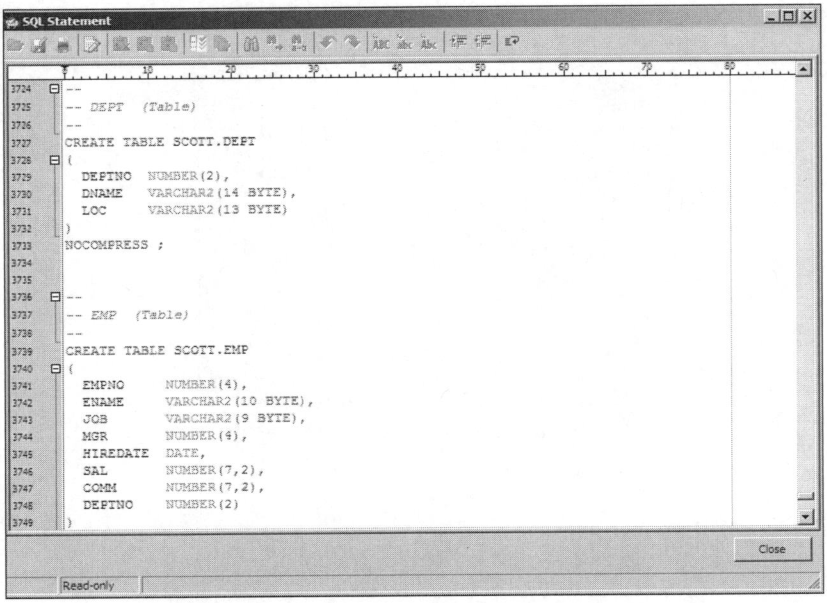

FIGURE 9.26   Generate Schema Script—SQL Display

Compare Databases

Sometimes you might need to compare and synchronize all your database-level objects (that is, those not owned by a schema, but rather required to build the database itself) between two different databases. For example, you might want to compare your test database to a production version to verify that both have the same basic foundation. Thus, you want the same tablespaces, roles, profiles, users, resource plans, resource consumer groups, and so on. In this situation, you want an easy way to compare and sync the database-level objects. Toad offers the Compare Databases screen for that purpose.

To launch the Compare Databases screen, choose Main Menu → Database → Compare → Databases. The screen shown in Figure 9.27 appears.

This screen includes five tabs; three are presented initially, and the fourth and fifth appear after you click the green arrow (the Execute button). The first tab, Databases, permits you to specify three critical pieces of information: the reference or source database, the comparison or target database, and where the synchronization SQL script will be written (scroll to the right of the target database where there is a column for the sync script). The order you choose here matters greatly, which explains the right-click menu option on a desired target that offers the choice for Switch with Source Database that enables you to switch or reverse the current selection. You can specify either a database connection or a previously captured snapshot file for both the reference and comparison database sources (refer to the earlier discussion for more information on snapshot files).

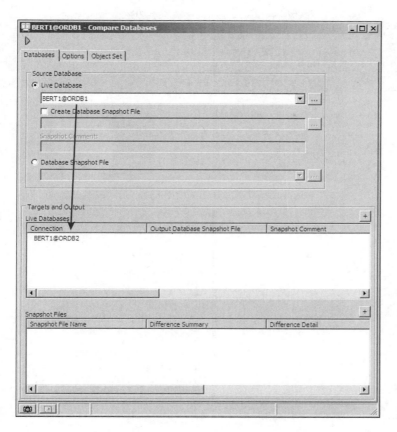

FIGURE 9.27   Compare Databases—Databases

The second tab, Options, enables you to choose those database-level objects that will have their DDL generated. The more database-level objects you pick, the longer the run time and potentially the larger the generated script.

After you click the green arrow (the Execute button) and the comparison processing has completed, the fourth and fifth tabs appear. The fourth tab, Results, presents a tree view showing the three types of objects: objects in the source and not in the target, objects in the target and not in the source, and objects that differ between the two databases (see Figure 9.28).

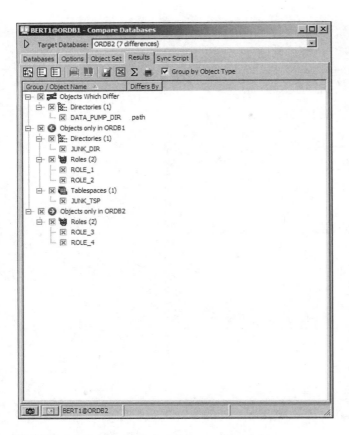

FIGURE 9.28   Compare Databases—Results

The fifth tab, Sync Script, shows the DDL necessary to sync the source to the target. If you feel the results are backward (a common error), then simply go back to the first tab and reverse the order of your prior selections.

Compare Schemas

On some occasions, you might need to compare and synchronize all of your schema-level objects (that is, those owned by a schema, and not by the database or PUBLIC) between two different databases. For example, you might want to compare your development database to a test version to verify that two MOVIES schemas are identical. Thus, you want the exact tables, indexes, sequences, views, procedures, functions, and packages. To complete this task, you want an easy way to compare and sync these schema-level objects. Toad offers the Compare Schemas screen for that purpose.

To launch the Compare Schemas screen, choose Main Menu ➔ Database ➔ Compare ➔ Schemas. The screen shown in Figure 9.29 appears.

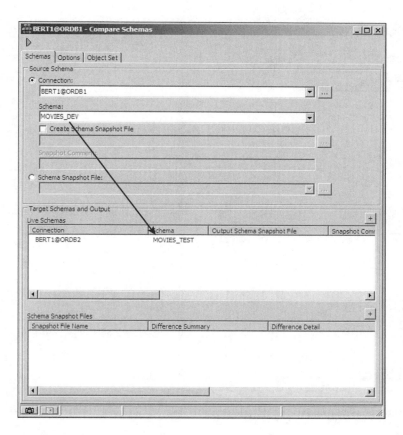

FIGURE 9.29   Compare Schemas—Schemas

This screen includes five tabs; three are presented initially, and the fourth and fifth appear after you click the green arrow (the Execute button). The first tab, Schemas, permits you to specify two critical pieces of information: the reference or source schema and the comparison or target schema. Both schema sources permit you to specify either a database schema or a previously captured snapshot file as the reference and comparison schema sources (refer to the earlier discussion of snapshot files for more information).

The second tab, Options, enables you to choose those schema-level objects that will have their DDL generated. The more schema-level objects you pick, the longer the run time and, potentially, the larger the generated script.

After you click the green arrow (the Execute button) and the comparison completes, the fourth and fifth tabs appear. The fourth tab, Results, presents a tree view showing the three types of objects: objects in the source and not in the target, objects in the target and not in the source, and objects that differ between the two schemas (see Figure 9.30). The fifth tab, Sync Script, shows the DDL necessary to sync the source to the target.

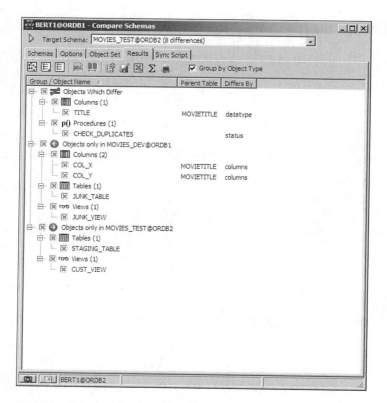

FIGURE 9.30   Compare Schemas—Results

Analyze All Objects

Starting with Oracle 10g, the database query optimizer has switched to being entirely *cost-based* (instead of *rule-based*, as was the case in Oracle 9i and earlier versions). That means that gathering accurate and up-to-date statistics and histograms has never been more critical than it is now. Whether the focus is your application's queries, third-party database applications, or even a tool like Toad, obtaining proper statistics is now a high-priority database administrative task. Luckily, Toad offers the Analyze All Objects screen to simplify that duty.

To launch the Analyze All Objects screen, choose Main Menu → Database → Optimize → Analyze All Objects. The screen shown in Figure 9.31 appears.

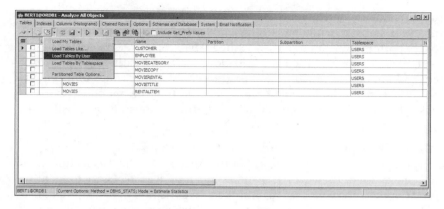

FIGURE 9.31   Analyze All Objects—Tables

By default, this screen launches with no data (that is, the tables, indexes, and columns tabs all contain empty data grids). In Figure 9.31, we have chosen to load the tables for the MOVIES schema by using the drop-down list and selecting Load Tables by User. A pop-up window then displays the schemas that we can choose. You can follow the same steps on the indexes and columns tabs if you want to gather index statistics and histograms as well. Note that for any of these, you must select the check boxes at the start of each row, as without a check there will be no analysis.

You should take time to investigate the fifth tab, Options, and its complex offerings. When you use the default statistics collection method of the Analyze command (which Oracle has deprecated), there's not too much to decide. However, specifying the use of DBMS_STATS opens up a whole new range of possibilities—and adds both additional tabs and sub-tabs (that is, tabs under tabs) to the Analyze All Objects screen, as shown in Figure 9.32.

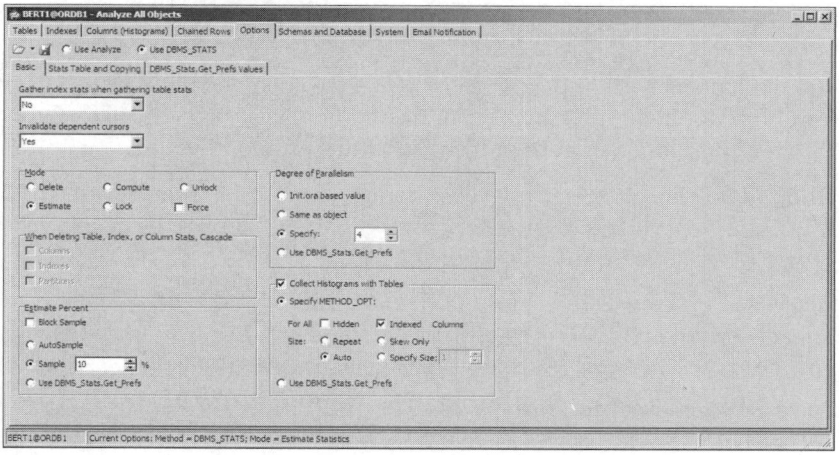

FIGURE 9.32   Analyze All Objects—Options

This approach supports the use of extended concepts such as statistics collection in parallel, gathering index statistics while processing a table, sampling, simplified histogram specification, exporting statistics to a user-defined table, copying statistics between schemas and/or databases, doing multi-schema statistics collections, gathering statistics for data dictionary and internal fixed tables, and partitioning statistics collections options. You should spend sufficient time and exercise care when selecting the options here for your specific needs—this is one place where blindly accepting the default values will not suffice.

Note in Figure 9.32 that the Options tab contains toolbar icons for saving and loading your options settings. This is an important aspect of the Analyze All Options feature, and you should learn to make use of these icons. Spend as much time as necessary to identify and select the correct options for your system, and then save them to a named file that you'll remember. That way you can expedite your use of this screen when you return to it in the future. After you've clicked the green arrow (the Execute toolbar icon), you'll see a message listed under each selected object that says Normal Successful Completion.

You may never actually need to run the Analyze All Objects screen via the main menu in the manner described in this section. Many users actually arrive at this point via the Schema Browser (introduced in Chapter 2). When you are browsing database objects for which statistics might exist, the Schema Browser offers a right-click menu item to automatically take you to this screen with all the proper objects already selected. For example, if you were browsing tables as shown in Figure 9.33, the Analyze Table option would send you to this screen for the selected tables.

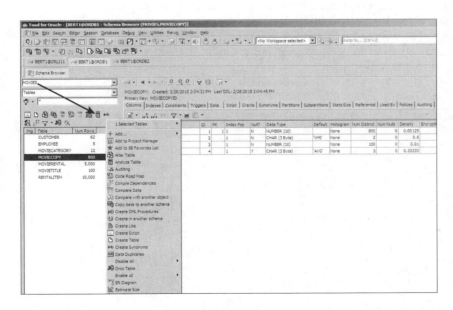

FIGURE 9.33   Schema Browser—Analyze Table

Rebuild Multiple Objects

One task that always seems to need doing at some point in any database is rebuilding or reorganizing objects. In fact, Oracle has provided a powerful PL/SQL package for handling this task. Unfortunately, the DBMS_REDEFINITION package is far too complex for casual use. And remember, it will re-create your objects—which means a wrong step could lose actual data as well as the objects. What you really need is a simple, effective, and safe interface into this complex package. Toad offers its Rebuild Multiple Objects screen for this purpose. With this facility, even the greenest novice can quickly and safely rebuild database objects like a pro.

To launch the Rebuild Multiple Objects screen, choose Main Menu → Database → Optimize → Rebuild Multiple Objects. The screen shown in Figure 9.34 appears.

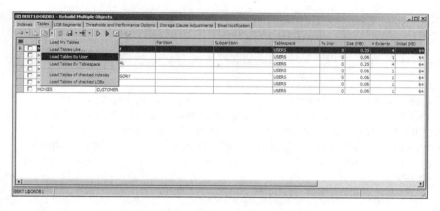

FIGURE 9.34   Rebuild Multiple Objects—Tables

You might have noticed that the Rebuild Multiple Objects screen (refer to Figure 9.34) looks a lot like the Analyze All Objects screen (refer to Figure 9.31). That's by design: The two look and function quite similarly, so review the prior section for additional insights into this screen's operation and behavior. Note that for any of these, you must select the check boxes at the start of each row, as without a check there will be no rebuild.

There are two areas where there are significant differences between the Rebuild Multiple Objects and Analyze All Objects screens—more specifically, where Toad's Rebuild Multiple Objects screen offers some highly specialized capabilities. Figure 9.35 shows the fourth tab, Thresholds and Performance Options, for specifying key rebuild thresholds and behaviors. We've chosen to rebuild only those objects whose size is 1GB or greater, that have 1000 or more extents, and that have indexes whose b-trees have become either too high or otherwise wastefully formed. Furthermore, we've chosen to perform the rebuild online using four-way parallel processing and no logging for speed, with both being reset back to the normal defaults after the object rebuild operation is complete.

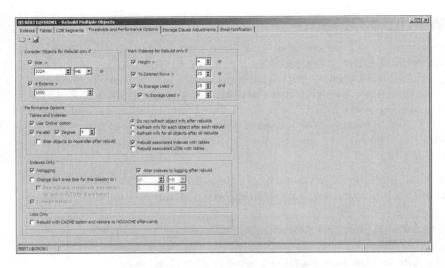

FIGURE 9.35   Rebuild Multiple Objects—Thresholds and Performance Options

The fifth tab, Storage Clause Adjustments, is even more complicated, and possesses sub-tabs. Here you can define small, medium, large, and huge tables, plus scale object storage clauses or place objects in tablespaces based on those definitions. Suppose you want to create standard object sizes and place such objects in tablespaces designed and optimized for an object of that size. This utility will completely automate the entire rebuild process to accomplish that goal.

You should take great care to review and carefully select from these two tabs' numerous offerings. You can generate very complex and valuable SQL scripts for performing amazing object reorganizations if you are willing to invest the time.

Summary

In recent years, Toad has emerged as much more than just a developer's tool; it has grown into something that offers numerous database administrative capabilities. Whether you're a DBA or just someone tasked with performing database administrative work, Toad now has much to offer you as you deal with these duties. You may need the optional Toad DB Admin Module to get many of the features covered in this chapter. After you have those features available, you will find that Toad can expedite all your various database administrative tasks—from the most mundane and routine to the most complex and unusual. For some people, Toad may well complement or even supplant other database administrative tools. Toad has grown up into a true one-stop, do-it-all tool.

Here's the current, complete listing of optional features provided by the Toad DB Admin Module, many of which were covered in this chapter (others are covered in Chapter 10, "Toad as a SQL Tuning Tool"):

- ▶ ADDM/AWR Report Generator
- ▶ Analyze All Objects
- ▶ ASM Manager
- ▶ Audit Objects
- ▶ Audit SQL/Sys Privs
- ▶ AWR Browser
- ▶ Code Road Map and ER Diagram
- ▶ Compare Databases
- ▶ Compare Schemas
- ▶ Control Files
- ▶ Database Browser
- ▶ Database Health Check
- ▶ Database Monitor
- ▶ Database Probe
- ▶ Data Pump Import/Export Wizards
- ▶ DBMS_FLASHBACK Interface
- ▶ DBMS_REDEFINITITION Wizard
- ▶ Export File Browser
- ▶ Generate Database Script
- ▶ Generate Schema Script
- ▶ Identify Space Deficits
- ▶ Index Monitoring
- ▶ Instance Manager
- ▶ Log Switch Frequency Map
- ▶ LogMiner Interface
- ▶ New Database Wizard
- ▶ NLS Parameters
- ▶ Operating System Utilities
- ▶ Oracle Parameters

6

- ▶ Pinned Code
- ▶ Redo Log Manager
- ▶ Resource Plan Scheduling
- ▶ Schema Browser
- ▶ Segment Advisor
- ▶ StatsPack Browser
- ▶ Tablespace Map
- ▶ Top Session Finder
- ▶ Trace File Browser
- ▶ Undo Advisor
- ▶ View Tablespaces

CHAPTER 10

Toad as a SQL Tuning Tool

IN THIS CHAPTER

▶ Toad and Explain Plans
▶ SQL Statistics
▶ Toad and SQL Trace
▶ Statspack Interface
▶ AWR Browser
▶ Toad and the PL/SQL Profiler
▶ Toad and the SQL Optimizer

This chapter covers various SQL performance tuning aspects of Toad. Toad has many features for finding and optimizing poorly performing SQL and applications and these features are covered in this chapter.

We start with the Explain Plan panel. This section covers how Toad interfaces with the PLAN_TABLE. We also make sure that you are using the correct PLAN_TABLE for your Oracle database environment.

The SQL Trace facility is covered next. Toad is a great tool for creating and working with trace files. The real hidden gem here is the Trace File Browser.

Toad also has cool interfaces to both the Statspack and AWR statistical analysis features of the Oracle RDBMS.

The Session Browser also has many SQL tuning items within it.

This chapter then covers the PL/SQL Profiler and concludes with information on automatic tuning features found only in Toad: the SQL Optimizer!

Toad and Explain Plans

Oracle explain plans are easily made visible via the Toad Editors Explain Plan output tab and by using the Explain Plan button 📇. (See the cursor position in Figure 10.1.)

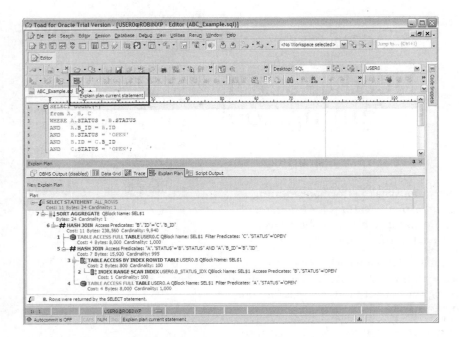

FIGURE 10.1   Toad Explain Plans

TIP

Explain plans and SQL performance tuning are covered in my Safari Books video course: *Oracle SQL Performance Tuning for Developers LiveLessons*. Set your browser to www.safaribooksonline.com or www.informit.com and search for this course.

Prior to Oracle10, a script was run to create the PLAN_TABLE in your schema. The PLAN_TABLE object is used heavily by Toad and other tools to display explain plan information (refer to Figure 10.1). Oracle10g+ has changed this script to a temporary table. You can reference it directly in Toad (see Figure 10.2) or have your DBA staff make a public synonym for it. In Oracle11 and above, the synonym has already been created. The owner and name of the table is SYS.PLAN_TABLE$. You can reference it easily in Toad by choosing View → Toad Options or clicking the Toad Options button; you will arrive at the window shown in Figure 10.2. Make sure the Oracle General Options panel Explain Plan option points to PLAN_TABLE.

> **NOTE**
>
> Make sure to drop the PLAN_TABLE in your schema, if there is one, as all the tools look in your schema first before looking for the synonym or the table elsewhere.

The Toad Explain Plan output tab will work with about any PLAN_TABLE but if the PLAN_TABLE is not the one for the release of Oracle you are using, you could be missing some useful information.

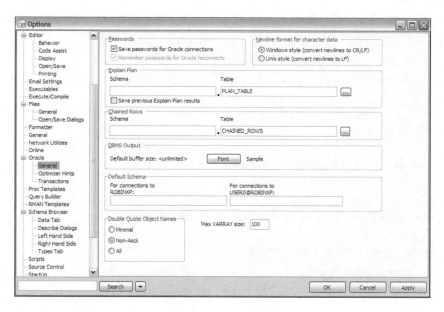

FIGURE 10.2   Toad Options for the PLAN_TABLE

To get an explain plan, or to populate the Explain Plan output tab, open a SQL statement from a file on your workstation, highlight a SQL statement in code in the Toad Editor (either in a script or in some PL/SQL code), and click the Explain Plan button (refer to Figure 10.1).

The content of this Explain Plan output tab can be highly customizable. Right-click the Explain Plan output in the Output tab panel and select Adjust Content as shown in Figure 10.3. The Execution Plan Preferences panel appears, as shown in Figure 10.4.

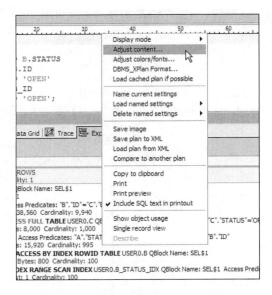

FIGURE 10.3   Adjust Explain Plan Content pop-up menu

Notice the various PLAN_TABLE columns that can be made visible and have their own column. Compare the columns checked with the output visible in Figure 10.1.

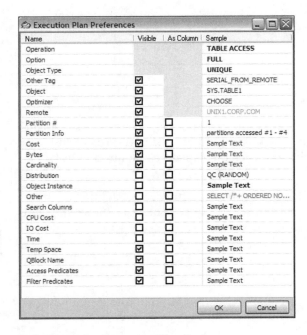

FIGURE 10.4   Execution Plan Preferences

NOTE

My preferences are selected in Figure 10.4.

Code Snippets, covered in Chapters 3 and 6, also pertain here. A SQL Optimizer Hints category allows you to drag and drop these performance enhancers into your SQL code as well. To make the Code Snippet autohide panel available, click Main Menu → View → Code Snippets. On the Code Snippets panel, change the category to SQL Optimizer Hints as shown in Figure 10.5.

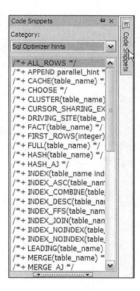

FIGURE 10.5   Code Snippets panel

SQL Statistics

A series of useful statistics are available for each SQL statement as well. The Auto Trace feature uses the Trace output tab, and you can enable the feature from this tab, as shown in Figure 10.6. For older Toad versions, right-click in the Editor window and select Auto Trace from the pop-up menu, and then execute the SQL again.

10

FIGURE 10.6   Enabling Auto Trace

This panel then becomes populated with runtime statistics about this particular SQL statement, as shown in Figure 10.7.

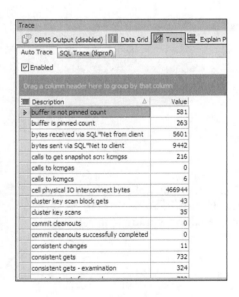

FIGURE 10.7   Auto Trace output

Toad and SQL Trace

SQL Trace, or the 10046 trace file, collects all the SQL and additional useful information

▶ For an individual session

▶ For a different user session than your own

▶ Across the entire database (if requested by Oracle Support)

NOTE

Discussing the technical content found in these SQL Trace files is beyond the scope of this book. This chapter merely shows how to use Toad to both run SQL Trace and get useful results and reports easily.

Toad can initiate these SQL Trace sessions and has two features that interpret the results:

▶ TKProf wizard (the interface to Oracle Corp's command-line interpreter)

▶ Trace File Browser (an additional purchased item)

NOTE

If a SQL Trace is initiated using Toad, when the SQL Trace is turned back off (we cover the syntax shortly), Toad will prompt you to use the Trace File Browser (if purchased) or the TKProf wizard. This feature makes viewing SQL Trace output very easy using Toad.

NOTE

The TKProf executable must be on your workstation and configured by choosing Main Menu ➔ Toad Options ➔ Executables. Toad will prompt you for this, though. You will need the following privileges:

   ▶ EXECUTE privilege on UTL_FILE

   ▶ SELECT on V$INSTANCE, V$SESSION, and V$PROCESS

   ▶ READ privilege on DIRECTORY Toad_TRACEFILE_DIR

      • which is an Oracle Directory object that will be created on the first attempt to read a trace file

   ▶ CREATE ANY DIRECTORY privileges

The Session Browser enables you to easily turn SQL Trace on and off...and to review the associated generated SQL Trace file. Figure 10.8 shows a SQL*Plus session running a SQL statement: Select count(*) from A,B,C ... and Figure 10.9 shows the Toad Session Browser illustrating this same SQL*Plus session and SQL. Notice that the mouse cursor is on the Session Browser button used to initiate this feature of Toad.

> **NOTE**
>
> The Session Browser is mostly for users with DBA-type privileges.

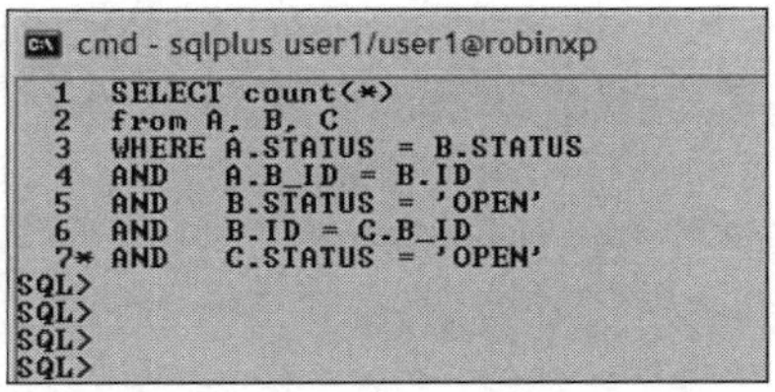

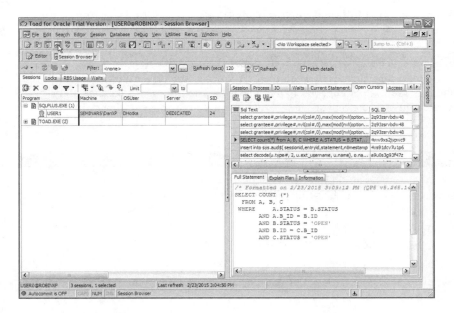

FIGURE 10.8   Sample SQL*Plus session

FIGURE 10.9   Toad Session Browser

Figure 10.10 shows the start (green) and stop (red) trace buttons for any session in this Toad Session Browser. Simply highlight the user for whom you want to initiate a SQL Trace in the left panel in Figure 10.9 and click the green button to initiate the SQL Trace process.

FIGURE 10.10   Toad SQL Trace start (left) and stop (right) buttons

Figure 10.11 shows the options for starting SQL*Trace. The three supported Oracle pack-ages that Toad can utilize are

► DBMS_MONITOR

► DBMS_SYSTEM

► DBMS_SUPPORT

These features each create the same identical trace file; there is simply more than one way to initiate a SQL Trace and Toad covers these options.

TIP

Dan always runs SQL*Trace to collect the additional bind and wait information.

FIGURE 10.11   Toad Start Trace options panel

For a nice example for this book, Dan started the SQL Trace by clicking on the OK button; Toad informed the user that a SQL Trace session had been started and the session being traced in the Session Browser would be highlighted in green.

Dan executed the SQL in the SQL*Plus session. In the real world, this is where you, the programmer running a test, or the Toad user working with an end user on an issue, would either start your test or have the user execute something in the application that has been causing issues.

Figure 10.12 shows the red button being clicked in Toad to stop the SQL Trace option.

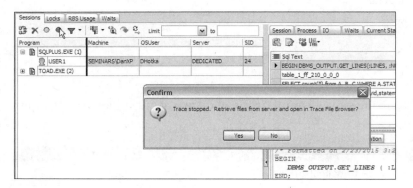

FIGURE 10.12   Stopping the SQL Trace using Toad

Notice Figure 10.12 is informing the Toad user that the trace has been stopped and is asking the user whether he wants to view the results. Dan used the trial version of Toad with permission from Dell Software Solutions. This trial version contains the Trace File Browser discussed later in this chapter. Your version of Toad may prompt you to view the results in the TKProf interface.

NOTE

SQL Trace can be initiated via syntax entered in SQL*Plus, from applications, or from other features of the Oracle RDBMS. Toad includes the capability to open these trace files as well, using either the TKProf wizard or the Trace File Browser (whatever you have purchased) from the Database → Diagnose menu item.

Figure 10.13 shows the SQL Trace of the ABC SQL in the Trace File Browser interface. Notice all the information that is available for this SQL Trace session. You can click the headings to sort the visible data into that particular descending order (worst offending items sort to the top). This interface shows great detail about the SQL collected from the SQL Trace.

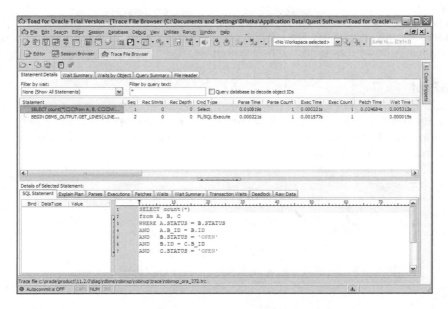

FIGURE 10.13   ABC SQL example in Trace File Browser

The Trace tab in the main SQL editor enables you to run a SQL Trace on the SQL in the current Editor window (the window can contain more than one SQL and they all will be traced), as shown in Figure 10.14. Like stopping the trace earlier (refer to Figure 10.12), Toad will run a SQL Trace on this individual SQL statement, and then prompt you asking whether you want to view the trace file results using either the TKProf wizard or the Trace File Browser (depending upon your Toad license options).

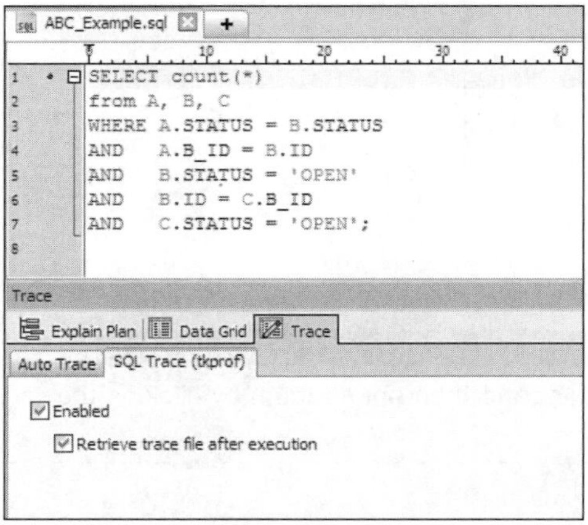

FIGURE 10.14   SQL Trace from Trace tab in Editor window

The next section of this chapter illustrates the TKProf wizard, and the later "Toad and Trace File Browser" section revisits the Trace File Browser, both sections showing the opening of existing SQL Trace files from the host computer.

Toad and TKProf

TKProf is the command-line interpreter for the Oracle RDBMS for SQL Trace files. It can be a bit difficult to use, but Toad makes it very easy with the TKProf wizard. Access this from Database → Diagnose → TKProf Wizard. The Files button (see Figure 10.15) enables you to access trace files from your workstation or by using FTP.

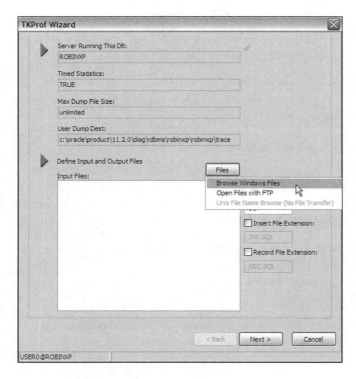

FIGURE 10.15   Toad TKProf wizard

TIP

Dan always gets these trace files to his workstation, and then opens them by clicking the Files button and selecting Browse Windows Files.

Fill out the sort grid as shown in Figure 10.16 (some knowledge of trace files is helpful) and Toad will then run the TKProf wizard tool and open the output using Notepad.

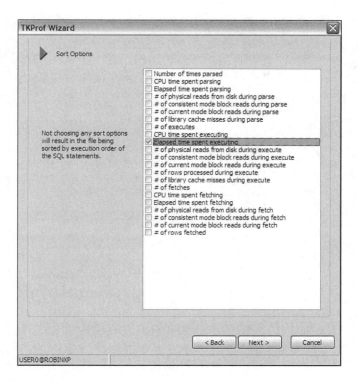

FIGURE 10.16   Toad TKProf wizard—Sort Options

TIP

Dan usually sorts in Elapsed Time Spent Executing. This puts the longest running SQL at the beginning of the output.

The final panel in the wizard controls the output. This page enables you to run TKProf and then view the output (see Figure 10.17). There is no reason to connect to the DB to run explain plans anymore. The first option limits the number of SQL statements to display. Usually, when you're selecting a sort option, displaying only 10 or 20 SQL statements is enough. You can choose to aggregate the common SQL statements together and you can also see the Oracle SQL executed on your behalf—called recursive SQL.

The center part of the wizard enables TKProf to be executed on your workstation, or the commands needed to execute your request are copied to the clipboard.

The final part deals with viewing the output and the closing of the TKProf wizard.

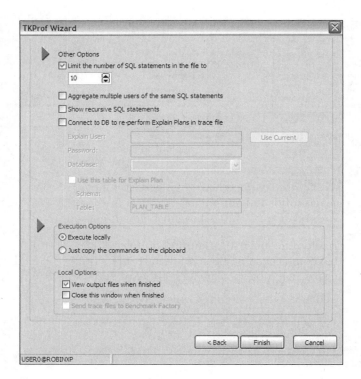

FIGURE 10.17   Toad TKProf wizard—Output Options

Dan usually sorts in Elapsed Time Spent Executing, displays 10 SQL statements, executes locally, and leaves the TKProf wizard open. This enables him to easily use the Back button to select a different sort order without having to start up the wizard and select the trace file again and again.

The content of this trace file is then displayed using Notepad (see Figure 10.18) on your workstation. You can change the display editor to a product other than Notepad on the Toad Options panel, Executables.

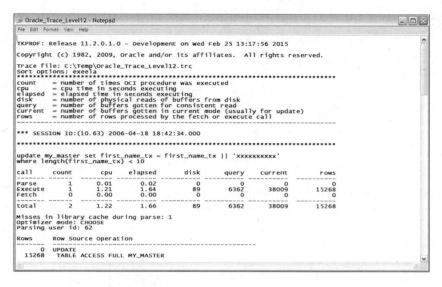

FIGURE 10.18   Toad TKProf output

Contact Dan (email: dan@danhotka.com) for information on interpreting the results of TKProf. These concepts are beyond the scope of this book.

Toad and Trace File Browser

The Toad DBA Pack has a unique tool for interpreting the results of SQL Trace files: the Trace File Browser. This interface is just under the TKProf wizard on the Database → Diagnose → Trace File Browser menu. Figure 10.19 shows the Trace File Browser with the same SQL Trace file opened (using the Open File button) as in the previous section on the TKProf wizard.

10

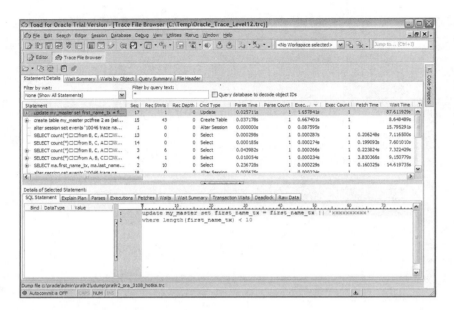

FIGURE 10.19   Toad Trace File Browser

Notice that this wizard enables you to sort by simply clicking on the report headings. This browser makes it possible for the SQL within the SQL Trace file to be quickly analyzed.

TIP

Dan first finds the longest running SQL, as shown in Figure 10.18, and then he clicks on the Wait Summary to see why the SQL is taking so long to run. Contact Dan for more information on the content of these SQL Trace files. Finding SQL performance problems is beyond the scope of this book.

Just about anything within the SQL Trace file can be easily visualized using this interface. The last tab on the lower-right part of the interface, Raw Data, would display any SQL bind variables that were used with the SQL statements.

NOTE

Either the TKProf wizard or the Trace File Browser will be automatically started when you stop a SQL Trace session using the Session Browser. The two preceding sections discussed starting the interfaces manually and supplying an existing SQL Trace file.

Statspack Interface

If your Oracle database has the older Statspack setup, then Toad has a wonderful interface to it. Check with your DBA staff before using this feature if you are unsure of its status in your environment.

Statspack is a collection of information about the Oracle database between two points in time. These points in time are called snapshots. The Statspack report compares two snapshots and displays the results. If Statspack is installed, these snapshots can be configured to occur automatically. DBAs usually set these up to be executed once per hour.

Toad's Statspack browser allows you to do the following:

▶ Initiate a snapshot

▶ View the results of any two snapshots using charts and data grids

▶ View the results of the Statspack report

To access this Statspack browser, choose Database ➔ Monitor ➔ Statspack Browser. The browser appears and the available snapshots for selection are made available—see the left side of Figure 10.20. Notice the lower left is where you can select information to display based on the snapshots selected.

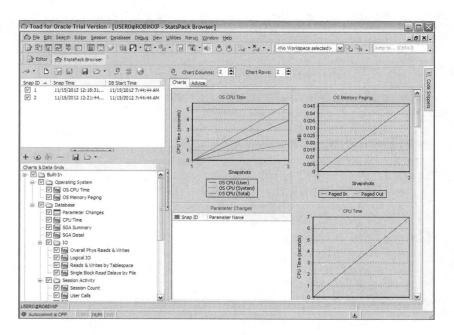

FIGURE 10.20   Toad Statspack Browser

The Statspack character-mode report can be executed by Toad by first selecting the two snapshots to apply the report on, and then right-clicking on the highlighted pair and selecting Run Statspack Report on Selected Snapshot Pair, as shown in Figure 10.21. Figure 10.22 shows the standard Statspack report.

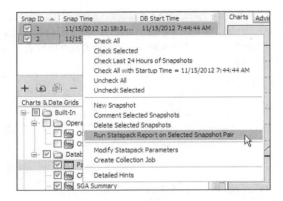

FIGURE 10.21   Toad Running the Statspack report

```
sp_report_ROBINXP_1_2 - Notepad
File  Edit  Format  View  Help

STATSPACK report for

Database      DB Id       Instance     Inst Num  Startup Time    Release      RAC
---------  ----------  -----------  --------  -----------  -----------  ---
           4181300236  robinxp             1  15-Nov-12 07:44  11.2.0.1.0   NO

Host Name             Platform                  CPUs Cores Sockets   Memory (G)
----------------  -----------------------  ----- ----- -------  ------------
      ROBINXP          Microsoft Windows IA (     1     1       1        1.0

Snapshot          Snap Id      Snap Time      Sessions Curs/Sess Comment
-----------     --------  ---------------  --------  --------  ----------
Begin Snap:            1  15-Nov-12 12:18:31        29       1.4
  End Snap:            2  15-Nov-12 12:21:44        29       1.5
   Elapsed:       3.22 (mins) Av Act Sess:        0.0
   DB time:       0.10 (mins)      DB CPU:      0.06 (mins)

Cache Sizes            Begin          End
-----------        ----------  ----------
     Buffer Cache:        92M                Std Block Size:        8K
     Shared Pool:        152M                   Log Buffer:    5,724K

Load Profile          Per Second    Per Transaction    Per Exec    Per Call
-----------        ---------------  ---------------  ----------  ----------
      DB time(s):            0.0               0.2          0.00        0.08
      DB CPU(s):            0.0               0.1          0.00        0.04
      Redo size:        8,479.3          58,446.3
   Logical reads:           94.4             650.9
   Block changes:           31.1             214.1
   Physical reads:           5.2              35.8
  Physical writes:           0.2               1.4
      User calls:            0.4               2.8
          Parses:            6.0              41.5
     Hard parses:            0.5               3.5
  W/A MB processed:          0.2               1.1
          Logons:            0.1               0.4
        Executes:           12.0              82.5
       Rollbacks:            0.0               0.0
    Transactions:            0.2
```

FIGURE 10.22   Statspack report

Contact Dan for information on interpreting the results of Statspack reports. These concepts are beyond the scope of this book.

AWR Browser

Oracle10g introduced Automated Workload Repository. It is like Statspack, but a lot more information is gathered and stored for just seven days (the range of saved data is configurable at the database level, not within Toad).

Viewing AWR information requires licensing from Oracle Corp. Check with your DBA staff to make sure your site has the proper licenses to view this AWR information.

You can run and review standard AWR reports using Toad. Use Database → Monitor → ADDM/AWR Reports to view the selections. See Figure 10.23 for a sample ASH report showing the information available via this interface. Notice that instead of the snapshots themselves, as selected in Statspack, the ASH report has begin and end times for the information to be viewed. Remember, AWR only stores information for seven days.

Notice the various ADDM and AWR reports, one per tab along the top in Figure 10.23.

Select the report for which you want to see data, adjust the time frame for the information you want to see, then click the green arrow button to initiate the report.

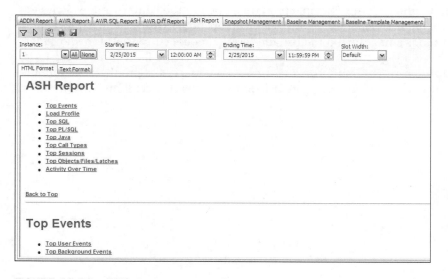

FIGURE 10.23   ASH report

10

TIP

Dan finds the information in the ASH report (Active Session History) useful for finding SQL performance problems.

NOTE

Contact Dan for information on interpreting the results of the AWR reports. These concepts are beyond the scope of this book.

Toad and the PL/SQL Profiler

Oracle introduced the PL/SQL Profiler back in Oracle8i. Toad has a nice interface to this feature.

The Profiler will gather execution times for each PL/SQL procedure or function being profiled, and execution time for each line of code. This information displays how long each module took to execute and how long each line of code took to execute.

This feature really saves a lot of developers' time when tuning PL/SQL.

NOTE

If the Profiler database objects are not set up, Toad will prompt you to set them up. If you need assistance when this information is requested by Toad, contact your DBA staff.

Figure 10.24 shows the Looping_Example procedure open in the Editor window. Refer to Chapter 6, "Working with PL/SQL," if you need help opening existing PL/SQL procedures. The Profiler button is along the top toolbar and has the mouse cursor positioned over it in Figure 10.24. This is a toggle button (it is up or down). Notice the Profiler tab at the lower part of the editor screen. This tab shows the current contents of the profiler table for our logged user. If this tab is not visible, right-click on the tabs and select Profiler from the pop-up list.

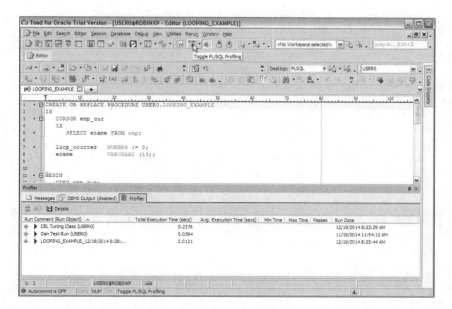

FIGURE 10.24   Using the PL/SQL Profiler

Click on the Toggle PL/SQL Profiling button 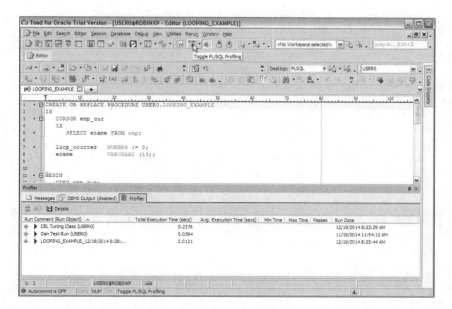 (see the cursor location in Figure 10.24). It will stay down. The Profiler is now gathering information.

Execute your PL/SQL by using the Execute PL/SQL Using Debugger button, found in the middle of the lower button menu bar (or press F11). You do not need to compile for debug to use this profiling feature. After your routine is done executing, again click the Toggle PL/SQL Profiling button and the profiling process is complete.

Review your profiled code using the Profiler tab (see Figure 10.25). The base information shows the routine executed and the total time of the execution. The next indented position shows each routine that was profiled. Clicking on each of these routines shows the output of the profiling session:

▶ Code line numbers

▶ Code execution time

▶ Number of times the code was executed

10

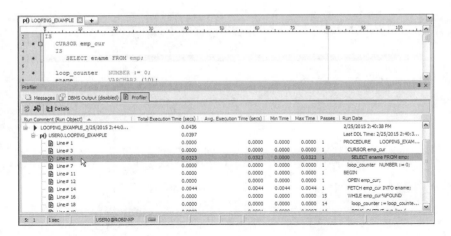

FIGURE 10.25   Profiler output tab

Notice each line of code is now visible, with how much time it took to execute. The long-running lines of code are easily sorted to the top by clicking on the report headings. Clicking on each line of code jumps the cursor to that code in the Editor window.

> **NOTE**
>
> If you happen to have a version of Toad older than Toad version 10, you can see similar information by choosing Database → Optimize → DBMS Profiler Analysis.

Toad and the SQL Optimizer

The SQL Optimizer is part of a larger SQL tuning tool sold by Dell Software. The Toad team put part of this package in Toad.

The SQL Optimizer runs your SQL with a variety of options that include various hints and SQL rewrites to find the optimal performing SQL rather automatically.

To start SQL Optimizer, click on the SQL Tuning button ▦ and select SQL Optimizer from the list of options that then appears or use Database → Optimize → Auto Optimize SQL (see Figure 10.26).

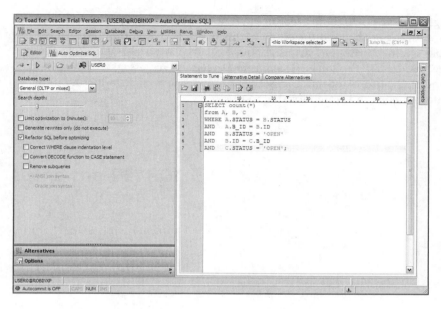

FIGURE 10.26   Auto Optimize SQL

TIP

Notice the SQL Refactoring tips on the left side of the Auto Optimize SQL panel. Toad can rewrite your SQL for possible better performance using these options.

The SQL Optimizer can quickly produce many options and run times for your SQL. You can choose to execute each one (good for shorter-running SQL) or just generate the various options, and you can decide to test and use the new code.

SQL Optimizer can compare the results as well.

Summary

This chapter covered various SQL tuning features that come with the base Toad or are available as options within Toad licensing. These features included the following:

- ▶ SQL explain plans
- ▶ SQL Trace options
- ▶ Statspack and AWR reports
- ▶ PL/SQL Profiling
- ▶ SQL Optimizer

This chapter highlights the SQL tuning features available within Toad; the concepts of SQL performance tuning are beyond the scope of this book. The co-author, Dan Hotka, has a Safari Books Online *LiveLessons* covering both explain plans and SQL performance tuning. It is titled *Oracle SQL Performance Tuning for Developers LiveLessons*. For details on explain plans and SQL performance tuning, set your browser to www.safaribooksonline.com or www.informit.com and search for this course.

Index

A

About screen, 5

Access file format, saving data in, 106

action code (Automation Designer), 183-187

Action Console, 171

Action toolbar (Editor), 126

Add Schema Name to Tables button (SQL Editor Query Builder), 67

Add Table Names to Column button (SQL Editor Query Builder), 67

Add/Delete Rows buttons (data grids), 104-105

Analyze All Objects screen, 220-222

Ansi button (SQL Editor Query Builder), 67

ANSI SQL, Query Builder (SQL Editor), 66

apps, launching from External Tools, 162

ASH reports, 245-246

Auto Add button (External Tools), 161

Auto Replace panel (SQL Editor), 63-64

Auto Trace tab (SQL Editor Output area), 49-50, 231-232

autocommit feature (data grids), 96

automation, 171

   Action Console, 171

   Automation Designer, 171, 180

      action code, 183-187

      adding action properties, 188-189

      availability, 188

      Command Line feature versus, 179

      Control tab, 188-190

      functionality, 180-181

      launching, 181

      main screen, 181-183

      programmatic controls, 189

Save/Load Window Snapshot, 180-181

scheduling, 183

toolbar, 182-183

Command Line feature, 171-172

Automation Designer versus, 179

command file example, 173-178

functionality, 172-173

running command files, 178-179

Save/Load settings, 173

shortcomings of, 180

auto-opening windows at startup, 34-36

AWR browser and SQL performance tuning, 245-246

B

Base edition (Toad), 4

BEGIN/END labels (Editor), 126

Bookmark Navigation buttons (data grids), 105

breakpoints (debugging code), 145, 147

conditional breakpoints, 150-152

modifying, 149-150

Breakpoints tab (SQL Editor Output area), 49

C

Calculate Selected Cells feature (data grids), 101

calculations, Query Builder (SQL Editor), 67

Call Stack tab (SQL Editor Output area), 49

call stacks, debugging code, 147

Cancel Query Execution or Fetch button (data grids), 104

cells (data grids), Calculate Selected Cells feature, 101

Check tab (Database Health Check), 193

choosing database connections, 27

Clear button (SQL Editor), 45

Code Analysis feature (Editor), 126, 139

functionality, 139

Halstead Volume, 142

Maintainability Index, 142

McCabe's Cyclomatic Complexity, 142

Report tab, 139

Toad Code Rating, 142

uses of, 139

code folding,126

Code Road Map, 157-158, 160

General tab, 159

Options tab, 159

Code Snippets, 133-134, 231

Code Snippets panel (SQL Editor), 58-60

Code tab (FastReport), 84

code templates, 127

building, 128-131

choosing, 127

Cursor Loop template, 127

modifying, 127-128

signaling, 127

substitution variables, 127

viewing, 127

color highlighting, Toad/database connections, 13

Command Line feature, 171-172

Automation Designer versus, 179

command files

example of, 173-178

running, 178-179

functionality, 172-173

Save/Load settings, 173

shortcomings of, 180

Commit/Rollback buttons (data grids), 96, 105

Compare Databases screen, 216-217

    Databases tab, 217

    Options tab, 217

    Results tab, 217

    Sync Script tab, 218

Compare Files utility, 163

Compare Schemas screen, 218-219

    Options tab, 219

    Results tab, 219

    Sync Script tab, 219

compiling objects for debugging, 147

conditional breakpoints (debugging code), 150-152

connection errors for bad passwords, 16

Content tab (HTML Documentation Generator), 116

Control tab (Automation Designer), 189-190

copying/pasting in Reports Manager (Schema Browser), 88

Create Table wizard (Schema Browser), 76-78

Cursor Loop template, 127

customizing

    Options screen

        finding new/unknown options, 37

        initial options to focus on, 38-39

        pop-ups in options, 39

    Toad, 18

        keyboard shortcuts, 33-34

        menus, 19

        Options screen, 19-21, 37-39

        Schema Browser, 34-36

        sharing options settings, 40

        SQL Editor, 34-36

        startup options, 36

        startup windows/screens, 34-36

        toolbars, 19, 30-33

        user settings, 40

    user settings (Toad), 40

D

Data Grid panel (SQL Editor Describe Objects panel), 56

Data Grid tab (SQL Editor Output area), 49

data grids, 93

    autocommit feature, 96

    Calculate Selected Cells feature, 101

    Cancel Query Execution or Fetch button, 104

    capabilities of, 93-95

    changing data and permissions, 95-96

    commit/rollback buttons, 96

    Export Dataset wizard, 102-103

        Dataset tab, 103

        Insert Statements tab, 103

        Options tab, 102, 103

        saving data, 106-111

    filtering/sorting data, 97-99

    functionality in, 96-97

    Master Detail Browser, 111-113

    permissions and changing data, 95-96

    pop-up menu, 95

    printing via FastReport, 79-80

        Code tab, 84

        Report wizard, 80-83

        saving reports, 84

        Style tab, 82

    Refresh Dataset button, 103

    refreshing data, 97

    rows

        Add/Delete Rows buttons, 104-105

        Bookmark Navigation buttons, 105

        Edit Row Set Control buttons, 105

        Row Set Navigation buttons, 105

    saving data

        Access file format, 106

        Delimited Text file format, 107

        Excel File format, 108

Excel Instance format, 108
Fixed Field Spacing option, 108-109
HTML Table file format, 109
Insert Statements file format, 109
Merge Statements file format, 109
ODBC Database file format, 110
SQL Loader option, 111
XML (with XLS) file format, 109
XML file format, 109
Show Detail Dataset button, 100
Show/Hide Columns menu, 100
Single Record Viewer button, 105
sorting
columns, 97
data, 97-99
SQL Editor, 95
View/Edit Query panel, 99
Data Pump Export wizard, 205-209
data tool palette (SQL Editor Output area), 48
database administration, 191
Analyze All Objects screen, 220-222
Compare Databases screen, 216-217
Databases tab, 217
Options tab, 217
Results tab, 217
Sync Script tab, 218
Compare Schemas screen, 218-219
Options tab, 219
Results tab, 219
Sync Script tab, 219
Data Pump Export wizard, 205-209
Database Browser, 197-202
Datafile IO tab, 200
Sessions tab, 199
Space Usage tab, 200-201
tablespace management, 210-212

Database Health Check, 192-193
Check tab, 193
Diffs Since Last Run tab, 194
Parameter screen, 193
Report Output tab, 194
Schemas tab, 194
Settings tab, 194
DB Admin Module, 4, 191-192, 224-226
Export Utility wizard
Data Pump Export wizard, 205-209
Generate Database Script screen, 212-214
Generate Schema Script screen, 214-215
simple exports, 202-204
Generate Database Script screen (Export Utility wizard), 212
Object Listing tab, 214
Object Types tab, 213
Script Options tab, 213
Source and Output tab, 212-213
Generate Schema Script screen (Export Utility wizard), 214
Object Types tab, 215
Script Options tab, 215
Source and Output tab, 215
SQL display, 215
Rebuild Multiple Objects screen, 223
Storage Clause Adjustments tab, 224
Thresholds and Performance Options tab, 223
Session Browser, 194-196
Locks tab, 196
tracing/killing sessions, 196
Waits tab, 197
tablespace management, 210-212
Database Browser, 197-202
Datafile IO tab, 200
Sessions tab, 199

Space Usage tab, 200-201

tablespace management, 210-212

database connections

choosing, 27

filtering, 28

grouping, 29-30

organizing, 25-30

sorting, 26

Toad operation (first time), 10

color highlighting, 13

connection errors for bad passwords, 16

Oracle Homes, 14-15

TNS tab, 10-11

TNSNAMES Editor, 11-13

database documentation

ER Diagrammer, 113-114

HTML Documentation Generator, 115-116, 118

Content tab, 116

HTML output and, 118

Object Descriptions tab, 117

Summary.html files, 116

Database Health Check, 192-193

Check tab, 193

Diffs Since Last Run tab, 194

Parameter screen, 193

Report Output tab, 194

Schemas tab, 194

Settings tab, 194

database security, common questions, 22

Databases tab (Compare Databases screen), 217

Datafile IO tab (Database Browser), 200

Dataset tab (Export Dataset Wizard), 103

datasets

Export Dataset wizard (data grids), 102-103

Dataset tab, 103

Insert Statements tab, 103

Options tab, 102, 103

saving data, 106-111

Master Detail Browser, 111-113

Refresh Dataset button, 103

DB Admin Module, 4, 191-192, 224-226

DBMS Output tab (SQL Editor Output area), 49

debugging code

adding privileges, 143

breakpoints, 145, 147

conditional breakpoints, 150-152

modifying, 149-150

call stacks, 147

changing

items "on the fly," 148-152

variable data, 148

compiling objects for debugging, 147

Editor, PL/SQL, 123-124

JIT (Just-In-Time) debugging, 152-153

keyboard shortcuts, 143

Looping_Example, 143, 144, 147

Menu bar options, 144

modifying variable data, 148-149

PL/SQL, 123-124, 142

advanced debugging, 148-153

basic debugging, 142-148

Run to Cursor feature, 143

Step Into button, 145

stopping code, 143

symbolic debugging, 142

advanced debugging, 148-153

basic debugging, 142-148

Terminate Execution button, 144

toolbar, 143

trigger code, 152

watches, 145, 147, 148

.DEF files, 213

deleting, rows in data grids, 104-105

Delimited Text file format, saving data in, 107

Describe Objects panel (SQL Editor), 51

    changing panel location, 52

    Data Grid panel, 56

    dragging/dropping columns, 51

    EMP Table Describe Panel buttons, 52

    Export DDL panel, 55

    Generate Statement panel, 56

    Script tab, 53

    viewing button functionality, 52-53

development of Toad, 2-3

    editions/suites, 3-5

    Oracle compatibility, 3

diagramming objects via Code Road Map, 157-158, 160

    General tab, 159

    Options tab, 159

Diffs Since Last Run tab (Database Health Check), 194

dragging/dropping columns in Describe Objects panel (SQL Editor), 51

E

Edit Row Set Control buttons (data grids), 105

editing

    objects in Schema Browser, 76

    reports in Reports Manager (Schema Browser), 88

    View/Edit Query panel (data grids), 99

Editor, 121

    Action toolbar, 126

    autohiding output tabs, 124

    BEGIN/END labels, 126

    Code Analysis feature, 126, 139

        functionality, 139

        Halstead Volume, 142

        Maintainability Index, 142

        McCabe's Cyclomatic Complexity, 142

        Report tab, 139

        Toad Code Rating, 142

        uses of, 139

    code folding, 126

    code templates, modifying, 127-128

    debugging code, 123-124

    Execute PL/SQL button, 123-124, 146-147

    Execute/Compile button, 123

    formatting code, 127

    full screen mode, 124

    highlighting code, 126

    IF/END IF labels, 126

    keyboard shortcuts, 135-137

    Load Database Object wizard, 122-123

    opening files in, 122

    saving code, 123

    Schema Browser, loading files from, 123

Editor button (SQL Editor), 44

EMP Table Describe Panel buttons, Describe Objects panel (SQL Editor), 52

ER Diagrammer, 113-114

Excel File format, saving data in, 108

Excel Instance format, saving data in, 108

Execute PL/SQL button (Editor), 123-124, 146-147

Execute/Compile button (Editor), 123

execution plans and SQL performance tuning, 229-231

Explain Plan tab (SQL Editor Output area), 49, 50

explain plans (SQL performance tuning), 227-229

    code snippets, 231

    execution plans, 229-231

Export Dataset wizard (data grids), 102-103

    Dataset tab, 103

    Insert Statements tab, 103

Options tab, 102-103

saving data, 106

    Access file format, 106

    Delimited Text file format, 107

    Excel File format, 108

    Excel Instance format, 108

    Fixed Field Spacing option, 108-109

    HTML Table file format, 109

    Insert Statements file format, 109

    Merge Statements file format, 109

    ODBC Database file format, 110

    SQL Loader option, 111

    XML (with XLS) file format, 109

    XML file format, 109

Export DDL panel (SQL Editor Describe Objects panel), 55

Export Utility wizard

    Data Pump Export wizard, 205-209

    Generate Database Script screen, 212

    simple exports, 202-204

External Tools program launcher, 160

    Auto Add button, 161

    configuration screen, 161

    launching apps from, 162

    Manual Add button, 162

F

FastReport data printing, 79-80

    Code tab, 84

    Report wizard, 80-83

    saving reports, 84

    Style tab, 82

Favorites list (Schema Browser), 73-74

filtering

    data grid data, 97-99

    database connections, 28

    objects, Schema Browser, 72

Fixed Field Spacing option, saving data in, 108-109

folding code in Editor, 126

formatting code in Editor, 127

full screen mode (Editor), 124

G

General tab (Code Road Map), 159

Generate Database Script screen (Export Utility wizard), 212-213

    Object Listing tab, 214

    Object Types tab, 213

    Script Options tab, 213

    Source and Output tab, 212-213

Generate Schema Script screen (Export Utility wizard), 214

    Object Types tab, 215

    Script Options tab, 215

    Source and Output tab, 215

    SQL display, 215

Generate Statement panel (SQL Editor Describe Objects panel), 56

Generated Query panel (SQL Editor Query Builder), 66-67

grouping database connections, 29-30

H

Halstead Volume (Code Analysis reports), 142

Halt button (SQL Editor), 45

Health Check, 192-193

    Check tab, 193

    Diffs Since Last Run tab, 194

    Parameter screen, 193

    Report Output tab, 194

    Schemas tab, 194

    Settings tab, 194

hiding/displaying

    output tabs in Editor, 124

    Show/Hide Columns menu (data grids), 100

    tabs in Output area (SQL Editor), 48-49

highlighting

    code in Editor, 126

    Toad/database connections, 13

HTML Documentation Generator, 115-118

    Content tab, 116

    HTML output and, 118

    Object Descriptions tab, 117

    Summary.html files, 116

        installer files, 6

        Windows prerequisites, 5-6

HTML Table file format, saving data in, 109

I

IF/END IF labels (Editor), 126

Insert Statements file format, saving data in, 109

Insert Statements tab (Export Dataset Wizard), 103

Insights panel (SQL Editor), 57-58

installing Toad, 6-8

J

JIT (Just-In-Time) debugging, 152-153

K

keyboard shortcuts

    debugging code, 143

    Editor, 135-137

    Toad shortcuts, 33-34

killing/tracing sessions (Session Browser), 196

L

launching programs. See External Tools

licensing Toad, installer license screen, 7

Load Database Object wizard, 122-123

Locks tab (Session Browser), 196

logins (multiple) in SQL Editor, 46

Looping_Example

    debugging code, 143, 144, 147

    profiling code, 154-156

M

Maintainability Index (Code Analysis reports), 142

Manual Add button (External Tools), 162

Master Detail Browser, 111-113

McCabe's Cyclomatic Complexity (Code Analysis reports), 142

Menu bar, debugging code options, 144

menus, customizing, 19

Merge Statements file format, saving data in, 109

Messages tab (SQL Editor Output area), 49

N

naming reports, Reports Manager (Schema Browser), 87

Navigator tab (SQL Editor Output area), 49

No Oracle Net Services error, 9

O

Object Descriptions tab (HTML Documentation Generator), 117

Object Listing tab (Generate Database Script screen), 214

Object Pallette, ER Diagrammer and, 113-114

Object Types tab

    Generate Database Script screen, 213

    Generate Schema Script screen, 215

objects

    Analyze All Objects screen, 220-222

    compiling objects for debugging, 147

    Describe Objects panel (SQL Editor), 51

        changing panel location, 52

        Data Grid panel, 56

        dragging/dropping columns, 51

        EMP Table Describe Panel buttons, 52

        Export DDL panel, 55

        Generate Statement panel, 56

        Script tab, 53

        viewing button functionality, 52-53

diagramming via Code Road Map, 157-158, 160

    General tab, 159

    Options tab, 159

ER Diagrammer, 113-114

Rebuild Multiple Objects screen, 223

    Storage Clause Adjustments tab, 224

    Thresholds and Performance Options tab, 223

Schema Browser

    adding objects, 73

    configuring object display, 70-72

    control buttons, 75

    Create Table wizard, 76-78

    creating objects, 76-78

    displaying objects, 70-72

    editing objects, 76-78

    enabling objects, 73

    Favorites list, 73-74

    filtering objects, 72

    grouping objects, 73

    maintaining objects, 73

    scheduling object creation, 78

    selecting objects, 73

    Show SQL button, 78

ODBC Database file format, saving data in, 110

Options screen, Toad customization, 19-21

    finding new/unknown options, 37

    initial options to focus on, 38-39

    pop-ups in options, 39

Options tab

    Analyze All Objects screen, 221-222

    Code Road Map, 159

    Compare Databases screen, 217

    Compare Schemas screen), 219

    Export Dataset Wizard, 102-103

Oracle
    Oracle Net Services
        No Oracle Net Services error, 9
        Toad connections (first time), 9-10
        sending SQL statements to, 44
    Toad compatibility, 3
Oracle Homes, Toad operation (first time), 14-15
Oracle SQL, Query Builder (SQL Editor), 66
organizing
    database connections, 25
        choosing, 27
        filtering, 28
        grouping, 29-30
        sorting, 26
    objects via Project Manager, 132
        adding objects to project folders, 132
        creating project folders, 133
        interface of Project Manager, 132
        maintaining Project Manager via Schema Browser, 132
        toolbar, 133
Output area (SQL Editor)
    Auto Trace tab, 49-50, 231-232
    Breakpoints tab, 49
    Call Stack tab, 49
    Data Grid tab, 49
    DBMS Output tab, 49
    Explain Plan tab, 49, 50
    hiding/displaying tabs, 48-49
    Messages tab, 49
    Navigator tab, 49
    Output area, data tool palette, 48
    Profiler tab, 48-49
    Query Viewer tab, 49
    REF CURSOR Results tab, 49
    Script Output tab, 49
    SQL Trace tab, 49-50, 233-238
    Trace tab, 49-50
    Watches tab, 49

P

Parameter screen (Database Health Check), 193
password connection errors, Toad/database connections, 16
performance
    SQL performance tuning, 227, 249-250
        AWR browser, 245-246
        explain plans, 227-231
        PL/SQL Profiler, 246-248
        SQL Optimizer, 248-249
        SQL Trace tab (SQL Editor Output area), 233-242
        statistics, 231-232
        Statspack browser, 243-245
        TKProf wizard, 238-241, 242
        Trace File Browser, 241-242
    Toad performance, common questions, 22
permissions, data grids, 95, 96
PL/SQL
    code snippets, 133-134
    code templates, 127
        building, 128-131
        choosing, 127
        Cursor Loop template, 127
        modifying, 127-128
        signaling, 127
        substitution variables, 127
        viewing, 127
    debugging code, 123-124, 142
        advanced debugging, 148-153
        basic debugging, 142-148

Editor
   Action toolbar, 126
   autohiding output tabs, 124
   BEGIN/END labels, 126
   Code Analysis feature, 126, 139-142
   code folding, 126
   debugging code, 123-124
   Execute PL/SQL button, 123-124,
      146-147
   Execute/Compile button, 123
   formatting code, 127
   full screen mode, 124
   highlighting code, 126
   IF/END IF labels, 126
   keyboard shortcuts, 135-137
   Load Database Object wizard, 122-123
   modifying code templates, 127-128
   opening files in, 122
   saving code, 123
   formatting code, 127
   profiling, 153-156
   saving code, 123
   Schema Browser, loading files from, 123
PL/SQL Profiler and SQL performance tuning,
   246-248
printing FastReport, 79-80
   Code tab, 84
   Report wizard, 80-83
   saving reports, 84
   Style tab, 82
Professional edition (Toad), 4
Profiler tab (SQL Editor Output area), 48-49
profiling PL/SQL, 153-156
program launchers. See External Tools
Project Manager, 132
   interface of, 132
   maintaining via Schema Browser, 132

project folders
   adding objects to, 132
   creating project folders, 133
   toolbar, 133

Q

queries
   Cancel Query Execution or Fetch button, 104
   View/Edit Query panel (data grids), 99
Query Builder (SQL Editor), 64-65
   Add Schema Name to Tables button, 67
   Add Table Names to Column button, 67
   Ansi button, 67
   ANSI SQL, 66
   calculations, 67
   Generated Query panel, 66-67
   Oracle SQL, 66
   subqueries, 67
   Update Diagram button, 67
   Update SQL button, 67
   WHERE clauses, 66
Query Viewer tab (SQL Editor Output area), 49
Quick Scripts, 167

R

Rebuild Multiple Objects screen, 223
   Storage Clause Adjustments tab, 224
   Thresholds and Performance Options
      tab, 223
REF CURSOR Results tab (SQL Editor Output
   area), 49
Refresh Dataset button (data grids), 103
refreshing data in data grids, 97

release history of Toad, 2-3

   editions/suites, 3-5

   Oracle compatibility, 3

Report Output tab (Database Health
   Check), 194

Report tab (Code Analysis feature), 139

Report wizard (FastReport), 80-83

Reports Manager (Schema Browser)

   adding reports to, 85-90

   adding scripts to, 90

   copying/pasting in, 88

   editing reports, 88

   naming reports, 87

   running reports, 90

   toolbar buttons, 86

Results tab

   Compare Databases screen, 217

   Compare Schemas screen, 219

Rollback/Commit buttons (data grids), 96, 105

Row Set Navigation buttons (data grids), 105

rows (data grids)

   Add/Delete Rows buttons, 104-105

   Bookmark Navigation buttons, 105

   Edit Row Set Control buttons, 105

   Row Set Navigation buttons, 105

Run to Cursor feature (Debugger), 143

running Toad (first time)

   database connections, 10-16

      color highlighting, 13

      connection errors for bad passwords, 16

      Oracle Homes, 14-15

      TNS tab, 10-11

      TNSNAMES Editor, 11-13

   No Oracle Net Services error, 9

   Oracle Net Services connections, 9-10

   Schema Browser, 17-18

   SQL Editor, 16

   Windows bit compatibility, 10

S

Save/Load Window Snapshot (Automation
   Designer), 180-181

saved database connection grid (Toad)

   choosing connections, 27

   filtering connections, 28

   grouping connections, 29-30

   sorting connections, 26

saving

   code in Editor, 123

   data

      Access file format, 106

      Delimited Text file format, 107

      Excel File format, 108

      Excel Instance format, 108

      Export Dataset wizard (data grids),
         106-111

      Fixed Field Spacing option, 108-109

      HTML Table file format, 109

      Insert Statements file format, 109

      Merge Statements file format, 109

      ODBC Database file format, 110

      SQL Loader option, 111

      XML (with XLS) file format, 109

      XML file format, 109

   PL/SQL code in Editor, 123

   reports, FastReport data printing, 84

scheduling

   Automation Designer, 183

   object creation in Schema Browser, 78

Schema Browser, 17-18, 69

   adding objects, 73

   auto-opening at startup, 34-36

   configuring, 70-72

   control buttons, 75

   Create Table wizard, 76-78

   creating objects, 76-78

editing objects, 76-78

Editor, loading files to, 123

enabling objects, 73

FastReport data printing, 79-80

    Code tab, 84

    Report wizard, 80-83

    saving reports, 84

    Style tab, 82

Favorites list, 73-74

filtering objects, 72

grouping objects, 73

maintaining objects, 73

maintaining Project Manager, 132

opening multiple Schema Browsers, 69

PL/SQL, loading files to Editor, 123

Reports Manager

    adding reports to, 85-90

    adding scripts to, 90

    copying/pasting in, 88

    editing reports, 88

    naming reports, 87

    running reports, 90

    toolbar buttons, 86

scheduling object creation, 78

selecting objects, 73

Show SQL button, 78

tabbed display, 70-72

Tables tab, 75

tree view, 70-72

Schemas tab (Database Health Check), 194

Script Manager, 165-166

    Quick Scripts, 167

    toolbar, 166-167

Script Options tab (Generate Database Script screen), 213, 215

Script Output tab (SQL Editor Output area), 49

Script tab (SQL Editor Describe Objects panel), 53

scripts

    Generate Database Script screen (Export Utility wizard), 212

        Object Listing tab, 214

        Object Types tab, 213

        Script Options tab, 213

        Source and Output tab, 212-213

    Generate Schema Script screen (Export Utility wizard), 214

        Object Types tab, 215

        Script Options tab, 215

        Source and Output tab, 215

        SQL display, 215

    Reports Manager (Schema Browser), adding scripts to, 90

    Sync Script tab

        Compare Databases screen, 218

        Compare Schemas screen, 219

security (database), common questions, 22

sending SQL statements to Oracle, 44

Session Browser, 194-196

    Locks tab, 196

    tracing/killing sessions, 196

    Waits tab, 197

Sessions tab (Database Browser), 199

Settings tab (Database Health Check), 194

sharing

    Toad options settings, 22, 40

    user settings (Toad), 40

shortcuts

    keyboard shortcuts

        debugging code, 143

        Editor, 135-137

        Toad shortcuts, 33-34

    SQL coding, Auto Replace panel (SQL Editor), 63-64

Show Detail Dataset button (data grids), 100

Show SQL button (Schema Browser), 78

Show/Hide Columns menu (data grids), 100

Single Record Viewer button (data grids), 105

snapshot (.DEF) files, 213

snippets (code). *See* Code Snippets panel (SQL Editor)

sorting

    data grids

        columns, 97

        data, 97-99

    database connections, 26

Source and Output tab

Generate Database Script screen, 212-213

Generate Schema Script screen, 215

Space Usage tab (Database Browser), 200-201

spellchecking, Auto Replace panel (SQL Editor), 63-64

SQL

    ANSI SQL, Query Builder (SQL Editor), 66

    code snippets, 133-134

    formatting code, 127

    Oracle SQL, Query Builder (SQL Editor), 66

    performance tuning, 227, 249-250

        AWR browser, 245-246

        explain plans, 227-231

        PL/SQL Profiler, 246-248

        SQL Optimizer, 248-249

        SQL Trace tab (SQL Editor Output area), 233-238

        statistics, 231-232

        Statspack browser, 243-245

        TKProf wizard, 238-241, 242

        Trace File Browser, 241-242

    shortcuts, coding in Auto Replace panel (SQL Editor), 63-64

SQL Editor, 16, 43

    Auto Replace panel, 63-64

    auto-opening at startup, 34-36

    button descriptions, viewing, 44

Clear button, 45

Code Snippets panel, 58-60

data grids, 95

data tool palette (Output area), 48

Describe Objects panel, 51

    changing panel location, 52

    Data Grid panel, 56

    dragging/dropping columns, 51

    EMP Table Describe Panel buttons, 52

    Export DDL panel, 55

    Generate Statement panel, 56

    Script tab, 53

    viewing button functionality, 52-53

Editor button, 44

functionality, 45

Halt button, 45

input options, 45

Insights panel, 57-58

multiple logins, 46

Output area

    Auto Trace tab, 49-50, 231-232

    Breakpoints tab, 49

    Call Stack tab, 49

    Data Grid tab, 49

    data tool palette, 48

    DBMS Output tab, 49

    Explain Plan tab, 49, 50

    hiding/displaying tabs, 48-49

    Messages tab, 49

    Navigator tab, 49

    Profiler tab, 48, 49

    Query Viewer tab, 49

    REF CURSOR Results tab, 49

    Script Output tab, 49

    SQL Trace tab, 49-50, 233-238

    Trace tab, 49-50

    Watches tab, 49

Query Builder, 64-65

    Add Schema Name to Tables button, 67

    Add Table Names to Column button, 67

    Ansi button, 67

    ANSI SQL, 66

    calculations, 67

    Generated Query panel, 66-67

    Oracle SQL, 66

    subqueries, 67

    Update Diagram button, 67

    Update SQL button, 67

    WHERE clauses, 66

sending statements to Oracle, 44

SQL Recall panel, 60-62

toolbars

    configuring, 46-47

    resetting options, 47

    standard toolbar, 45

SQL Loader option, saving data in, 111

SQL Optimizer and SQL performance tuning, 248-249

SQL Recall panel (SQL Editor), 60-62

SQL Trace tab (SQL Editor Output area), 49-50, 233-238

startup options (Toad), customizing, 36

startup windows/screens (Toad), customizing, 34-36

statements

    Generate Statement panel (SQL Editor Describe Objects panel), 56

    Insert Statements file format, saving data in, 109

    Insert Statements tab (Export Dataset Wizard), 103

    Merge Statements file format, saving data in, 109

Statspack browser and SQL performance tuning, 243-245

Step Into button (debugging code), 145

stopping code during debugging, 143

Storage Clause Adjustments tab (Rebuild Multiple Objects screen), 224

Style tab (FastReport), 82

subqueries, Query Builder (SQL Editor), 67

suites (Toad), 4-5

Summary.html files (HTML Documentation Generator), 116

symbolic debugging, 142

    advanced debugging, 148-153

    basic debugging, 142-148

Sync Script tab

    Compare Databases screen, 218

    Compare Schemas screen, 219

T

Tables tab (Schema Browser), 75

tablespace management, 210-212

templates (code), 127

    building, 128-131

    choosing, 127

    Cursor Loop template, 127

    modifying, 127-128

    signaling, 127

    substitution variables, 127

    viewing, 127

Terminate Execution button (debugging code), 144

testing data, Show Detail Dataset button, 100

Thresholds and Performance Options tab (Rebuild Multiple Objects screen), 223

TKProf wizard and SQL performance tuning, 238-241, 242

TNS tab, Toad/database connections, 10-11

TNSNAMES Editor, 11-13, 164

Toad
    About screen, 5
    Base edition, 4
    common questions, 21
        database security, 22
        functionality, 21-22
        performance, 22
        sharing options settings, 22
    connection screen, 10
    customizing, 18
        keyboard shortcuts, 33-34
        menus, 19
        Options screen, 19-21, 37-39
        Schema Browser, 34-36
        sharing options settings, 40
        SQL Editor, 34-36
        startup options, 36
        startup windows/screens, 34-36
        toolbars, 19, 30-33
        user settings, 40
    database connections, 10
        choosing, 27
        color highlighting, 13
        connection errors for bad passwords, 16
        filtering, 28
        grouping, 29-30
        Oracle Homes, 14-15
        organizing, 25-30
        sorting, 26
        TNS tab, 10-11
        TNSNAMES Editor, 11-13
    database security, common questions, 22
    DB Admin Module, 4
    .DEF files, 213
    functionality, common questions, 21-22

installing, 6-8
    installer files, 6
    installer license screen, 7
    Windows prerequisites, 5-6
licensing, installer license screen, 7
Options screen
    finding new/unknown options, 37
    initial options to focus on, 38-39
    pop-ups in options, 39
Oracle Homes, 14-15
Oracle Net Services connections, 9-10
performance, common questions, 22
prerequisites, 5-6
Professional edition, 4
release history, 2-3
    editions/suites, 3-5
    Oracle compatibility, 3
running (first time)
    connection screen, 10
    database connections, 10-16
    No Oracle Net Services error, 9
    Oracle Net Services connections, 9-10
    Schema Browser, 17-18
    SQL Editor, 16
    Windows bit compatibility, 10
saved database connection grid
    choosing connections, 27
    filtering connections, 28
    grouping connections, 29-30
    sorting connections, 26
Schema Browser, 17-18, 34-36
sharing options settings, common
    questions, 22
SQL Editor, 16, 34-36
suites, 4-5
Windows prerequisites, 5-6
Xpert edition, 4

Toad Code Rating (Code Analysis reports), 142

Toggle PL/SQL Profiling button (PL/SQL profiling), 153

toolbars

    Action toolbar (Editor), 126

    Automation Designer, 182-183

    customizing, 19, 30

        displayed toolbars, 30

        toolbar layouts, 31-33

    debugging code toolbar, 143

    Project Manager, 133

    Reports Manager (Schema Browser), 86

    Script Manager, 166-167

    SQL Editor

        configuring, 46-47

        resetting options, 47

        standard toolbar, 45

Trace File Browser and SQL performance tuning, 241-242

Trace tab (SQL Editor Output area), 49-50

tracing/killing sessions (Session Browser), 196

tree view (Schema Browser), 70-72

trigger code, debugging, 152

tuning SQL performance, 227, 249-250

    AWR browser, 245-246

    explain plans, 227-229

        code snippets, 231

        execution plans, 229-231

    PL/SQL Profiler, 246-248

    SQL Optimizer, 248-249

    SQL Trace tab (SQL Editor Output area), 233-238

    statistics, 231-232

    Statspack browser, 243-245

    TKProf wizard, 238-241, 242

    Trace File Browser, 241-242

U

UNIX Monitor, 167-168

Update Diagram button (SQL Editor Query Builder), 67

Update SQL button (SQL Editor Query Builder), 67

user settings (Toad), sharing, 40

V

View/Edit Query panel (data grids), 99

W

Waits tab (Session Browser), 197

watches (debugging code), 145, 147, 148

Watches tab (SQL Editor Output area), 49

WHERE clauses, Query Builder (SQL Editor), 66

Windows (Microsoft)

    bit compatibility and Toad operation, 10

    Toad prerequisites, 5-6

wizards

    Create Table wizard (Schema Browser), 76-78

    Data Pump Export wizard, 205-209

    Export Dataset wizard (data grids), 102-103

        Dataset tab, 103

        Insert Statements tab, 103

        Options tab, 102-103

        saving data, 106-111

    Export Utility wizard

        Data Pump Export wizard, 205-209

        Generate Database Script screen, 212-214

Generate Schema Script screen, 214-215

simple exports, 202-204

Load Database Object wizard, 122-123

Report wizard (FastReport), 80-83

TKProf wizard and SQL performance tuning, 238-241, 242

X - Y - Z

XML (with XLS) file format, saving data in, 108

XML file format, saving data in, 108

Xpert edition (Toad), 4